THREE WORLDS *of*
MICHELANGELO

THREE WORLDS *of* MICHELANGELO

JAMES H. BECK

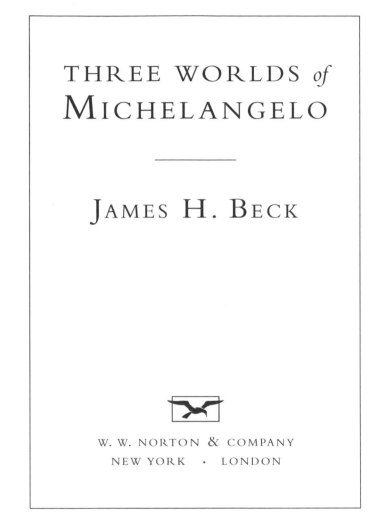

W. W. NORTON & COMPANY

NEW YORK · LONDON

For information about permission to reproduce
selections from this book, write to
Permissions,
W. W. Norton & Company, Inc.,
500 Fifth Avenue,
New York, NY 10110.

The text of this book is composed in Bembo
with the display set in Bembo Italic
Composition by Allentown Digital Services Division of R.R. Donnelley & Sons
Company
Manufacturing by the Maple-Vail Book Manufacturing Group
Book design by BTD/Sabrina Bowers

LIBRARY OF CONGRESS CATALOGING-IN-PUBLICATION DATA

Beck, James H.
Three worlds of Michelangelo / James H. Beck.
p.   cm.
Includes bibliographical references and index.
ISBN 0-393-04524-2
1. Michelangelo Buonarroti, 1475–1564—Criticism and interpretation.
2. Michelangelo Buonarroti, 1475–1564—Friends and associates.
I. Michelangelo Buonarroti, 1475–1564. II. Title.
N6923.B9B38 1998
709'.2—dc21   98-21538
CIP

W. W. Norton & Company, Inc.
500 Fifth Avenue, New York, N.Y. 10110
http://www.wwnorton.com

W. W. Norton & Company Ltd.
10 Coptic Street, London WC1A 1PU

2 3 4 5 6 7 8 9 0

This book is dedicated to my three worlds:
Darma, Nora, and Larry.

Contents

⬚⬚⬚

ILLUSTRATIONS   ix

PREFACE   xiii

A MICHELANGELO CHRONOLOGY   xix

Prologue: *A Divine Mission*   1
I: *Michelangelo and Lorenzo il Magnifico*   11
II: *Michelangelo and His Father, Lodovico*   77
III: *Michelangelo and Pope Julius II*   141
Epilogue: *A Celestial Triangle at Macel de' Corvi*   215

A NOTE ON SOURCES   233

BIBLIOGRAPHIC NOTE   235

NOTES   239

ACKNOWLEDGMENTS   253

CREDITS   255

INDEX   259

Illustrations

✠

Donatello, *Marzocco*.   5

Michelangelo's horoscope.   7

Michelangelo, study of *Madonna and Child*, detail.   9

Donatello, bronze *David*.   15

Leonardo da Vinci, Lorenzo il Magnifico, profile head.   18

Martin Schongauer, *Temptation of St. Anthony*, detail.   19

Donatello, *St. George*.   22

Roman artist, *Marsyas*.   27

Michelangelo, copy after *Profile Portrait of Alessandro, Count of Canossa*, detail.   29

Michelangelo, study for the *Battle of Cascina*.   30

Marcantonio Raimondi, *Three Figures* (from Michelangelo's *Battle of Cascina*). Engraving.   31

Bertoldo di Giovanni, *Medal of the Pazzi Conspiracy*, obverse with the head of Lorenzo il Magnifico.   41

Farnese Cup.   47

Masaccio, *Shivering Boy*. Detail from *Baptism of the Neophites*.   49

Daniele da Volterra, *Portrait Bust of Michelangelo.* 50

Michelangelo, study after Masaccio's *Tribute Money.* 53

Piero di Cosimo, *Portrait of Giuliano da Sangallo,* detail. 56

Michelangelo, block sketches for reclining figures. 58

Michelangelo, *Battle of the Centaurs.* 64

Madonna of the Steps. 68

Michelangelo (?), *Hercules.* 71

Botticelli, *Adoration of the Magi,* detail. 74

Jacopo della Quercia, *Creation of Eve.* 82

Michelangelo, letter to his father. 102

Anonymous, *Portrait of Savonarola.* Bookplate from *Oracolo della renovatione della chiesa.* 106

Anonymous, *Savonarola Preaching.* Bookplate from the *Compendio di revelatione.* 110

Leonardo da Vinci, detail of a map of Tuscany showing the Arno River. 114

Rustichi, drawing of Florence Duomo. 117

Michelangelo, drawing for the bronze *David.* 121

Raphael, study after Michelangelo's *David.* 122

Donatello, *Judith and Holofernes.* 126

Leonardo da Vinci, drawing of Michelangelo's *David.* 132

Michelangelo, *Doni Tondo.* Head from frame of *Doni Tondo.* 137

Michelangelo, *Bacchus,* detail of foot. 153

After Michelangelo, project for the Julius Tomb. 156

Raphael, *Portrait of Julius II,* detail of head. 160

Michelangelo, studies for the *Slaves* for the Julius Tomb. 162

Laocoön detail, head. 173

Michelangelo, study for the *Bruges Madonna.* 175

Engraving of the Sistine Chapel before Michelangelo's ceiling. 179

Full view of the Sistine Chapel ceiling. 182

After Michelangelo, copy of Michelangelo's Sistine Chapel
ceiling. Detail: *Lunette with Ancestors of Christ.* 185
Michelangelo, composition sketch for the Sistine Chapel
ceiling. 186
Michelangelo, studies for three *Ignudi.* 189
Michelangelo, detail of God the Father from *Creation of
Adam.* 192
Michelangelo, *The Flood.* 200
Michelangelo, *Ignudo.* Detail from Sistine Chapel ceiling. 204
After Michelangelo, copy of Michelangelo's Sistine Chapel
ceiling. Detail: female "putto" supporting inscription. 205
Michelangelo, male head in profile. 206
Michelangelo, *Judith and Holofernes.* 206
Michelangelo, detail of the head of Holofernes from *Judith
and Holofernes.* 206
Michelangelo, drawing of a kneeling woman. 208
Michelangelo (?), possible self-portrait. 213
Michelangelo, shopping list. 227
Michelangelo, drawing of hand holding book. 232

Preface

◼◼◼

A HANDFUL OF INDIVIDUALS in the history of Western culture have evolved into universal symbols for the entire civilization. They are, in effect, the civilization. Although the foundation of their primacy rests upon extraordinary accomplishments, with the passage of time their lives have become the stuff of mythology. We scrutinize them and their work in limitless detail, seeking to participate in their raw genius and, thus, in the best of humankind's achievements. To be sure, each generation necessarily writes its own unique interpretation of the deeds of its heroes, although within a single generation, the conclusions may diverge according to diverse orientations or points of view.

In the case of Michelangelo Buonarroti, we deal with an individual without parallel—painter, sculptor, architect, poet all rolled into one. We approach him with trepidation, for even in his own lifetime he was regarded (at least rhetorically) as "divine." Concentrating on Michelangelo offers distinct advantages over treating another genius simply because of the ample quantity of reliable contemporary data available to us. Although Michelangelo was born more than five hundred years ago, we can readily consult over five hundred letters that he wrote as well as hundreds of others written to him. In addition, a vast body of so-called indirect correspondence in which he or his works are discussed by third parties has been collected over the centuries. Supplementing this correspondence are unself-conscious notations known as *ricordi,* or memoranda, written by Michelangelo, his father, and others close to him, which are often of the most basic sort, like a shopping list—including herring or the medications he was wont to purchase, inevitably herbal—or records of payment for clothing such as breeches, a jacket, hose, or a French-style cap. In an entirely different category are business records and notarial acts regarding land purchases and, less frequently, contracts for his artistic productions, all of which can be consulted for additional authoritative information.

And two biographies of the master were written during Michelangelo's lifetime. The earlier is by his admirer Giorgio Vasari and was printed in 1550 as part of Vasari's influential collection of lives of Italian artists. Vasari, himself a painter and architect who had affectionate dealings with the master, gave Michelangelo a privileged place in the *Lives.* But despite Vasari's high regard for his subject, Michelangelo had serious reservations about what Vasari had written, especially concerning the early phases of his life and how his career had unfolded. Besides, he was not quite satisfied with the overall thrust of Vasari's account. Determined to correct what he regarded as errors in it, Michelangelo urged his pupil Ascanio Condivi to compose a new biography. Michelangelo supplied information based upon his recollections, correcting and emending Vasari when he considered it appropriate. Much of Condivi's *Life of Michelangelo,* which was published in 1553, should be considered a virtual autobiography of the then seventy-eight-year-old Michelangelo, who revealed himself to be deeply concerned about how future generations would perceive him. Unquestionably, Michelangelo had a sharp sense of history, especially his own.

The literary evidence surrounding Michelangelo is augmented by and takes on physical reality from the body of his work: sculptures, paintings, plans, drawings, buildings, and poems. Unlike Leonardo da Vinci, for instance, whose finished paintings are restricted to a handful in number, Michelangelo produced a substantial oeuvre over his long life (he was almost eighty-nine when he died).

This mass of material is not just luxury, but a challenge for anyone who seeks to penetrate Michelangelo's core of creativity and reach the quality that lies behind both his life and his work—his humanity. Such is the goal of this enterprise. A warning should be drawn while plotting the route: however great the temptation, the human being, the artist, should never be confused with his creations. An artist—any artist—I suggest, is not his work; an artist is a person who makes works. Of course, his work, thoughts, and actions derive from the identical reservoir of forces and currents that, collectively, I have designated as his humanity. This is the case with Michelangelo, although he was undoubtedly compulsive when it came to his art. When not painting or carving, Michelangelo, it is said, would sleep with his boots on like a crazed general so that he could snap into action at a moment's notice.

The intention of this book is to search out and get in touch with Michelangelo. We will observe him during the nearly four decades from his birth in 1475 to the completion of the Sistine Chapel ceiling in 1512 and the death of Pope Julius II in 1513, in the context of three men who had a decisive impact on his life and career: Lorenzo de' Medici, Lodovico Buonarroti Simoni, and Pope Julius II. Although this span represents less than half his life and much less than half his professional activity, it covers a solid segment of his surging creativity.

The first of these individuals, Lorenzo de' Medici, called "il Magnifico," headed Europe's most powerful bank and was, effectively, the ruler of Florence until his death in 1492. He provided Michelangelo with a challenging setting in his adolescence. The second, Lodovico di Lionardo Buonarroti, was Michelangelo's biological father, to whom Michelangelo was deeply attached and whose impact on Michelangelo's life seems to have been especially strong following Lorenzo's death. The third, the "terrible" pope Julius II, born Giuliano della Rovere, proved to be Michelangelo's most remarkable patron, commissioning sculptures for his tomb, including *Moses,* and the unequaled frescoes on the ceiling of the Sistine Chapel.

These men were Michelangelo's three "fathers," who pointed him toward artistic accomplishment and personal development. They affected Michelangelo in distinctive ways, but all three were crucial for the fulfillment of Michelangelo's mission as it unfolded during those eventful years. Each formed for the artist an epicenter for discovery and expansion.

Lorenzo, who could be considered Michelangelo's intellectual father, implicitly represented the whole Medici clan, not least Giovanni and Giulio, Lorenzo's son and nephew, respectively, who became Michelangelo's patrons when they were elected pope, the former as Leo X and the latter as Clement VII. The other members of Lorenzo's household, including prominent philosophers and poets, also helped to refine the young Michelangelo's thinking. Even after his death, Lorenzo continued to haunt Michelangelo, whose close connection to the Medici weakened when Lorenzo's oldest son and heir, Piero, known as "Piero the Unfortunate," turned out to be a disappointment to the blossoming artist.

Michelangelo's father, Lodovico, stood at the core of a cluster of connections that embraced Michelangelo's four brothers, other relatives near and far, and an impressive group of loyal friends and companions. Until the execution of the charismatic Dominican preacher

Girolamo Savonarola in 1498, and even after, the aura of his sermons and his awesome predictions hung over the Buonarroti family and was never forgotten by Michelangelo.

Julius II, pope from 1504 to 1513, was the individual who had the greatest influence over Michelangelo's art. He was not merely a patron father to Michelangelo, he was the Holy Father, *"il Papa."* Michelangelo's involvement in the vast papal, and especially Roman, world, which he sometimes found frustrating, came from his rapport with Julius. During the years he was active at the Vatican, Michelangelo became associated with others who were employed by the pope, such as the architects Donato Bramante and Giuliano da Sangallo.

Michelangelo's interactions with Lorenzo the Magnificent, with his father Lodovico, and with Pope Julius II may be regarded as corresponding to the three phases in the artist's life up to its midpoint, concluding with the triumph of the Sistine Chapel ceiling.

Cajoled, castigated, and caressed by these three strong individuals, Michelangelo Buonarroti in his unprecedented artistic journey never swerved from his self-defined goals. Their personalities each had unique properties of their own. The Hamlet-like Lorenzo il Magnifico operated in the long shadow of his brilliant grandfather, Cosimo il Vecchio, and the memory of his beloved brother Giuliano, murdered in a failed political plot in the prime of life. The self-centered and self-indulgent Lodovico Buonarroti had to raise five sons virtually on his own. He seems to have had difficulty in expressing his emotions toward Michelangelo, and when he did so, they often proved harsh and damaging. Pope Julius II was a determined warrior and fearless general, who had inherited religious and lay authority from his uncle, Pope Sixtus IV. To his credit, Julius willingly patronized the artist and inspired him to create his finest works, but in the end, failed to dominate him.

A Michelangelo Chronology

▨▨▨

6 March 1475★   Michelangelo is born in Caprese.

8 March 1475   Michelangelo is baptized in the Church of San Giovanni in Caprese, in the diocese of San Sepolcro.

1 April 1475   Lodovico's term as *podestà* being concluded, he and his family return to Florence.

11 December 1475   Birth of Giovanni de' Medici, Lorenzo il Magnifico's second son, who will become Pope Leo X.

26 May 1479   Birth of Giulio, son of Giuliano de' Medici, brother of Lorenzo il Magnifico, who will become Pope Clement VII.

6 December 1481   Michelangelo's mother Francesca dies in Florence at the age of about twenty-six and is buried at Santa Croce.

★ Years are given throughout by the modern calendar.

1485	Lodovico Buonarroti marries again, this time to Lucrezia degli Ubaldini da Gagliano.
28 June 1487	Michelangelo, age twelve, performs an errand for the Ghirlandaio shop of painters *(bottega)*.
1 April 1488	Michelangelo is officially apprenticed to the Ghirlandaio shop.
ca. March 1490(?)	Michelangelo leaves Ghirlandaio's studio and goes to work in the Medici Gardens.
8 April 1492	Lorenzo il Magnifico dies at the family villa in Careggi.
24 September 1494	The humanist and poet Angelo Poliziano dies in a room in the garden of Clarice Orsini, next to the Medici Gardens.
10 October 1494	Michelangelo leaves the house of Piero de' Medici.
ca. 14 October 1494	Michelangelo departs from Florence for Venice, then goes to Bologna, where he settles for about a year, working on the *Arca of San Domenico.*
ca. November 1495	Michelangelo returns to Florence and remains about seven months.
17 February 1496	Girolamo Savonarola preaches at the Duomo in Florence.
Late June, perhaps 25 June 1496	Michelangelo arrives in Rome.
2 July 1496	Michelangelo writes from Rome to Lorenzo di Pierfrancesco de' Medici in Florence, his first extant letter.

18 July 1496	Payment recorded to Michelangelo for the *Bacchus;* the final payment to come the following year.
13 May 1497	Pope Alexander VI excommunicates Savonarola.
November 1497	Michelangelo receives a significant advance from a French cardinal for his *Pietà*.
23 May 1498	Savonarola dies at the stake on Piazza Signoria in Florence.
27 August 1498	The contract for the marble *Pietà* is signed.
3 July 1500	The final payment for the *Pietà* is apparently made on this day, although the work was finished during the previous year.
18 March 1501	Michelangelo is recorded back in Florence after a five-year stay in Rome.
5 June 1501	Contract for the Piccolomini Altar statuettes for the Duomo of Siena.
16 August 1501	Commission to Michelangelo from the officials of the Cathedral for the marble *David:* he is given two years to finish it, beginning on 1 September 1501.
12 August 1502	The Signoria contracts Michelangelo for a bronze *David* for a French patron.
25 April 1503	Michelangelo is commissioned to produce twelve *Apostles* for the interior of the Cathedral to replace painted ones.
1 November 1503	Giuliano della Rovere elected pope as Julius II.

?1504–05   Michelangelo completes the *Doni Tondo*—a circular picture of the Holy Family commissioned by Angelo di Francesco Doni upon his marriage in January 1504 to Maddalena Strozzi.

25 January 1504   A meeting *(pratica)* is convened to discuss the placement of the marble *David*.

28 May 1504   The Signoria publicly authorizes that the *David* be installed on the low wall *(ringhiera)* in front of the palace in the spot where the *Judith* by Donatello had been placed.

August 1504   Michelangelo is commissioned to paint the *Battle of Cascina* for the Palazzo Signoria, for which he has first to produce a cartoon.

8 September 1504   The marble *David* is "unveiled" on the occasion of a new gonfaloniere taking office that morning.

27 March 1505   By this date Michelangelo is back in Rome, and in the weeks that follow he makes drawings for the monumental tomb of Julius II.

30 (or 31?) August 1505   Michelangelo's cartoon for the *Battle of Cascina* is placed in the Palazzo Signoria.

14 January 1506   The *Laocoön* is discovered in Rome and Michelangelo goes to see it with Giuliano da Sangallo. Two months later it is purchased by the pope.

13, 14, 15, 16 April 1506   Michelangelo goes daily to the Vatican to speak with the pope and each time is told to return.

17 April 1506   (Friday) Michelangelo is sent away (or "thrown out") from the papal office; the next day, he leaves Rome.

ca. 19 April to 27–28 November 1506	Michelangelo is back in Florence, working on his projects there.
30 (or 29?) November 1506	Michelangelo, in Bologna, has a reconciliation with the pope.
17 February 1508	The newly finished bronze statue of Pope Julius II by Michelangelo is brought to San Petronio and installed in Bologna on the 21st.
9 March 1508	Michelangelo, fresh from Bologna, is recorded back in Florence.
27 March 1508	Michelangelo returns to Rome.
10 May 1508	Michelangelo formally begins painting the Sistine Chapel ceiling.
July–August 1508	The assistants who are supposed to come from Florence to help paint the ceiling are mentioned.
ca. 27 February (or May–June) 1509	Michelangelo writes to his father, who had implied that in Florence people were saying Michelangelo was dead: "I care very little about it because I am surely alive." Then he advises his father "not to speak about me to anyone because there are nasty people around."
24 June 1509	Michelangelo obtains a payment of 500 ducats, one of several, for the Sistine ceiling.
July–August 1510	Michelangelo writes to his brother Buonarroto about finishing the first half of the Sistine Chapel frescoes.
26–28 September 1510	Michelangelo goes to Bologna to see the pope.

24 May 1511   Cardinal Alidosi, seeking out the pope in Ravenna, is slain by the pope's nephew, Francesco Maria della Rovere.

14 August 1511   Eve of Assumption Day. The pope goes to see the newly uncovered frescoes in the Sistine Chapel—the first half of the work.

4 October 1511   In a letter to Lodovico in Florence, Michelangelo writes that none of his things should be touched by anyone.

30 December 1511   Michelangelo's bronze statue of Julius II in Bologna is destroyed by an angry mob.

28 May 1512   Michelangelo buys a large farm called "Macia" from the Hospital of Santa Maria Nuova.

4–19 July 1512   Duke Alfonso d'Este of Ferrara ascends the scaffolding and sees the ceiling that Michelangelo is still painting.

24 July 1512   Michelangelo writes to Buonarroto, lamenting, "I am having more difficulty than any man there ever was, in poor health and the greatest fatigue. And yet I have the patience to achieve the desired end."

31 August 1512   Piero Soderini flees Florence and Giuliano di Lorenzo de' Medici enters (1 September), marking the end of the republic and the restoration of the Medici, which occurs on 14 September.

18 September 1512   Michelangelo writes to Buonarroto, giving advice about his conduct in the new political situation in Florence. The Medici are back

and the danger from the Spanish troops has dissipated. "So stay there in peace and don't make friends or be familiar with anyone except God; and speak neither good nor ill about anyone, because one doesn't know the outcome of things. Concern yourselves only with your own affairs."

early October 1512   In a letter to Lodovico, Michelangelo writes that the Sistine Chapel ceiling is finished and that the pope seems quite satisfied.

1513   Luca Signorelli, the painter from Cortona, asks and obtains money from Michelangelo in the form of a loan.

21–22 February 1513   Julius II dies in Rome after presiding as pope for nine years, three months, and twenty-one days.

11 March 1513   Cardinal Giovanni de' Medici is elected pope. He takes the name of Leo X.

25 March 1513   Giovanni de' Medici is inaugurated as pope on this day, the Florentine New Year.

★★★

12 February 1564   Michelangelo works all day on the *Rondanini Pietà*.

15 February 1564   Michelangelo is prescribed a long list of medications.

18 February 1564   Michelangelo dies. In a *ricordo,* his nephew, Lionardo, writes: "On this day today, Friday, the 18th of February, 1564 [modern style] at 23½ hours, Michelagnolo di Lodovico di Lionardo Buonarroti Simoni left this present

life, having died in Rome. He was eighty-eight years, eleven months, and fourteen days old. His body was deposited in the Church of the Apostoli on February 19 and it remained there until March 2. After that, the shipper Simone de' Berna brought his body to Florence, where it arrived on March 10 and was deposited at San Piero Maggiore, resting there for two days. Then it was carried to Santa Croce by the Florentine Academicians of painting and sculpture. . . ."

19 February 1564   A Roman official takes an inventory of the contents of Michelangelo's house at Macel de' Corvi.

THREE WORLDS *of*
MICHELANGELO

Prologue:
A Divine Mission

In addressing Michelangelo Buonarroti, a daunting epithet has to be confronted: one that encompasses his activities as painter, sculptor, architect, and poet. Michelangelo was often referred to as "divine" during his lifetime, and increasingly so thereafter. The grand master Titian, by contrast, never was. Even the painter-friar Fra Angelico could not attain such status, although he was—and is—lovingly called the "Beato [Beatified] Angelico." Leonardo, superhuman in scope, intellect, and accomplishment, inexplicably never achieved such classification. Nor did Raphael. "Divine" is appropriate, uniquely among his contemporaries, only for Michelangelo.

The designation fits Michelangelo effortlessly—no flight of fantasy is required. In one of the most moving, if high-flown and rhetorical, passages in his *Lives of the Artists,* Vasari states:

> The most generous Ruler of Heaven mercifully cast his eyes down to earth, and seeing the vain infinitude of so much enormous effort, the arduous studies that fail to bear fruit, and the presumptuous opinions of men who are farther removed from truth than darkness

is from light, resolved to send a spirit to earth who was universally skilled in every art and in every profession: a person capable of demonstrating on his own perfection in the art of outlining, in shading, and in lights, giving three-dimensional efforts to his pictorial images. And a person who could work in sculpture, in making buildings comfortable and secure, healthy, happy and with good proportions, as well as rich in diverse architectural ornaments, all with excellent judgment. Moreover, He willed to endow that man with true moral philosophy and with the adornment of sweet poetry, so that the world might recognize and admire him for his more singular vision in life, in his art, in morals, and in the sanctity of all human endeavors. And for all these things we would regard him as being more of heaven than of earth.

And in Lodovico Ariosto's *Orlando Furioso* (1516), Michelangelo is singled out from Leonardo, Giambellino, Titian, and Raphael as being "more than mortal, a divine angel" *(più che mortale, angel divino),* a play, of course, on his name. But the label—not easily explained since no family member seems to have had it before—was also sometimes the source of ridicule and jests: the sharp-tongued writer Pietro Aretino took Michelangelo to task for his alleged divinity, while the poet Francesco Berni of Lamporecchio poked friendly fun at the artist.

In 1513, Luca Signorelli, the Umbrian artist whose brilliant frescoes in Orvieto served more than any others as inspiration for Michelangelo, sought out financial help from his younger colleague in Rome. Michelangelo, who was ill at the time, did not disappoint him. Years later, Michelangelo recalled the words of the old painter from Cortona on the occasion of the loan: "I have no doubt but that Angels from the sky will take you up in their arms and help you." The play on his name, Michael Angelo, was a factor; indeed, Michelangelo once signed a letter by drawing two angel wings—presumably in jest. In conversation, Michelangelo maintained that it was not enough for a painter to render the holy image of Christ and to be an excellent master. An artist, he is quoted as saying, "must maintain a good life, and if possible be holy, so that his intellect can be inspired by the Holy Spirit."

The circumstances surrounding Michelangelo's death in Rome on Friday evening, February 18, 1564, and the funeral service conducted in Florence a few weeks later, emphasize the intensity of perceptions about his assumed divinity. Michelangelo died at 11:30 P.M., sixteen days short of his eighty-ninth birthday, attended by two dear friends, the artist Daniele da Volterra and another longtime Roman intimate, Tommaso Cavalieri, as well as two medical doctors. Although Michelangelo never bothered to prepare a will, he left ample instructions over time for his nephew Lionardo, son of his favorite brother Buonarroto, and to the others at his deathbed. He wished to be laid to rest in his beloved Florence—to return home after an absence of over thirty years.

The artist could hardly have been unaware of the popular saying, "We know where we are born but not where we will die" *(Si sa dove si nasce, ma non si sa dove si muore)*. To make his reentry more momentous, the Florentine Fine Arts Academicians posthumously elected him Prime Academic, the "head, father and master of everyone" *(capo, padre et maestro di tutti)*, upon learning of his death.

Michelangelo's body was first laid out for observances in Rome until March 2 in the Church of the Holy Apostles, tended to by the Confraternity of San Giovanni Decollato. Since John the Baptist was Florence's patron saint, Michelangelo, not surprisingly, belonged to the confraternity when he lived in Rome, as did Leonardo da Vinci. After two weeks, the body was meticulously wrapped, set into an expressly constructed casket, and shipped by horse to Florence for Michelangelo's final journey home. The body arrived in the city on the Arno on April 10. The remains were brought to the room assigned to the Company of the Assumption *(Assunta)* beneath the Church of San Pier Maggiore, a mere stone's throw away from the Buonarroti family's old residence on the narrow, curving Via dei Bentaccordi, and not far from their new one on Via Ghibellina.

After funeral arrangements were completed two days later, the academicians ceremoniously accompanied the draped coffin to the spacious Franciscan basilica of Santa Croce nearby. While the older members of the Academy held torches, the younger ones were assigned to support the bier. Happy indeed were those who could shoulder the body and in times to come could boast of having borne the corporeal remains of the greatest man that ever existed in their profession. Propelled by a "divine frenzy" *(furor divino)*, as a contemporary account has it, crowds unexpectedly gathered. As word spread throughout the city that the body of the fabled Michelangelo was being carried to Santa Croce, the numbers constantly expanded. Once at the church, the coffin was transported into the sacristy and the lid was solemnly raised. To the amazement of the participants, instead of the stench of decay properly to be expected—after all, it had been fully three weeks since Michelangelo's death—only sweet smells emanated from the coffin. This was a sure sign of saintliness, observers said; besides, not the slightest sign of bodily disfigurement was noticeable *(non era trasfigurato)*. Michelangelo lay dressed in a black damask gown, boots with spurs, and his habitual French-style silk cap with a smooth black velvet ribbon. Even in death, he followed his father's advice to take special care of his head: "keep it moderately warm and don't wash it ever!"

Solemnly, one by one, the academicians touched the soft and lifelike forehead and cheeks. Artists of every age trusted that a shred of Michelangelo's artistic power could be passed on to them. A simple inscription on the temporary tomb summarized common sentiment: "The Divine Michelangelo" *(Il Divino Michelangelo)*.

By chance or mysterious design, Michelangelo the Florentine was born not in Florence but in Caprese, a rugged Apennine hill town 2,000 feet high, not far from Arezzo and La Verna, the spot where St. Francis received the wounds of Christ. Lodovico had been sent there by the Florentine government, presumably on the recommendation of a (distant) relative of his wife's, none other than Lorenzo de' Medici, as *podestà* or chief official of Caprese, as well as of another nearby castle town, Chiusi. When Lodovico's six-month term ended on April 1, 1475, less than a month after Michelangelo's birth, the family returned to Florence.

The circumstances connected with any child's birth were regarded with utmost seriousness. For exam-

DONATELLO, *Marzocco*, c. 1419.

ple, mysterious portents surrounded the birth of Leo X, Lorenzo de' Medici's second son, born with the name Giovanni in the same year as Michelangelo. While his mother Clarice Orsini was pregnant, she dreamt that she gave birth in Florence's vast Duomo (Cathedral) to an oversized lion of exceptional gentleness. Thus, the lion (*Leone* is the name he chose as pope), the symbol of Florence, was to be saved by Giovanni, who would lead the Medici family to its glorious destiny. No such premonition was recorded for Michelangelo's birth, although his mother Francesca had taken a severe fall from a horse while carrying him.

Astrologically, however, Michelangelo's birth was interpreted as extremely positive for a career in art. Though there is no particular evidence to suggest that Michelangelo was unusually superstitious about such matters, he was, after all, a man of his times. We know that he retained the chart of his nativity among his Florentine possessions and that, in later life, when planetary aspects were on his mind, he asked his nephew Lionardo to send the horoscope on to him in Rome.

Michelangelo's biographer Ascanio Condivi reports—surely on the basis of what Michelangelo had told him, which he, in turn, had learned from an astrologer—that March 6, 1475, four hours before daybreak between Sunday and Monday, provided an excellent nativity. It demonstrated what was to become of the boy child and with what creativity *(ingegno)* he would operate. Still, according to Condivi's account, the prediction was possible because Mercury and Venus were in the second house, in a favorable aspect to Jupiter. Condivi added, not without hindsight, that the prediction had been proven correct because with that configuration, Michelangelo would succeed in whatever enterprise he undertook, but especially in those arts that delight the senses: painting, sculpture, and architecture.

Contrary to widely accepted opinion, Michelangelo was almost certainly first breast-fed by his mother, Francesca, the daughter of Neri di Miniato del Sera and of Bonda Rucellai. She was an honest and noble woman from a good family, as Vasari puts it. Indeed, his mother's attributes as he knew them seem to have affected Michelangelo's thinking about women and marriage, although she died when he was only six. A half century later, in advising his nephew Lionardo by letter about the kind of wife he should seek out, Michelangelo wrote him that she "should be of noble family and well brought up, but better without a dowry than a large one, in order to be able to live in peace"—a rare if oblique reference to his mother, Francesca.

Only after the family left Caprese and returned to Florence could

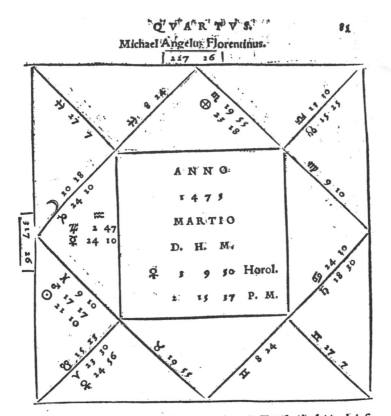

| 217 | 26 |

```
                    A N N O.
                    1 4 7 5
                  M A R T I O
                  D.  H.  M.
              ♀   3   9   50  Horol.
              ♌   15  37  P. M.
```

M ercurius eous a Sole 27. gradibus elongatus, in Falciferi hofpitio, ab ipfa Venere irroratus exagona radiatione platica, effecerunt ipfum Michaelem Angelum fculprorem, & pictorem eminentifsimum; Phidia, & Praxitele clariorem cum opibus affluentifsimis, quam foelicitatem affirmare videtur Iuppiter fecundæ domus hofpitator in horofcopo platice fupputatus, & a Venere foeliciter irrigatus. Ex fui genij doribus thefauros af fluentifsimos cumulauit, & a Principibus ecclefiafticis honores clarifsimos.

Michelangelo's horoscope. A horoscope shows the position of the stars at the time of birth divided equally into the twelve houses. Modern usage arranges the houses as segments of a circle, while during the Renaissance they were represented as twelve triangles within a square, four of which formed another square in the middle by their long sides. These four were regarded as the most important of angular houses of the horoscope and began on the left at the middle which is the ascendant.

Michelangelo have been boarded out in Settignano, a pleasant, hilly area noted for its farms and stone quarries. Overlooking the city to the south, it was a leisurely hour's walk from the Duomo in central Florence. He must have been nursed by his own mother before the family returned home from Caprese and for some time thereafter, until he was actually sent to Settignano, perhaps a matter of weeks or even months. If there was a separation, it could not have been immediate. Besides, even the fact that the child had been handed over to a wet nurse does not necessarily signify that he was totally separated from his natural mother. Francesca may well have established herself on the Buonarrotis' farm in Settignano while Michelangelo was being nursed. Long owned by the Buonarroti, the property in Settignano, in the area called the Popolo of Santa Maria, included a gentleman's house *(una casa da signore)*—something, that is, more than a mere farmhouse. At the least, Francesca could easily have made regular visits to her second son from the city.

Of course he did have a wet nurse, as did nearly all children from his social class (though, incidentally Raphael, did not). Who was the surrogate mother? According to Michelangelo, his wet nurse was the daughter of a stonemason who was married to a man who practiced the same trade. In later life, the artist asserted to Condivi that it should hardly come as a surprise that he delighted in the chisel, since, as he explained, the milk of his wet nurse had so much power that it changed the "temperament" of his body, actually introducing a different nature or inclination than that found at birth. Even if the family genes might have precluded his becoming a painter or a sculptor, Michelangelo asserted that his nurse's milk had modified his nature, whether Lodovico liked it or not. Michelangelo left the graphic image of metaphorically "sucking from the milk of my wet nurse the chisels and the hammer with which I carve figures" *(come anche tirai dal latte della mia balia gli scarpegli e il mazzuolo con che io fo le figure)*.

At some point, perhaps when he was around five and ready for schooling, Michelangelo was brought back from Settignano to the family's city house on the Via dei Bentaccordi. There seems to be no doubt that his very earliest years spent in the countryside had an effect upon his character. His formal schooling, which began with a tutor from Urbino, lasted until he was contractually apprenticed at the age of thirteen in the painting workshop of the Ghirlandaio brothers.

One detail stands out from his boyhood. Michelangelo stubbornly insisted on becoming a painter, a resolve which so enraged his father Lodovico and his uncle Francesco that they sought to dissuade him by intermittent cajoling and beatings. Half a century later, Michelangelo was to recall bitterly that the two literally "hated" the art of painting. The Buonarroti Simoni family was impoverished, and Lodovico could hardly tolerate the idea of his son's being little more than a common artisan, a mere decorator. But so unwavering was Michelangelo's sense of mission, even as a child, that his tormented father eventually had no choice but to assent.

Michelangelo was at heart a Tuscan, and specifically a Florentine. At the same time, he had more than his share of the

MICHELANGELO, study of *Madonna and Child,* detail.

country, if not the barnyard, in his veins. Throughout his career, he would continue to maintain cordial contact with local stone workers at Settignano. This country background, together with his Tuscan sense of humor, were distinguishing components in his identity. He relied upon the wisdom contained in aphorisms like those that circulated Settignano; they seemed to consolidate Michelangelo's natural tendency toward the practical and the commonsensical. And later, once his fortunes turned favorable, he invested all his not inconsequential earnings in rural properties, after buying a fine city residence on the Via Ghibellina. He knew full well that "A kiss on the mouth often does not touch the heart" *(Bacio di bocca spesso cuor non tocca)* and that "He who praises you to your face, curses you in your absence" *(Chi ti loda in presenza, ti biasima in assenza)*. And he once referred to a disloyal assistant as "that piece of dry dung" *(questo merda seca di questo fanciullo)*.

Michelangelo's all-encompassing commitment to family, which was lifelong, also may be ascribed to his experience in the country. As an adult, he would find himself supporting an aging father, several brothers, and even a nephew and a niece, and their welfare would always remain an encompassing personal priority.

Years later, in a letter of 1542 written from Rome, Michelangelo responded to a friend in Florence who had commented that the artist was what God wanted him to be. Michelangelo, then approaching seventy, claimed to be nothing but "a poor man and of little value, a man who goes along laboring in that art which God has given me [*quell'arte che Dio m'à data*] for as long as I possibly can."

I

Michelangelo and
Lorenzo il Magnifico

※※※

THE DREAM

I N A DREAM one early fall night in 1494, perhaps on October 4, the
feast day of St. Francis, Lorenzo di Piero di Cosimo de' Medici,
"the Magnificent," appeared to a disconcerted Michelangelo Buonarroti. The vision proved unsettling to the young sculptor because
Lorenzo had died two and half years before. Besides, Michelangelo
was highly strung. And the death of his unofficial adviser, the poet
Angelo Poliziano, only days before must have made the young sculptor especially tense.

Through Condivi, Michelangelo narrated that Lorenzo had appeared to him in the dream clad only in a ragged black gown over his
naked body. Lorenzo ordered Michelangelo to advise his first son,
Piero de' Medici, that he would soon be thrown out of Florence and
never again allowed to return. Piero would lose the reins of government, inherited from his father.

Constitutionally robust and physically strong, Piero was regarded

by the people of Florence as a haughty and even cruel man, who preferred to be feared rather than loved. He was judged as possessing neither the goodness of his brother Giovanni, the cardinal, who would
become pope as Leo X, nor the courtesy and humanity of his other
brother, Giuliano, the future duke of Nemours. Despite the admiration the Florentines held for his father and his two younger brothers,
Piero lost first their affection and then their support for Medici rule.
Hated by his enemies, who were many, Piero even managed to dis-
please his friends and natural allies.

The "dream" or "vision" seemed straightforward enough to
Michelangelo. Among details that were inexplicable, however, he tells
us that Lorenzo had appeared nude under his shabby gown. How
could Michelangelo know this? Yet in dreams things happen that do
not follow "normal" waking logic. Perhaps it occurred to Michelangelo that here was a reference to "naked truth," even though Truth
was regularly portrayed as female—as a master painter of the previous generation, Sandro Botticelli, had depicted her. Michelangelo
interpreted the overall meaning of the dream or, in his words, the "di-
abolical illusion or divine prediction or intense imagination, whatever
it was," as an admonition from beyond the grave, directed ostensibly
at Piero, but in reality at himself. After all, Piero could do nothing to
change things; but Michelangelo could and did.

Although the dream had been engraved on his memory, the
nineteen-year-old Michelangelo never openly claimed it as his own,
even to intimate friends. Instead, he ascribed it to someone else who
also had lived in the Medici Palace on Via Larga, a fellow called "il
Cardiere," the significance of which is uncertain. Lorenzo the Magnificent had prized Cardiere, whose real name no one, not even
Michelangelo, seems to have known, as a musician. To the delight of
dignitaries who were frequent guests, as well as his own sons and
daughters, Lorenzo regularly called upon Cardiere to play the lyre and
sing, improvising as he went along. Lorenzo himself was wont to join
in, singing with "divine furor," according to one witness. And, of

course, Michelangelo was frequently present as well, according to legend at least, prominently seated beside Lorenzo. Yet it was Cardiere, said Michelangelo, who had passed on to him the particulars of the dream. Evidently Michelangelo sought to appear uninvolved in what could have become a sensitive, strictly Medici family matter.

In fact, fearing Piero's unpredictable temper—he was known to explode over a trifle without warning—Michelangelo at first opted not to transmit Lorenzo's solemn warning. Angered, the distraught apparition returned some nights later in a fresher, even more vivid dream, wearing the same ragged gown as before. Lorenzo's shade slapped Michelangelo's cheek smartly for failing to warn Piero as he had been directed.

This time Michelangelo took his mentor's commandment to heart, overcoming, if only temporarily, concern for his personal safety. He set out from Florence on foot intent upon finding Piero at Careggi, where the Medici had a country villa—and where both Cosimo and Lorenzo had died. Careggi, set a few miles from Florence in the foothills of the Apennines, and known for its gentle climate, was the nearest of four Medici villas, all within a radius of twenty miles or so from the Palazzo Signoria. Halfway to Careggi, Michelangelo encountered Piero, who was en route back to the city. Without formalities Michelangelo hailed him, blurting out exactly what he had been instructed to say.

Piero, who had little respect for artists in general and hardly any for Michelangelo, construed the warning as a joke *(beffa)*. He belittled Michelangelo in front of his entourage, leaving the artist deeply ill-at-ease. The encounter made Michelangelo even more apprehensive of Piero, who the previous winter, after Michelangelo had been hanging around the palace for months awaiting a fitting commission, had ordered him to sculpt a snowman in the courtyard of the Medici Palace following an unprecedentedly heavy snowstorm on January 20, 1494.

Piero's chancellor, the severe and humorless Piero Dovizi da Bibbiena, who had earlier served Lorenzo, responded on behalf of his benefactor, suggesting that Michelangelo must have lost his mind. He asked whether the sculptor thought that the great Lorenzo had loved him more than his own flesh and blood, and volunteered that Lorenzo would have appeared to Piero rather than any other person in the entire world. In effect, Bibbiena, known for possessing a sharp tongue *(huomo superbo et maligno)*, told Michelangelo to be off; he may have even added depreciatingly, to get back to his dusty studio and gross tools. The question of il Magnifico's affection for Michelangelo is revealing and confirms claims that such an attachment did indeed exist; whether he preferred Michelangelo or Piero is not the issue. Clearly, he had a genuine affection for Michelangelo in the mind of the artist.

The dream episode came to an abrupt end. Lorenzo never again appeared to Michelangelo or to anyone else. Predictably, Piero de' Medici paid no heed to the warning transmitted by Michelangelo, just as his brother Cardinal Giovanni's advice shortly after their father's death to be "beneficent, liberal, affable, and humane" fell on deaf ears.

Michelangelo, for his part, took the dream with utmost seriousness. After agonizing for two days, he reached a drastic decision. Gathering up his belongings, he left the Medici Palace where he had spent the better part of five years, nearly three with Lorenzo and two with Piero. With Lorenzo's sober warning resounding in his brain, Michelangelo seems to have realized that if the vision were true, Florence was hardly a safe place for him. He abandoned not only the Medici Palace but his beloved Florence, in this the first of many unwelcome separations.

With two companions, Michelangelo crossed the Apennines and headed straight to Venice. After a brief stay in the city on the lagoons, he partially retraced his steps, stopping at Bologna. Not many weeks after his departure, the haughty Piero de' Medici, along with the branch of the family headed by Cosimo il Vecchio, known as *Pater Patriae,* were expelled from the city by its furious residents, and political control of Florence was transferred to populist republicans, including two of Lorenzo's cousins, Giovanni and Lorenzo di Pierfrancesco de' Medici, known as the *Popolani,* who opposed autocratic rule.

Piero was never again to return to Florence—a bitter confirmation of the accuracy of Michelangelo's vision. According to the account of a trusted Medici supporter, Piero de' Medici secretly slipped out of Florence on November 9, 1494, a Sunday, having previously brought valued possessions from the palace down the street to the Medici Gardens in preparation for a hurried departure. His party came first to Bologna. Michelangelo from time to time must have encountered Piero, the very person he had sought to avoid, on Bologna's main square, the expansive Piazza Maggiore, perhaps along with Cardinal Giovanni, who came a little later, as well as Giuliano de' Medici.

The Medici did not remain in Bologna for long, opting to reside in Venice, as their ancestor and the effective founder of Medici power, Cosimo, had done earlier in the century when exiled. Lorenzo's gardens, where Michelangelo had thrived, were sold to the rulers of Bologna, the Bentivoglio, in order to raise cash for Piero's expenses and to protect the family possessions from possible confiscation. Donatello's bronze statues, the *David* and the *Judith and Holofernes,* which had been placed in the palace gardens, were appropriated by the new government in Florence the following year.

DONATELLO, bronze *David,* c. 1435.

Michelangelo must have interpreted the dream warning as Lorenzo's final act of loyal guardianship and goodwill toward him. Even from the grave, Lorenzo reached out to deliver Michelangelo from injury or possible death at the hands of his "enemies."

ARTISTIC ORIGINS

From the start, Michelangelo had to battle his family elders to become an artist. Despite the efforts to set him on the "right" track by giving him a decent education, one that might lead to a decorous and well-compensated position such as that of notary, lawyer, government employee, or shopkeeper, Michelangelo mutinied. He neglected his schooling, lamenting that all he wanted to do was become a painter. (We should remember that his tuition was not an entirely lost cause; he spent about six years at it and must have learned something, including some rudimentary Latin, and he certainly knew how to read and write.) But instead of paying attention to his tutor, Francesco Galatea of Urbino, Michelangelo's mind was focused on drawing, according to his own recollections. His father and his uncle Francesco, who lived in the household, by an admixture of calm reasoning and angry beatings, sought to turn the boy's head from painting. Although in poor straits, the Buonarroti Simoni claimed ancient, noble lineage, and for centuries not a single ancestor had been an artisan. To have a son become a painter was nothing less than a disgrace. Ironically, Michelangelo himself later in life complained about having a brother, Gismondo, who, he wrote, spent his time at the back end of a pair of oxen plowing the fields on the family farm at Settignano.

As the confrontation over the boy's career intensified, his father, Lodovico, a sometime bureaucrat in Florentine governmental service, turned to Lorenzo de' Medici for advice and material assistance. After all, he was a distant relative by marriage of il Magnifico. Presumably the consultation over Lodovico's second-born's future took place in February 1488, shortly before Michelangelo's thirteenth birthday on March 6. Il Magnifico arranged for Michelangelo to be placed in the workshop *(bottega)* of Domenico Ghirlandaio and his two brothers, who conducted the best organized and most profitable painters' shop in the city. The alternatives were the *bottega* of Cosimo Rosselli, who was a fine and upstanding man but not a particularly good painter, or that of Sandro Botticelli, a very good painter indeed, but a man who did not seem to deal effectively with pupils. (In future years, Michelangelo would enjoy cordial relations with the painter of the *Birth of Venus* and the *Primavera,* although Botticelli's vision as an artist differed dramatically from his own.)

Lorenzo de' Medici would have encouraged Lodovico to make the best of his son's determination. He likely explained to the distraught father the futility of opposing the boy's aspirations and at the same time offered practical help by arranging to provide him with the very best training available. In this way, even as a painter, Michelangelo would be primed for economic success. For il Magnifico, that meant finding an apprenticeship with Domenico Ghirlandaio. As luck would have it, Ghirlandaio was at that very moment frescoing the immense choir of Santa Maria Novella under the patronage of the Tornabuoni, the family of Lorenzo's mother. Thus il Magnifico could negotiate to place the boy with Ghirlandaio—and Domenico was in no position to refuse. Lorenzo saw to it that Lodovico Buonarroti would obtain decent compensation for the boy's services, totaling 24 florins over three years: the first year 6, the second 8, and the third 10, the equivalent of the rental of a modest studio for that length of time. For a beginner, such significant compensation was uncommon. The contract, Lorenzo must have intended, would placate Lodovico and at the same time offer Michelangelo a certain dignity in the eyes of the family. The Ghirlandaio brothers, for their part, were required to teach him to paint.

Even before the arrangements were codified, Michelangelo had been hanging around the bustling work area *(cantiere)* at Santa Maria Novella, where the Ghirlandaios had installed scaffolding so they could fresco the imposing choir with stories from the lives of John the Baptist and Mary. Francesco Granacci, Michelangelo's good friend from his neighborhood, the quarter of Santa Croce, was al-

LEONARDO DA VINCI,
Lorenzo il Magnifico, profile head, c. 1480.

ready an advanced apprentice with Ghirlandaio, and the previous year, as a boy, Michelangelo had made himself useful by running an errand for the shop. Domenico may already have been familiar with Michelangelo's ambitions, for Granacci would have praised his friend's talent and his desire to become a painter.

It was Granacci who gave Michelangelo an engraving of the *Temptation of St. Anthony* by Martin Schongauer to copy. The German printmaker and painter was much admired in those days for his fertile imagination in depicting esoteric creatures. Granacci also provided Michelangelo with a gessoed wooden board, tempera colors, and brushes, proposing that he try his hand at creating a painting from Schongauer's work, which he eagerly did. Around the contorted, long-bearded Anthony in the print was a collection of strange flying demons and devils who were tormenting the harried hermit saint. Michelangelo searched high and low among the stalls in the fish market, scrutinizing the colors of eyes and bodies for tones he could import into Schongauer's monochromatic invention. He rendered the creatures' wings to conform to the gills of diverse fish he found on display.

Apparently this, Michelangelo's first excursion with colors and brushes, was generated before he was officially enrolled in the shop and may even have been a demonstration. The picture, which has long since disappeared, was considered marvelous, leading Domenico Ghirlandaio to brag that it was produced by one of his pupils, Michelangelo recalled proudly a half century later, perhaps with some exaggeration.

Despite Granacci's encouragement, Michelangelo felt uncomfortable with Domenico Ghirlandaio almost from the beginning of his apprenticeship, for he sensed (unjustifiably, Domenico's son, Ridolfo Ghirlandaio, adamantly asserted in retrospect) that the master was jealous of the pupil's talent. Michelangelo, on his part, could easily have conjured the Tuscan proverb: "Jealousy is the sin of the small-minded" *(L'invidia è un peccato da minchioni)*. Even after Michelangelo had been taken into the shop, Domenico seemed reluctant to

MARTIN SCHONGAUER, *Temptation of St. Anthony,* detail, 1470s.

lend the new apprentice the *bottega*'s copybooks, containing drawings gathered for the purpose of teaching. Either he feared that Michelangelo would make fun of their efforts or that he would seek not to imitate but to improve upon what he found.

On one occasion, Ghirlandaio did turn over to the boy a portrait head he had painted years before, for copying, an exercise that was part of the normal routine. Michelangelo, to demonstrate his own brilliance and perhaps to embarrass the master in the process, switched his copy with the original portrait. To make the counterfeit more effective, Michelangelo even doctored his panel with smoke so that it would appear the same age as Ghirlandaio's. This trick, while it might have enhanced Michelangelo's reputation with the other apprentices *(garzoni),* could hardly have endeared him with the master.

From the evidence that has come down, and his total failure to give any credit whatsoever to Ghirlandaio, we may assume that Michelangelo was an unappreciative and, very likely, an unteachable pupil, at least for Ghirlandaio. As history has also concluded, Michelangelo must have regarded Domenico, along with his brothers (Davide and Benedetto), as skillful painters who were nonetheless pedestrian when it came to invention and expression. Besides, while in the shop, Michelangelo's interest shifted from painting to sculpture, and the Ghirlandaios knew nothing whatsoever about marble carving. They excelled at producing prestigious, highly finished and handsomely wrought altarpieces and lucrative, brightly colored frescoes.

Michelangelo was unbending in all matters related to art, especially as the demands of his mission became clearer. We might also guess that fresco painting, which was then the principal activity of the Ghirlandaio *bottega,* increasingly bored him; he may have disliked the built-in uncertainties and limitations of the medium, in which one is never quite certain exactly how the colors will appear when dry and where adjustments and corrections are difficult to make once the paint is applied. This youthful inattention would later prove costly when Michelangelo was forced to compensate for the lessons he neglected while in the shop. In working for Pope Julius II in Rome on the ceiling of the Sistine Chapel (1508–12), the artist had to fall back on trial and error, indistinct recollections, imprecise pointers by temporary assistants, and the advice of architect and mason friends. Had he been more attentive when apprenticed to the Ghirlandaios, technical problems that caused him considerable distress in Rome could undoubtedly have been avoided.

Michelangelo's realization that sculpture rather than painting was the medium best suited to his natural inclinations probably came upon him gradually, as his study of the human figure evolved into a fixation. He must have became increasingly impatient in the painters' shop, but the fault was not all that of the Ghirlandaios. It probably mattered little with which master painter Michelangelo had been placed, although in terms of temperament he might have preferred to have shared company with a painter like Piero di Cosimo, a confirmed eccentric who lived like a hermit in the middle of bustling Florence. The Ghirlandaios must have seemed too unimaginative, too conventional, too tiresome for the budding Michelangelo. Nor were they risk-takers like Piero di Cosimo or Botticelli; nothing about them was the least strange or bizarre. Instead, the Ghirlandaio brothers were predictable, profit-oriented craftsmen. On his part, Domenico, as head of the shop, might have resented Michelangelo's presence, since the boy probably had been thrust on him by Lorenzo de' Medici, though Granacci may have had a hand too. Seen in these terms, a tense, potentially explosive situation was defused when Michelangelo was permitted to break the contract in a city where business contracts were sacred; surely, both parties had reason to celebrate. And once again Lorenzo il Magnifico must have interceded behind the scenes on Michelangelo's behalf.

If his father and his uncle hated painting, we can imagine what they must have thought about Michelangelo's change of heart in

favor of sculpture. For them, being a sculptor really meant being a stone carver *(scarpellino)*, a manual laborer who produced window frames, pediments, balustrades, and carved decorations, and yes, a statue or two. There were many such men, like the neighbors in Settignano, a zone famous for precisely this activity. They had disfiguring calluses on their hands and were covered with powered marble dust from head to toe at the end of a day's work. A sculptor looked like a baker, Leonardo da Vinci was to observe disparagingly— possibly with Michelangelo in mind—and would have been on the same social level as the husband of Michelangelo's wet nurse.

Again, Michelangelo was unswayable. When he went off to the Medici Gardens after leaving the Ghirlandaios' *bottega,* the objections at home may well have subsided, partly out of exhaustion and partly because they recognized that Michelangelo was being taken under the wing of Florence's most influential citizen. Still, his father Lodovico continued to harbor his disapproval, which surfaced in correspondence from time to time over the next decades.

We do not know exactly what caused the change in Michelangelo's aspirations. Somewhere along the line, perhaps when Michelangelo went about the city to draw, a conversion took place. In the center of town he would have seen an unprecedented collection of majestic statues, including some impressive figures by Donatello—a refined *St. George,* an imposing *St. Mark,* a grim but expressive *Zuccone* (the figure that the Florentines used to swear by), and the dramatic *Abraham,* all carved in Carrara marble. These formed a kind of informal school of their own, and when Raphael came to Florence for the first time, he was also very much taken by them.

Michelangelo began to recognize that painting was a kind of lie, an illusion, a visual but ingenious and engaging trick. As Benvenuto Cellini would write in the next century, "An excellent painter is like

DONATELLO, *St. George,* c. 1415–17.

a liar, who feigns the appearance of veracity, hoping that his lie is very beautiful and very pleasing. . . ." Painting could make a representation appear to be three-dimensional, but a painted fresco or picture was truly a flat surface. Sculpture, on the contrary, was by definition three-dimensional, so a sculptural image was precisely what it appeared to be. To make sculpture signifies creating figures that occupy the same space as the carver and that compete and combat with the spectator for their spatial existence. Michelangelo had to leave the Ghirlandaios. And where better to develop his inclination toward sculpture than in the Medici Gardens?

THE MEDICI GARDENS

Michelangelo was now drawn into a Medici family circle where he seems to have shared a place of near equality with Lorenzo's closest blood relatives, his sons Piero, Giovanni, and Giuliano; his nephew Giulio; and his four daughters; not to mention his mother's relations, the Tornabuoni. Also within easy reach were a cluster of philosophers and poets, including Marsilio Ficino, Angelo Poliziano, and Giovanni Pico della Mirandola—all of whom must have been familiar to Michelangelo, though to what degree can only be guessed. Ficino, the oldest of the three, had astrological interests, although an ordained priest. He had an impact upon an entire generation of Medici children, including Lorenzo, whom he outlived (Ficino died in 1499). A devoted translator and a reviver of Plato, he spearheaded the formation of the Platonic Academy in Florence and conflated Greek and Egyptian religious ideas with Christianity.

Poliziano, who was a particularly accomplished Greek scholar, also served as a teacher in the household, being the master of Piero di Lorenzo; Poliziano wrote an important poem about

Lorenzo il Magnifico's brother Giuliano, entitled *Stanze per la giostra del magnifico Giuliano de' Medici,* and he composed the first Italian pastoral drama, *La favola d'Orfeo.* The nobleman Pico della Mirandola, the youngest of the three, was the most daring, esoteric, and wide-ranging in his thoughts, some of which were considered heretical.

The impact on Michelangelo's part of rubbing shoulders with these intellectuals at the Medici "court" is easily overestimated. He was not only totally preoccupied with the challenges of his art but was very young and relatively uneducated by their standards, in that he seems to have known only a little Latin. Yet the presence of such remarkable luminaries, and Lorenzo himself, must have been exhilarating. Besides, il Magnifico was for Michelangelo a fountain of ideas: for his sculpture, his poetry, and his mind. Each heady day would have been rich in discoveries for the young Buonarroti. Lorenzo was much more than a mentor: he must have been a prestigious guide during Michelangelo's crucial adolescent years.

The Medici Gardens, protected from city noise and the prying eyes of inquisitive passersby by formidable walls, were purchased by Lorenzo in 1475, the same year his son Giovanni (and Michelangelo) were born. The gardens stood at the corner of the Piazza San Marco, opposite the church, and consisted of a group of low masonry structures. We can imagine that the main quarters—a country house or casino of sorts—were surrounded by cypresses, which made the area particularly agreeable in summer. Several loggias provided space for the young and aspiring artists to work in. Sleeping quarters were also available, and Michelangelo probably lived in a room on the property along with several other young men until he was brought into the palace.

Angelo Poliziano had rooms in the garden attached to the Medici Gardens that belonged to Lorenzo's wife, Clarice Orsini. Known as the "new Homer," and a regular companion to the young men who worked in the Medici Gardens, Poliziano offered them erudite explanations of classical mythology. It may have been Poliziano who explained to Michelangelo the story of Laocoön, the clairvoyant priest of Troy who distrusted the giant wooden horse the Greeks had placed outside his city. Virgil recounted that as punishment, Laocoön's two young sons were crushed by sea snakes, who then squeezed him to death, too. The myth was rendered in a collaboration between three Greek sculptors. Michelangelo must have been particularly impressed by the literary description of the sculpture and the assumption that the group was carved from a single block of marble (although, in reality, it is not), which he would recall a decade later when the statue was unearthed in Rome.

Presumably the artists of the gardens were provided with small stipends as well as meals. They spent hours drawing from the antiquities, but also in copying contemporary sculptures gathered there. Some of the objects had already been collected by Cosimo, others by Piero the Gouty, while the remainder were acquired by Lorenzo il Magnifico. Headless, armless, and legless torsos or torso-less heads, chiefly Roman, all inevitably without noses, were scattered throughout the area. Sometimes missing portions had been appended by expert sculptors like Verrocchio and Mino da Fiesole, or for the sake of practice by the young aspirants themselves.

Two fairly complete life-size ancient statues of *Marsyas,* one of red marble and the other of white, seem to have been favored by Michelangelo in his early explorations in the gardens and in the Medici Palace gardens down the street, to which he also must have had access. Marsyas, a flautist and a primitive deity of the woodlands, had challenged Apollo to a musical contest, only to be skinned alive for his hubris. The representation of a flayed body, stretched by its own weight, hanging from a tree had rich potentialities for a budding sculptor just starting to study human anatomy. Michelangelo would easily have realized that the body could also be effectively transposed into a crucified Christ, hanging from the arms of the Cross. The

Roman artist, *Marsyas.*

Marsyas statues continued to reverberate in the artist's mind. Forty years later, in the *Last Judgment* fresco on the altar wall of the Sistine Chapel, he depicted St. Bartholomew. On the skin that he holds, Michelangelo roughly sketched in his own face; the saint's body as he painted it actually shows no raw flesh, perhaps indicating that the saint's skin had miraculously grown back since he had been flayed.

Soon after seeing the two *Marsyas* statues, one of which is thought to have been restored by Donatello and the other by Verrocchio or Mino da Fiesole, Michelangelo had ample opportunity to question Poliziano about the myth. He could have identified with the hapless Greek satyr: like Marsyas, Michelangelo was prepared to make any sacrifice in the name of art.

Together with the Roman sculptures, a smattering of original Greek work was available in the gardens for study—marbles

Cosimo's agents had purchased directly in the Greek isles, upon the advice of Cosimo's sculptor friend, Donatello. But of still greater attraction for Michelangelo must have been works by contemporary Tuscan sculptors, especially those by Donatello himself. Michelangelo knew nearly every work by Donatello available in Florence. His own precocious explorations tended toward marble carving, and to the extent that he ever directly emulated anyone, it was Donatello. This is not to say that Michelangelo was above criticizing his hero for, of all things, not finishing his sculptures.

Michelangelo would have been familiar with Donatello's enviable friendship with Cosimo *Pater Patriae:* sculptor and patron, both about the same age, seem to have been distantly related, and Cosimo had provided that his companion be buried near his own final resting place in the crypt of San Lorenzo, below the main altar. Donatello came from an ancient family, the Bardi, much as Michelangelo claimed for Buonarroti Simoni, the Canossa. During those days in the gardens Michelangelo could have aspired to establish a relationship with Cosimo's grandson, Lorenzo, much like the one Donatello had achieved with Cosimo, in spite of the twenty-six-year difference in age between Michelangelo and Lorenzo.

From hearsay, Michelangelo must have been aware that another artist once active in the Medici Gardens had had a familiar rapport with the same patron some years before. Leonardo, son of the notary ser Piero di Antonio from nearby Vinci, was a painter who had won Lorenzo il Magnifico's recognition years before. Since Leonardo left the city back in 1482 to settle in Milan, no one in Florence seemed to have much concrete information about him. Rumor had it that he had been sent by Lorenzo, as a personal representative or possibly even a spy for Florence. He was known to have been in Verrocchio's workshop back in the late 1460s and 70s, where he received a wide-ranging introduction not only to painting but to sculpture and the goldsmith's art as well. Leonardo apparently made occasional trips

MICHELANGELO, copy after *Profile Portrait of Alessandro, Count of Canossa*, detail, 1520s. • In a learned witticism, Michelangelo drew a dog gnawing on a bone on the count's helmet. Canossa actually regarded Michelangelo as a relative and this was a reference to the name—*cane* (dog) and *ossa* (bone)—that serves to solidify Michelangelo's claims to a noble origin.

back to Florence, and in one instance, he offered advice about the construction of the main hall of the Palazzo Signoria shortly after the expulsion of Piero. But all in all Leonardo remained a mystery to his Florentine contemporaries until he resettled there. As it happened, Michelangelo's first face-to-face encounter with him could not have taken place until after Leonardo's definitive return to Florence from Milan via Venice, which more or less coincided with Michelangelo's reentry from Rome in 1501.

Both Leonardo and Michelangelo of course made gigantic contributions to the definition of art in their time and ever since, although it should be stressed that Leonardo (born in 1452) was twenty-three years older and consequently belonged to the previous generation. On only one project, the mural decorations for the Hall of the Great Council in the Palazzo Signoria, did their activities overlap. Both were awarded commissions by the Florentine government for a large wall painting in mid-1504: Leonardo for a depiction of equestrian combat, the *Battle of Anghiari;* Michelangelo for the *Battle of Cascina,* illustrating Florentine foot soldiers being alerted

MICHELANGELO, study for the *Battle of Cascina,* 1504.

MARCANTONIO RAIMONDI, *Three Figures* (from Michelangelo's *Battle of Cascina*). Engraving.

to an imminent enemy attack in a Pisan campaign. The head-on confrontation afforded by the assignment of analogous subjects could have been one of the most spectacular artistic competitions imaginable. But in the end, neither artist completed his work.

During the years Michelangelo was growing up, a confusing and imprecise account of the mythical Leonardo circulated in Florence. His pictures were practically unknown. The finest painting he left behind was never finished: a squarish altarpiece depicting the *Adoration of the Magi,* originally projected for a monastery a few miles outside Florence, at San Donato a Scopeto, but which ended up in a Florentine palace. Florentine artists knew that Leonardo had secured a place in the court of Lodovico il Moro, ruler of Milan, and that there he produced a painting, the soft and atmospheric *Madonna of the Rocks,* which caused quite a stir among his Lombard colleagues. All in all, however, Leonardo was regarded as more of a wizard than a painter, famed for knowing about every imaginable subject from geology to comparative anatomy. He even had a certain talent as a musician.

The drawings, paintings, and models Lorenzo made available to the habitués of the Medici Gardens were mostly created by artists who had worked for the Medici family. They were part of an art collection, most of which was housed in the palace on Via Larga. Among the pieces were works by such artists as Filippo Brunelleschi, affectionately known as "Pippo," who was the first architect to operate in the new "Renaissance" style, and the creator of the new Church of San Lorenzo for the Medici. Brunelleschi also engineered the majestic cupola of the Duomo and he is regarded as the inventor of modern linear perspective.

Masaccio, a young friend of Brunelleschi's, almost single-handedly formulated the Renaissance painting style, and was a particular Michelangelo favorite. Other examples included paintings by Paolo Uccello, a master the Medici favored for their palace, who was much taken with potentialities of perspective for rendering figures in space. Of a more delicate artistic flavor, and especially revered by the Medici, was the Dominican Fra Angelico, who had decorated the Medici-sponsored Church of San Marco, and frescoed the cells in the convent attached to it, on the square not far from the Medici Gardens. These masters from an earlier generation were properly regarded as being the founders of the new language of art, and their work must have offered Michelangelo many lessons, as well as pride in his Florentine origins.

More recent pictures by the popular Florentine Sandro Botticelli and by Andrea Mantegna, the highly respected painter from northern Italy who was still active in the Mantuan court of the Gonzaga, were also available among the Medici holdings. A handful of Flemish paintings executed in the new medium of oil were there as well. Since the Italians remained attached mainly to painting in tempera (in which ground pigment was mixed with an egg binder), the luminous oil paintings created considerable fascination, and a few Italian masters tried to emulate the technique. Jan van Eyck's tiny *St. Jerome in His Study* was among the prizes that Lorenzo il Magnifico might have ceremoniously unveiled from time to time. Meticulously protected in a specially fashioned leather pouch, it could easily have been brought to the gardens in his pocket.

The Medici Gardens have been referred to loosely as a school for painters and sculptors. Yet there was no curriculum and those in attendance were of varying ages and stages in their respective careers. A few were already masters in their own right. Rather than a school, much less an art academy, the gardens really functioned as a dignified place to work under the discerning eye of Lorenzo, a refuge where full-fledged and aspiring artists could have space and tranquility together with a degree of privilege. One can reconstruct conditions in which the younger artists were encouraged by Maestro Bertoldo di Giovanni—whom Lorenzo had placed in charge of the antiquities the Medici had collected—to draw, as Bertoldo's teacher Donatello was known to have advocated. *Disegno* (loosely meaning "drawing"), long regarded as the basis of the visual arts, as the bridge between hand and mind, encompasses the concept of form making or imaging. Later, when he himself was in a position to guide aspiring artists, Michelangelo insisted on the importance of drawing. In exasperation, he once scribbled on a scrap of paper a reminder to a particularly doltish pupil, Antonio Mini: "Draw Antonio, Draw Antonio, Draw Antonio, and don't waste time" *(disegnia Antonio, disegnia Antonio, disegna* [sic] *e non perder tempo).*

Strict distinctions between moderns and the ancients probably were not always maintained in the gardens. Bertoldo, a modeler and bronze caster with limited if any experience in stone carving, was regarded as a specialist in Greek and Roman sculpture. Yet he would have called the young men's attention to Donatello's marble statues all over Florence, and especially those in niches on the Duomo, on the bell tower, and on the exterior of Orsanmichele, the Florentine Guild's chapel: the self-assured *St. Mark* and the lithe, intense *St. George.* Donatello's reputation saw a robust revival toward the end of the fifteenth century, coinciding with Michelangelo's evolution as an artist.

Considering his orientation as a caster, Bertoldo also must have admired Lorenzo Ghiberti's complex bronze reliefs on the so-called *Gates of Paradise,* the name Michelangelo is said to have used to describe the east doors of the Baptistery, those facing the Duomo. Ten gilt bronze historical panels depicted events from the Old Testament: scenes from the Creation, and others showing Solomon, which were incidentally to serve Michelangelo in good stead as he later plotted out the Sistine Chapel ceiling frescoes. Michelangelo could hardly have failed to prize Ghiberti's craft, his control over bronze as a medium, for he knew all too well the intricacies and unpredictability of casting. About fifteen years later, Michelangelo would experience his share of tribulations when casting a huge portrait of Pope Julius II and a *David* in bronze for a French official, neither of which has survived.

LORENZO IL MAGNIFICO

Michelangelo's life changed fundamentally when in the winter of 1489–90 he entered the orbit of Lorenzo il Magnifico, and eventually became a frequenter of the Medici Palace on the Via Larga, known today as Via Cavour. Access to the palace was the consequence of Michelangelo's frequent communion with il Magnifico, which is assumed in a hypothetical reconstruction of events. The personalities of the two men harmonized, despite the differences in their age and social status. Legend has it that the older man relished demonstrating and explicating to the younger, as a skilled teacher might to an appreciative and talented pupil.

From what can be deduced in hindsight, the older ruler and the young artist had an uncommon, though short-lived, rapport, at a formative time in Michelangelo's life as an impressionable adolescent. Michelangelo does not seem to have been especially dazzled by il Magnifico's worldly authority. He may have been too young and inexperienced fully to appreciate political realities and his relationship with Lorenzo was, in essence, private, personal, of the mind. Lorenzo was not only Florence's first citizen but one of the most prestigious heads of state in Europe. His impact rested partly on uncommon gifts of statesmanship, partly on Florence's central position as a balance among conflicting interests in Italy. The power he wielded far exceeded that of the sword, however: behind him stood the mighty Medici bank, with branches from Barcelona, Lyon, and Paris to London and Naples, at a time when banking was at the heart of all commerce.

Through informal and private encounters, Lorenzo managed to exert a tangible impact upon the entire fabric of Florentine society as his father and grandfather had done before him. He cultivated a faithful clientele—one that extended far beyond the bounds of clan and *amici*. Loyalty, an essential component of Medici power and of the maintenance of an authority based upon unwritten agreements rather than constitutional provisions, was expected in return.

Lorenzo was the nexus of innumerable requests for favors, for jobs, for money, for advice each year in his unofficial but very real capacity as universal *patronus* and, more pointedly, as Florence's *Maestro della Bottega,* as he was frequently called—literally, "head of the place." Marsilio Ficino, the philosopher, dubbed him "servant of the country."

Physically, Lorenzo was of medium height, with broad shoulders and a solid and robust body; probably he was a shade taller than the young Michelangelo. Of dark complexion, Lorenzo's appearance was essentially somber, betraying a grave countenance. His voice was unpleasantly rough, since he talked through his nose, which was narrow, sloping distinctively upward at the tip and flattened at the base. This attribute, especially noticeable in profile, seems to have been inherited from his mother, Lucrezia Tornabuoni. Moreover, he lacked a sense of smell. Among other defects, Lorenzo was myopic, his eyes bulging outward; his poor eyesight was a genetic characteristic that he, in turn, passed on to his second son, Giovanni.

Lorenzo spent as much as five hours every day dictating his vast correspondence, of which nearly twenty thousand letters for recommendations written to Lorenzo are still extant. At times he became so exhausted that he would have his brother Giuliano (until he was murdered in the Pazzi uprising of 1478 by local enemies of the Medici family) take over. Among Lorenzo's more delicate tasks was seeing to it that dowries were provided for young women from impecunious families. Can it be pure coincidence that Michelangelo, in his own philanthropy later in life, was to do the same, albeit in secret and on a more modest scale? Lorenzo also sought to ensure that the humble members of society would be treated well in the courts. Indeed, there was hardly a facet of the social, cultural, and, of course, the political life of Florence where Lorenzo failed to exert his presence. He especially enjoyed the company of biting and witty men *(faceti e mordaci)*, and childish games, more than might be expected from a man of his position.

Lorenzo operated strategically to attain one prime objective: the continuation and reinforcement of the Medici family's power in Florence and Italy. He genuinely loved his seven children—three sons, Piero, Giovanni, and Giuliano, and four daughters, Lucrezia, Maddalena, Contessina, and Luigia—and he kept a sharp eye on them from infancy to adolescence. Lorenzo was particularly concerned with their education, despite the heavy commercial and political demands upon his time.

To ensure the future well-being of the family, Lorenzo sought to place his children in positions of influence. He prepared the oldest, Piero, to take over the family banking business together with the governance of Florence. (A strategy not successful for long, due to Piero's unsavory character, the shifting political realities in Florence, and the entrance of foreign powers into Italy.)

Lorenzo was strikingly successful in arranging for his second son, Giovanni, to be created cardinal on March 9, 1489, which he did by skillfully manipulating the pope, Innocent VIII. The operation was necessarily carried out in secret because Giovanni was only thirteen at the time, notoriously young to achieve such dignity. Lorenzo had prepared the ground well. Michelangelo must have been amazed that the rotund Giovanni, with whom he often sat at table, and who was his junior by nearly a year, had already been so honored. Although the appointment was only made official in a public ceremony a few weeks before Lorenzo died three years later, there was a good deal of talk in Florence about Giovanni's new position, which must be regarded as the crown of il Magnifico's family achievements. Lorenzo was well aware of the magnitude of his accomplishment: in Machiavelli's words, the cardinalate was recognized as the "stairway to power which could raise the family fortunes to the heavens" *(Il che fu una scala da potere fare salire la sua casa in cielo)*. Giovanni not only went on to become Pope Leo X, but his cousin Giulio, the illegitimate son of Lorenzo's murdered brother Giuliano, whom Lorenzo also raised in his household, became Clement VII, further cementing the family's power.

Lorenzo's third son, Giuliano, named after the uncle who was murdered, was less illustrious, perhaps due to the limited time that Lorenzo had left to provide for him. Like his father, Giuliano tried his hand at writing poetry and was something of a patron of the arts: he had the good sense to have picked up his father's sponsorship of the unpredictable Leonardo da Vinci. Il Magnifico once guardedly related an evaluation of his sons, which effectively coincides with history's, to a Venetian friend: "I have three sons, a decent one, a wise one, and a crazy one. The decent one is Giuliano, the wise one Giovanni, and the crazy one, Piero with a swelled head."

Of Lorenzo's four daughters, Lucrezia, the eldest, was married to the powerful Jacopo Salviati; Maddalena, the second, to Franceschetto Cibò, the natural and thoroughly disagreeable son of Pope Innocent VIII, who had provided for the unprecedented appointment of Giovanni as cardinal; and the sensitive, gentle Contessina to Piero Ridolfi. Luigia, the youngest, was intended to marry Lorenzo's cousin Giovanni di Pierfrancesco de' Medici, but she died prematurely, at age eleven. Giovanni went on in another marriage to have a son known as Giovanni dell Bande Nere, a professional soldier who was the father of another Cosimo, the duke, giving rise to the new branch of the Medici in the sixteenth century. The marriages, as was il Magnifico's intention, functioned to expand the Medici interconnections with influential and prosperous families, and had Luigia not died, he would also have succeeded in reuniting the Medici branches.

If Lorenzo il Magnifico did extremely well on the whole in providing for the glory of the Medici line, guaranteeing himself an ample niche in history, his friendship and early connection with Michelangelo would prove equally momentous for his historical reputation. Through the persona of Michelangelo, for whom he created the appropriate conditions for the artist's early development, Lorenzo managed to leave (almost by default) as lasting a mark on the cultural landscape of Italy as he had done on the political one.

How did Lorenzo's efforts compare with those of his illustrious grandfather, Cosimo? In terms of architectural patronage, the *Pater Patriae* must be given the nod. Cosimo was responsible for prestigious buildings and churches, including the very palace on Via Larga where Lorenzo lived, as well the total rebuilding of the Medici church, San Lorenzo. The Old Sacristy proved a potent model for later Renaissance architecture. Begun around 1420, the Old Sacristy functioned as a repository for the tomb of Cosimo's mother and father, Picarda Bueri and Giovanni de' Medici. Designed by Filippo Brunelleschi, decorated with sculptures by Donatello, an unbeatable combination, it became the template for Michelangelo one hundred years later when designing the New Sacristy for the same church, in which he created the Medici Tombs. The Library at San Marco was also built under Cosimo's patronage. And he saw to the rebuilding of the church and the historic monastery of San Marco, where Fra Angelico was to paint, where Cosimo himself maintained a cell, and where decades later the preacher Savonarola was to live.

Lorenzo's main attempt at large-scale construction was a fairly remote country villa at Poggio a Caiano, and even that remained incomplete at the time of his death. If second to Cosimo in architectural patronage, Lorenzo did devote considerable energy to the expansion of Florence. Recognizing that significant empty spaces within the city walls were still without habitation, he arranged for new streets and new housing.

The times, the roles, and the accomplishments of grandson and grandfather were understandably distinct. Lorenzo established the family in a pan-Italian rather than a more strictly Tuscan context and he performed at a diplomatic level unthinkable for Cosimo. In contrast to his grandfather, too, Lorenzo was endowed with eloquence, notwithstanding his unpleasant voice. Cosimo is said to have been rather inept in his speech and rarely spoke in public, perhaps for that reason.

To increase the security of the Florentine state, Lorenzo sought to shore up defenses on all sides. He strengthened the Apennine town of Firenzuola, which faced the Bolognese on the north in a direct line with the Medici family seat at Caffaggiolo. Toward the south, Lorenzo fortified Poggio Imperiale, a castle in the Val d'Elsa, offering protection from any potential threats from Siena in an area not far from where Michelangelo was to purchase a farm. Besides, Lorenzo acquired the towns of Pietrasanta and Seravezza, with their valuable marble quarries which Michelangelo was to frequent in later decades, thereby effectively closing off the coast road to the Genoese or other menace emanating from that direction. As for potential threats from the Arno Valley, he was able by means of clever arrangements with the established political powers such as the rulers of Perugia to maintain peaceful relations. His reign was a period of peace and security in which the people were united and lived in relative harmony. Tournaments, theatrical performances, and triumphal displays in the style of the Romans were regularly offered, giving the Florence of Michelangelo's youth a festive atmosphere.

Lorenzo respected anyone who excelled in art, but he gave special consideration to the writers, poets, and philosophers. He founded a university in Pisa, a commercial city that became part of the Florentine state in 1406, where young men could be educated. Further, he patronized the poet Poliziano, who tutored his children, and Cristofano Landino, the Dante specialist. Another intellectual whose company Lorenzo relished was the young nobleman Pico della Mirandola, whom even the pragmatic historian Machiavelli was able to describe as practically divine *(uomo quasi che divino)*. Pico had come to Florence in 1484 so as to be close to Lorenzo and the Medici favorite, Marsilio Ficino. Lorenzo also sponsored poetry, his own favored expression, as well as music, and to a lesser extent, painting and sculpture, which were encouraged by his "infinite liberality and abundant provisions for able men," according to another contemporary historian, Francesco Guicciardini. But it was his prudence *(prudenzia)*, which increased year by year, that was Lorenzo's most admired attribute.

Though a lively commentator in public and in private, Lorenzo had his enemies, too. Indeed, some thought him arrogant or vainglorious, determined to win at all costs, even in trivial children's games. After the Pazzi uprising, in which his beloved brother Giuliano was killed and he barely escaped with his own life, Lorenzo became fundamentally distrustful. He kept a tighter rein on the government, a change that gave rise to accusations of tyranny. Among other weaknesses, many argued, was his failure in the management of the bank-

BERTOLDO DI GIOVANNI, *Medal of the Pazzi Conspiracy,* obverse with the head of Lorenzo il Magnifico, 1478.

ing business, which again reveals a contrast to Cosimo. When Lorenzo ran short of money, he borrowed substantial sums from his cousins, the sons of Pierfrancesco de' Medici, and was required to cede important properties to them.

As Guicciardini put it, "He was libidinous, amorous and faithful in his loves, which would last for a number of years." Lorenzo's detractors accused him of having been inordinately devoted to the joys of Venus, beginning with an adolescent romance with a newly married woman, Lucrezia Donati. She became his Beatrice, his Laura. Gossip concerning Lorenzo's alleged passion for Bartolomea de' Nasi, wife of Donato Benci, supposedly his last great love, also circulated in the city and may have reached Michelangelo's ears. Though said to be gracious and charming, the woman was anything but beautiful. Lorenzo was nonetheless described as being so obsessed with her that he would ride out in the middle of the night for illicit encounters. Unsympathetic observers thought it absurd that a man of such reputation and prudence should be infatuated in his fortieth year with a woman neither young nor beautiful. However, the account of this affair with Bartolomea may have been the pure invention of Lorenzo's enemies to discredit him.

THE MEDICI PALACE

The Medici Palace was known as "Cosimo's palace" because it had been originally designed for Cosimo by Michelozzo di Bartolommeo, Donatello's longtime partner, provided an abundance of rewards. The boundless contents were equal to the fine physical structure. A treasure trove of mysterious and exotic objects was laid open to Michelangelo by Lorenzo, who, we can guess, unfolded their secrets patiently but not without considerable ceremony.

Lorenzo never tired, we must assume, of introducing Michelangelo to the splendors of his collection. This exposure to things rare and beautiful—unicorn horns, elephant tusks, exotic instruments constructed from animal trophies—constituted a vital component in Michelangelo's visual preparation as an aspiring artist. Contemporary works of art, together with the Greek and Roman sculptures, were far and away the most valued Medici possessions (with the exception of jewelry); they included figures, heads, vases, cameos, medals, coins, and relief plaques.

Although he had only a smattering of Latin and no Greek at all as far as we know, Michelangelo would have encountered the classical world formally through the Medicis' collection of ancient gems and cameos. Both Lorenzo's grandfather and his father had acquired rare manuscripts and precious objects from the ancient world.

The collection also contained pictures by the best masters of earlier times, including the immortal Giotto, the first "modern" Italian painter, whose memorial marble portrait in the Duomo had been commissioned by Lorenzo; and even some wonderful miniature mosaic paintings by Near Eastern artists constructed of fine stone chips. A pair of wood tempera panels depicting *St. Peter* and *St. Paul* by Masaccio, now lost, were regarded as remarkably lifelike; the sturdy proportions and dignified composure of the figures would have further confirmed Michelangelo's exalted estimate of his predecessor's vision.

The main sitting room on the ground floor *(la camera grande terrena detta la camera di Lorenzo),* where Lorenzo often received dignitaries as his father and his grandfather had done before him, was dominated by huge paintings by Paolo Uccello. These striking panels illustrated the Battle of San Romano, in which Florentine forces defeated a military coalition led by the Sienese, marking a singular victory under Cosimo's rule. Uccello, the devotee of pictorial perspective, rendered the battle like a parade leading up to a ceremonial joust, an activity relished by Lorenzo and his brother Giuliano, who kept armor, lances, together with fanciful helmets, swords, daggers, and gloves, scattered about the room and indeed throughout the palace. Michelangelo could have recalled these later when he had to depict Medici commanders for the tombs in the New Sacristy of San Lorenzo. In another room Michelangelo could have seen a painting set into the back of a chair *(spalliera)* showing a tournament in which Lorenzo had taken part, which, tradition had it, had been painted by Masaccio's brother (Lo Scheggia).

Uccello arranged the earth-colored horses and their riders in complicated configurations within expansive, unnaturalistic landscapes. Located well above eye level in the ample chamber, the bloated images seemed to float illusionistically off the walls and intrude upon the actual space of the room. These could hardly have been among Michelangelo's favorites, however. When, a decade and a half later, he was assigned by the Florentine government to produce a scene of his own depicting the Battle of Cascina for the main hall of the Palazzo Signoria, Michelangelo's solution was altogether different from Uccello's emblematic, decorative, and fanciful treatment.

Part of the same series as the *Battle of San Romano* were two other large pictures by Uccello, a *Judgment of Paris* and a *Battle Between Dragons and Lions,* which might have appealed to Michelangelo somewhat more. They have not survived. Magnificent marquetry, inlaid slivers of different-toned wood, embellished all four walls beneath the level of Uccello's paintings, with closets and shelving built in. This decoration, much like that found in the Old Sacristy of San Lorenzo, was full of wondrous perspectives, depictions of still lifes, animals, views of the countryside, and the emblems of the Medici family, golden balls or *palle,* decorated with a diamond ring and three feathers. Jutting from the walls were several elaborate pewter sconces, also decorated with Medici symbols.

One of the most impressive pictures in the room was a large, circular painting *(tondo)* by Fra Angelico, showing the Madonna and Child with the Magi giving offerings. Other pictures were scattered about, including a portrait of the duke of Urbino, the famous Federico da Montefeltro, warrior, humanist, and sometime professional general *(condottiere)* of the Florentine armies, and another of the elegant Duke Galeazzo Maria Sforza of Milano, once a guest in the palace.

The dominant piece of furniture was a *lettuccio*, a massive nine-foot-long bed with closets at either end, four sets of drawers, marquetry decorations with Florentine lilies and Medici balls, and an embroidered canopy with damask curtains. With a modicum of imagination one can envisage Lorenzo reclining on the bed, chatting with guests and perhaps even an attentive Michelangelo from time to time.

Wooden decorated chests *(cassoni)*, found throughout the house, usually embellished with pictures, held their own secrets: decorated cloths, rare Asian carpets, Flemish tapestries with hunts and ubiquitous tournaments along with depictions of mythological scenes.

Two pictures in the Palazzo Medici that must have sparked Michelangelo's attention in particular were cityscapes by Filippo Brunelleschi, one showing the Duomo and the Baptistery, the other a view of the Piazza and Palazzo Signoria. From these panels, Michelangelo would have been able to penetrate the experiments of the developing style in architecture, whose explorations in perspective lay at the basis of the new art.

Many of the objects in the collection were specifically related to the Medici family. One that Lorenzo must have pointed out to a wide-eyed artist on an early visit to the Palazzo was a plate or salver painted on the occasion of Lorenzo's birth, and which he kept, as his father Piero had done before him, in the private suite on the second floor of the palace. The circular wooden plate, two feet in diameter, was painted on one side showing three feathers emerging from a diamond ring, Piero's heraldic device, and on the other with a representation of the "Triumph of Fame," based upon an interpretation of the fourteenth-century writer, Petrarch. According to the message on the salver, a path had been plotted for Lorenzo even before he saw the light of day on January 1, 1449, at the fifteenth hour. Lorenzo could very easily have interpreted the message as both a prognostication of his achievement and a constant reminder of his obligation to the aspirations of his ancestors.

Michelangelo must have recognized other reminders of family destiny scattered throughout the house. Lorenzo's apartments, known as the *sala grande di Lorenzo,* contained marble portraits above the doorways of his mother, Lucrezia Tornabuoni, and his father, Piero. Other treasures that might have engaged Michelangelo were kept in these rooms, in particular, the *camera della sala grande.* This contained three large canvas paintings—*Hercules Squeezing Antaeus to Death, Hercules Killing the Hydra,* and *Hercules Victorious Over the Lion*—by the Pollaiuolo brothers, as well as several small sculptures, including a little marble nude that could readily be understood as a *Hercules* because it held a club, and a marble relief of the *Ascension of Christ* by Donatello. Other works by Donatello included a *Madonna and Child* relief with Mary shown in perfect profile; a distinctive marble relief of the *Feast of Herod* within a brilliantly invented perspectival stage; and a gilt bronze *Madonna.*

Far and away the grandest object among the Medici possessions was also one of the smallest: a Hellenistic cameo in the form of a flattened cup, known today as the *Farnese Cup* (*Tazza Farnese,* now in the National Archeology Museum, Naples). The interior is decorated with esoteric Egyptian fertility symbols; a luxurious head of Medusa is carved on the outside. While the imagery does not seem to have had much impact on Michelangelo, he certainly could not have failed to have been impressed by the cup's value: 10,000 florins represented an immense sum at the time, more than a fine farm or country villa would cost in Settignano. In his wildest dreams, he could not aspire to earn a tenth part of that sum for one of his sculptures.

THE TORRIGIANI INCIDENT

The many frescoes dispersed around Florence served as capital exemplars for budding artists frequenting the Medici Gardens, offering a veritable handbook of figural poses, types, and expressions. Here, too, an introduction to aerial or atmospheric together with mathematical perspective was to be found, as well as an assemblage of solid,

Farnese Cup.

convincing compositions. One favorite location was the Brancacci Chapel, the last chapel down the right aisle of Santa Maria del Carmine, located on the side of the Arno opposite the Cathedral and the Palazzo Signoria. Almost from the moment that Masaccio executed his frescoes in 1427 dealing with the life of St. Peter, which were introduced by the *Temptation and Fall of Adam and Eve* and the *Expulsion of Adam and Eve from Paradise,* they became a magnet for other painters. Even Fra Angelico, older than Masaccio, is thought to have pondered them. It would hardly be surprising, then, that the young men at the gardens studied these remarkable demonstrations of excellence in much the same way that Michelangelo's *Battle* cartoon became an inspiration for youth of the following century. Michelangelo copied Masaccio's groundbreaking frescoes, where both types of perspective are found for the first time in large-scale narratives in which majestic figures circulate in a comprehensible pictorial stage, a convincing extension of the real world.

One of the sculptors at the gardens, Pietro Torrigiani, of aristocratic stock, must have been incurably jealous of Michelangelo's special status with Lorenzo. Torrigiani expressed doubts over Masaccio's ability as a painter, probably in order to provoke the younger Michelangelo. Although Masaccio was thought to have died of poisoning seventy years before, at age twenty-six in Rome, and had produced relatively few works during his short life, Michelangelo held this artist in the highest regard. I imagine that one gray day, as a group of men from the Medici Gardens were drawing intently in the Carmine church, Torrigiani commented loudly to his companions that copying Masaccio was a waste of time. Masaccio, Torrigiani claimed, had made unpardonable errors in anatomy and in the proportions of his figures. Torrigiani called attention to the nude boy shivering with cold who is awaiting baptism by St. Peter, an anatomically impossible rendering: arms too short, legs too thick, generally awkward proportions. Instead, Torrigiani reserved his praises for the exacting and scientific standards of the leading artists of his own day—Andrea Verrocchio, who had just died; Antonio Pollaiuolo and his brother Piero; and Domenico Ghirlandaio, whose mere mention would have put Michelangelo on alert.

Torrigiani's vilification of Masaccio, who, along with Donatello, formed Michelangelo's ideal from his Florentine heritage, angered Michelangelo to the point that, in a breach of all the unwritten rules that governed such matters, the young man began to heap insults upon Torrigiani, three years his senior. Others who were likely present could have included Michelangelo's best friend and companion, the painter Francesco Granacci, as well as budding sculptors like Baccio da Montelupo. Torrigiani, losing his patience, pummeled his smaller, frailer companion with a single shattering blow to the bridge of the nose, crushing the cartilage and unleashing an abundant flow of blood.

Benvenuto Cellini, Michelangelo's self-styled supporter and confidant, reports in his lively autobiography a conversation he had with Torrigiani, who had come down from England much later on a brief trip to search for Florentine assistants for his work for the king. So we have Torrigiani's own account of this famous incident: "This Buonarroti and I as youngsters were studying in the Carmine church in Masaccio's chapel, and because Buonarroti was in the habit of joking with everyone who was drawing, one day among many, he annoyed me, I became more angry than usual, and I extended my hand, giving him such

MASACCIO, *Shivering Boy.* Detail from *Baptism of the Neophites,* Brancacci Chapel, c. 1427.

a hard punch on the nose that I felt the bone and cartilage of the nose give way, as if it were sponge cake; and thus, marked by me, he will remain for the rest of his life."

Cellini described Torrigiani as a robust and audacious man, who had more the menacing air of a soldier than a sculptor.

The flattened nose, a visible reminder of Masaccio's merits, remained with Michelangelo for the rest of his life. Aesthetically distracting, it affected his breathing and even changed the resonance of his voice. All this pain in defense of Tommaso di ser Giovanni, known as Masaccio ("big Tom"), who lived back in the early decades of the century. Masaccio had changed the way people saw the world, extending Giotto's breakthroughs of the previous century. Michelangelo may well have been

DANIELE DA VOLTERRA, *Portrait Bust of Michelangelo,* c. 1560.

proud of his battle scar and could have thought of the flayed *Marsyas:* everything in the name of art.

He could probably not avoid having to tell Lorenzo what had happened. Il Magnifico consoled Michelangelo, he was unforgiving toward the talented Torrigiani, who eventually left Florence altogether. The sculptor managed to obtain a commission for a series of marble statuettes for an altar in the Cathedral of Siena from the Piccolomini, a potent clan wont to embarrass the Florentines at every opportunity. Ironically, a few years later the project was turned over to Michelangelo, who had the distinct pleasure of "finishing" the figure of *St. Francis* started by his arch rival. He did so by entirely obliterating the slightest trace of Torrigiani's work. The paths of the two men crossed again in Rome years later when Torrigiani obtained marble that had once belonged to Michelangelo. Eventually (as we have seen) Torrigiani ended up in England, of all places, where he produced work for the royal court, including a portrait of Henry VII in painted and gilded terra cotta.

LEARNING ON HIS OWN

The painted copy of Schongauer's print and the portrait Ghirlandaio lent him, the earliest works about which we know (both have since disappeared), cannot be regarded as independent creations by Michelangelo. Instead, they must be considered as the equivalent of art school productions, or more accurately, the pre–art school exercises of a talented child. Because of his later achievements and because the two copies no longer exist, they command scant critical attention. Still, they are significant efforts in the course of the learning process. In the Schongauer copy, Michelangelo's effort must have been a relatively free interpretation because of the drastic shift in medium from engraved original to a painting. Besides the introduction of color, Michelangelo probably also expanded the size in his version. In the case of the portrait, Michelangelo had copied the head so well that instead of returning the original, he claims to have substituted his own replica, tricking Ghirlandaio into accepting the copy for his own. If in the first instance Michelangelo embellished and annotated a print, in the second he counterfeited his model. These two efforts must have been part of a larger corpus, which undoubtedly included drawn copies of compositions and painted figures. Claimants to this category have cropped up from time to time, but they cannot be readily dated or attributed to Michelangelo.

In fact, no painting or sculpture of convincing authenticity from Michelangelo's very first years has been identified. Nothing from his two-year stint with Ghirlandaio can be confidently associated with him, even among the hundreds of figures produced by the workshop in Santa Maria Novella. Indeed, it is highly unlikely that he worked in any recognizable capacity on these frescoes simply because one cannot expect that a thirteen- or fourteen-year-old beginner would have been allowed meaningful latitude. And in the remote chance that he had been assigned independent passages, he would have been restrained by inexperience—if by nothing else—from deviating noticeably from the overall style of the shop, thus making any identification problematical.

The attraction of very early efforts by a genius, even one of Michelangelo's caliber, is more a question of curiosity than artistic delight. The two lost "copies" would have revealed little stylistic integrity. Like all beginners, even brilliant ones, Michelangelo must have struggled to cope with fundamental tasks, such as learning to control the medium and to render the human figure. Just at the stage at which he might have been expected to take a slightly larger role in the Ghirlandaio shop and to become more conscious of pictorial style in general and his master's specifically, he had left. Michelangelo's early pen and ink drawings do reveal a generic connection with Ghirlandaio's drawing style. The marble reliefs executed shortly after he left, on the other hand, fail to exhibit even the slightest hint that the artist had been with Ghirlandaio.

In contrast, Leonardo da Vinci had been totally immersed in his master Verrocchio's style. In fact, Leonardo's earliest identifiable independent efforts, much later than those by Michelangelo, are virtually identical with Verrocchio's. In his writings, Leonardo would later advise students to do likewise with their teachers.

Raphael, too, was deeply impressed by his teacher, Perugino, remaining associated with him until about the age of seventeen and painting in his manner. This sophisticated observation was made by none other than Pope Leo X, whose portrait Raphael painted. Both Raphael and Leonardo went through what might be characterized as a "normal" apprenticeship. Leonardo actually had trouble cutting the cord, staying on with Verrocchio for approximately nine years all told, first as an apprentice and then as an independent member of the shop. Not so with Michelangelo. After moving out of range of Ghirlandaio, Michelangelo abandoned painting altogether for almost a dozen years, a gap which makes it especially diffi-

MICHELANGELO, study after Masaccio's *Tribute Money*, from the Brancacci Chapel, c. 1488.

cult to reconstruct anything like a stylistic pattern between what he might have done at the apprentice stage and what he actually painted in a mature one.

The Medici Gardens functioned quite differently from a master's workshop, whether for painting or sculpture. The gardens were no *bottega*. There was no head, no master whom an apprentice might be required to follow. Collaborations on commissions, for example, or the farming out of all or portions of a particular contract to a pupil or assistant *(garzone)*, did not occur in the gardens. Michelangelo's training and early evolution were therefore markedly unlike those of his contemporaries, who learned their craft in the studios of other artists. Effectively, Michelangelo had no master, no teacher after he left Ghirlandaio, as in fact he claimed.

Bertoldo di Giovanni was in charge of the antiquities in the gardens, as we have seen; he may have had contact with the young men there, including Michelangelo, and perhaps was available for advice and guidance, but nothing like a teacher-pupil relationship can be claimed. Bertoldo was by then living in semiretirement in the Medici Palace and was available to Michelangelo for only about two years, 1490 and most of 1491; he died in the very last days of that year, when Michelangelo was not yet seventeen. (We might speculate further that in the months or more before his death, Bertoldo was not especially active at the gardens, anyway.)

Bertoldo was a sculptor who produced medals, small bronzes, and plaques for the Medici and other patrons; and two extensive cycles of reliefs—one in stucco for Bartolommeo Scala's palace on Borgo Pinti and the other, in glazed terra cotta, for Lorenzo's country villa at Poggio a Caiano—are regarded as his. One of il Magnifico's most trusted artist friends, and among the more learned when it came to Roman lore, Bertoldo was pressed into service by Lorenzo to oversee the antiquities as a kind of sinecure in old age. With his classical inclinations (and an interest in cooking), Bertoldo epitomizes the culture of the Medici court, balancing a devotion to the Florentine artistic revolution of the *quattrocento* (the 1400s) with his own visually rigid interpretation of the ancient world. Vasari was ungenerous toward Bertoldo (his opinion possibly reflecting Michelangelo's assessment), relegating him to a role as merely an artistic creature of Donatello, who finished Donatello's bronze pulpits for San Lorenzo.

Compared to Donatello, Bertoldo was more cerebral, an artist-scholar; he never attained Donatello's artistic grandeur. All his life Bertoldo had been a modeler, never to our knowledge a carver of stone, whereas Michelangelo was by choice a carver. For this and the other circumstances, Bertoldo can be ruled out as Michelangelo's sculpture teacher.

But if neither Bertoldo nor Ghirlandaio was his teacher, was Michelangelo then really self-taught, as he claimed? And if so, what does that tell us about his modes of expression and representation, and his rapport with other artists and with patrons?

There are several candidates who might have introduced Michelangelo to carving in marble. One was Giuliano da Sangallo; after all, he is well documented as Michelangelo's loyal friend in the years after 1500. Although Giuliano eventually became exclusively an architect and military engineer, he began as a sculptor in wood and stone, creating highly respectable relief carvings, including those for the Sassetti Tombs in Santa Trinità, as well as impressive wooden crucifixes in Florentine churches. It is worth pausing over the possibility of an early connection between Michelangelo and Giuliano, who was born around 1445, that is, like Bertoldo a full generation older than Michelangelo. Giuliano was prominent in Florence during the hegemony of Lorenzo the Magnificent and had access to the Medici Palace, regularly supplying Lorenzo with antiquities. As an architect, he designed a palace for the Gondi and began construction of the New Sacristy at San Lorenzo, destined to house the Medici Tombs, when Lorenzo's death interrupted the work. In his distinguished career, Giuliano served as chief of works *(capomaestro)* of the Florentine Duomo.

Giuliano da Sangallo's brother Antonio was also a ranking architect with connections to Michelangelo, while Giuliano's son Francesco, a sculptor, maintained cordial relations with Michelangelo for decades. Given Michelangelo's fame, however, had he actually been trained by Giuliano da Sangallo, some hint should be expected in the biographies or the letters. The total silence on the matter is tantamount to evidence that such was not the case. The Sangallos constituted a powerful clan in Rome, and Giuliano's nephews became well known in the arts. Since the Sangallos were Florentines by origin, a camaraderie between them and Michelangelo developed over time in Rome: Michelangelo visited Giuliano's Roman house

Piero di Cosimo, *Portrait of Giuliano da Sangallo,* detail, c. 1500.

frequently, and Giuliano served as Michelangelo's consultant for the Sistine Chapel frescoes when technical problems arose. At the end of his life, Giuliano da Sangallo was made the architect of St. Peter's, a position that Michelangelo acquired decades later, toward the end of his own life. While Giuliano da Sangallo cannot be regarded as Michelangelo's teacher, he was a loyal older colleague, countryman, and friend, who had a significant effect upon Michelangelo's professional life.

Another, better-known practitioner of sculpture has also been suggested as Michelangelo's teacher, the marble and wood carver Benedetto da Maiano; but Benedetto's competent marble and wood figures reveal little affinity to Michelangelo's early explorations, and there is not a single hint of a connection in surviving documents and commentaries. In the final analysis, no master fits, even hypothetically, as Michelangelo's sculpture teacher.

By insisting that he was self-taught, Michelangelo makes his spectacular artistic accomplishments even more spectacular. Yet there is little reason to doubt his claim. To be sure, Michelangelo's peculiar method of addressing the marble block—when creating in-the-round statues—was unprecedented. He carved as if the object were a massive relief, and he worked from an ideal front position to the back, instead of working all around the figure at the same time. Such an odd procedure serves to confirm his claim that he was self-taught, since no formally trained sculptors operated this way. But if Michelangelo did not have a flesh and blood teacher in the conventional sense, or a personal Virgil who led him through the intricacies of art, he found another sort of guide in the example of Donatello, the greatest sculptor of the earlier period.

In other words, among Renaissance artists, Michelangelo had an unorthodox if not unique education; one is hard-pressed to find an analogous case. We can readily imagine that the effect of being self-taught, while creating a certain uneasiness due to the absence of solid,

dependable, formal instruction in contrast to his fellows, was also a
source of freedom. Without a master to guide or limit him, or a studio style to emulate, Michelangelo was in the position of being able
to pick and choose approaches and ideas from a vast range of possi-
bilities. While the same examples were available to his contemporaries, they were constrained by the usual practice of pupil-teacher
relations. Michelangelo had no restrictions except those that he established for himself.

Among other sculptors from the recent past he admired was the

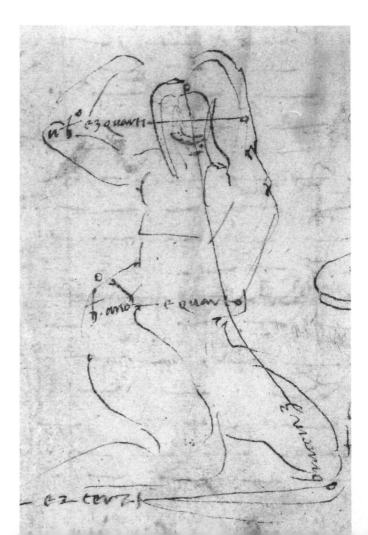

Sienese master Jacopo della Quercia, whose sculptures on the main entrance (the *Porta Magna*) of the Basilica of San Petronio in Bologna he saved from certain destruction during a new facade campaign. Besides Donatello, other Florentines included Nanni di Banco and

MICHELANGELO, block sketches for reclining figures, c. 1525. • These drawings are notations, probably for a marble supplier for a sculpture intended for the *Medici Tombs* in San Lorenzo but never carried out. They show two views of the same planned carving and offer insight into Michelangelo's conceptual process.

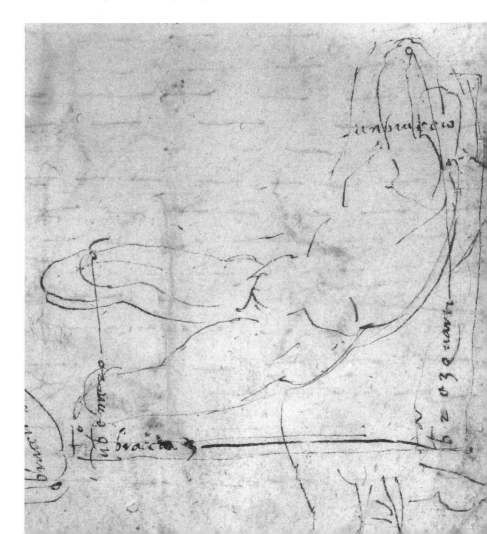

Desiderio da Settignano. But for Michelangelo, there were never strings attached; he could easily reject ideas proposed by those sculptors he favored most without batting an eye. Even his chosen surrogate teacher Donatello could be criticized and improved upon. In this regard, Michelangelo was singularly positioned to operate with greater flexibility than any of his contemporaries, and he did so.

Michelangelo appears to have decided to relive the tradition of Tuscan sculpture, beginning with the distant contributions of Nicola Pisano and his son Giovanni back in the thirteenth century. In this exercise, Michelangelo explored the history of his chosen craft at will, without constraint or prejudice. As for Greek and Roman models, once mature, he never mimicked classical art in the strict fashion that we find with Bertoldo, for example. Michelangelo felt free to recreate to whatever extent his inclinations would allow. This liberty, especially for an artist just starting out, could have easily degenerated into anarchy. But Michelangelo's self-restraint and his ability to focus on his own goals were admirable; for a less disciplined artist the results could have been disastrous.

The freedom of action afforded by Michelangelo's unusual training, combined with his overarching sense of mission, gave him a decided advantage over his sculptor contemporaries. Because he operated without dogma, each situation called for its own unique solution. Further, his early switch from painting to sculpture and then later on back again to painting, as well as the opportunity to work at times in both media simultaneously, offered him other advantages. He came to examine the human form from the viewpoint of both painter and sculptor, or, if you will, as neither painter nor sculptor, overcoming the boundaries of medium. Beyond the impact of talent, which Michelangelo obviously had in abundance, the ease with which he could move back and forth from two dimensions to three was exceptional. Behind Michelangelo's approach to both painting and sculpture lay an unconventional learning process and a personal demand for absolute rigor in drawing *(disegno),* which was an irreducible component of his creativity.

THE EARLIEST SCULPTURES

We learn from Vasari and Condivi that Michelangelo produced three sculptures in the Medici Gardens following the termination of his connection with Ghirlandaio. This period in the gardens must have roughly spanned the years 1490 until mid-1492, beginning when Michelangelo was still fourteen and ending when he was just seventeen. The marbles carved in the gardens are properly regarded as exercises, possibly suggested to him by Bertoldo, il Magnifico, or a colleague for the purpose of exploring the three basic categories of stone sculpture: in-the-round (the *Head of a Faun*); high relief (the *Battle of the Centaurs*); and low relief (the *Madonna of the Steps*). The last two were preserved by Michelangelo himself and are now in the Casa Buonarroti. They show that step by step the artist approached technical and aesthetic problems inherent in the distinct categories of sculpture. His explorations were exclusively in stone, leaving modeling clay or wax aside, except perhaps for preparatory stages as three-dimensional "sketches."

These marble sculptures, like the two painted efforts produced before he came to the gardens, were, roughly speaking, copies appropriate to an artist-in-training. But could it have been otherwise, considering his age and his experience? However, each of the objects has its own private pattern and separate rules of procedure. Of the three, the *Head of a Faun* was copied from an ancient prototype, most likely bronze; the *Battle* was based at least generically upon the bronze relief by Bertoldo; and the *Madonna of the Steps* was a free imitation/counterfeit of Donatello.

The *Faun* has disappeared without trace, although later painters often proposed fanciful reconstructions when illustrating the Michelangelo saga. As with so many works by Michelangelo, fable has been grafted onto myth. One anecdote would have it that Lorenzo il Magnifico, when he saw Michelangelo's newly carved head, criticized it because the faun had a full set of teeth, which would have been quite impossible since he was old. Factual or apocryphal, this droll account embodies an artistic lesson. Grandfather Cosimo's friend, the humanist, theoretician, artist, and architect Leon Battista Alberti, had insisted in his treatise on painting on the propriety of all aspects of a figure, and of an entire narrative, for that matter. Old persons should not run like children, and old men (old fauns included) have missing teeth. Lorenzo's criticism, which in retrospect seems quite reasonable, confirms that il Magnifico retained an ongoing curiosity about Michelangelo's progress.

The *Head of a Faun* must have been the first of the three works Michelangelo carved in the Medici Gardens, since he had to borrow not only the marble but the tools for carving, not having any of his own. He based it on an ancient bronze head he found among the antiquities in the gardens. His model was probably a Roman copy after a Greek original, and must have been an object that had seen better days, requiring that Michelangelo supply or really invent missing details and lost refinements. Thus, what he finally offered could not have been a true copy; besides, the shift in medium, from bronze to marble, also called for improvisation. The *Faun* was Michelangelo's first effort in carving in-the-round, the category of sculpture that could not have been more distant from painting and from the recent memories of Domenico Ghirlandaio.

Like the *Faun,* the *Madonna of the Steps* and the *Battle* reliefs were produced in the gardens, and all three, at least obliquely, should be regarded as being "for" Lorenzo de' Medici, but under no circumstances were they commissions. Michelangelo retained the two reliefs throughout his long life, as artists frequently do with juvenilia, being profoundly attached to early works; of the two he appears to have preferred the *Battle,* which in late life he uncharacteristically regarded as "perfect." But which of the two came first? Significantly diverse in appearance, there is no strict stylistic coherence between them, largely because the self-constructed problems posed by each were so dissimilar. The best assumption, effectively eliminating the need to award one or the other an absolute chronological priority, is that the two were carved simultaneously over an extended period of time. One is rendered in extremely low relief *(schiacciato),* the other in a high relief *(mezzo relievo)* with portions decisively projecting from the matrix of the block. The two subjects belong to different if not conflicting cultures; the traditional Christian theme of the Madonna and Child, and a classical narrative of esoteric if not completely indecipherable interpretation in the guise of a battle. Michelangelo through Condivi credits the mythological theme to Poliziano.

Some thirty-five years after he left the Medici Gardens, Michelangelo showed the *Battle* relief to a representative of the duke of Mantua who was anxious to purchase a work from the master's hand. In conversation, the artist averred that the *Battle* then in his Florentine studio had been destined for an important lord *(un gran signore)* who had died. Although the Medici name did not come up in the conversation, the reference to Lorenzo the Magnificent is inescapable. Michelangelo may have avoided mentioning Lorenzo because at that point the Florentine republicans, whom Michelangelo supported and actually collaborated with in designing defenses for the city, had once again chased the Medici from Florence, temporarily to be sure, and Michelangelo was deeply involved in their political maneuverings. But we can be sure that Michelangelo did not have a commission as such from Lorenzo to produce the *Battle* relief. More in character with his situation and in harmony with the moment, Michelangelo probably intended, upon completion, to present his

patron and mentor the *Battle* as a gift, but was foiled by Lorenzo's un-
timely death. In this way, he could have properly considered it "for"
Lorenzo.

The relief, carved from a squarish thick block that had been
shaved at the back, is an impressive achievement, even in its imperfect, that is, unfinished state. One finds a wealth of figural poses and
postures, types which critical hindsight claims he was to "reuse" later
on in his career. In other
words, one may be tempted
to see in the *Battle of the Centaurs* a kaleidoscopic prediction of what Michelangelo
would be producing in future
decades. Besides the portrayal
of the male nude, the most
suggestive element connect-
ing the *Battle* with the mature
Michelangelo is its unfinished
state, the widely heralded
"non finito," which has become a synonym for the
artist, in what amounts to a
simplistic and not always rewarding theorem.

Because of the composi-
tional complexity, really the
confusion, surrounding the
Battle, several speculations are
appropriate. The upper center is dominated by the figure
of a youthful centaur(?),

MICHELANGELO,
Battle of the Centaurs, c. 1492.

whose bare human torso is turned slightly in space as he raises his right arm, with the hand behind his head. Standing confidently, he looks to his right, perhaps to the figure shown in profile holding a massive rock in his right hand. The poses and the placement of the two imply potential confrontation, while a vanquished version of the centaur in the center is repeated on the bottom edge of the relief. Once such a compositional triangularity is postulated, other rela-

tionships become blurred, certainly in terms of a guiding narrative urgency. The single representations are quite marvelous, especially those accomplished with substantial undercutting, such as the bald old man who grasps a rock with both hands at the center of the left border, or the fatally wounded youth directly beneath him. These figures are close to becoming in-the-round statuettes and confirm the technical approach to sculpturing that Michelangelo had developed for himself.

In spite of its strengths and even its perfection in the eyes of its creator, the *Battle* cannot be regarded as the product of a polished artist. Rather, it is the work of an advanced student, though surely one at the head of the class and probably without equal in the history of any art academy. Characteristically, the ambition of the *Battle* is boundless, although the incidents, the subgroupings, are not fully integrated into a significant whole, while connections between the more projecting portions of the relief and the figures in the second plane betray indecisive transitions. The carver seems to have aimed to fill the entire available relief space with active narration, a strategy that exposes Michelangelo's immaturity, or more precisely, his lack of experience. The problem of creating a narrative in the antique manner is an exceptionally arduous one, and Michelangelo never again approached it.

Undoubtedly, the artist must have kept a keen eye out for Roman sarcophagi, which were readily available in Florence and elsewhere in Tuscany. A classical flavor, along with a familiarity with Bertoldo's bronze *Battle* relief (which is also based upon meditations of ancient reliefs), defined the cultural ambiance of Michelangelo's brilliant student effort in high relief.

Did Lorenzo the Magnificent ever see the *Battle* relief while Michelangelo was laboring over it? If so, the patron would have quickly recognized how wise he had been to single the young Michelangelo out for special attention. More than anything else,

Michelangelo's *Battle* manifests enormous creative potential. These figures, 10 or 12 inches high, would soon enough burst forth, expand twenty-fold, and evolve into massive three-dimensional creatures. The *Battle of the Centaurs* has to be regarded as an essential and inevitable milestone on the road to Michelangelo's artistic independence.

Like so many of his works, the *Battle* relief has been regarded as "unfinished." This was not an artistic decision. In fact, Michelangelo left works in differing states of finish for a variety of reasons, but we cannot support the belief that any of them were aesthetic. The *Battle,* essentially a study piece anyway, did not require high finish, much less polishing, and since there was no client (and the intended recipient had died), finishing it was superfluous. Besides, decisively freeing limbs from the central mass of the stone any more than he did would greatly increase the risk of breakage, another reason to leave the piece as it was. And as a student exercise, bringing it to what is regarded as "completion" was an irrelevancy anyway. Much the same was true for the *non finito* state of its sister relief, the *Madonna of the Steps.*

Like the *Battle of the Centaurs,* the *Madonna of the Steps* was a student undertaking, not derived from a commission. The issue of working on commission, to be sure, was to become a moral consideration for Michelangelo later on, for he always contended that he was not an artist "of the *bottega*" (did he mean like Ghirlandaio?) and he did not provide objects for the art trade. Instead, he worked either on order or, occasionally, for his own pleasure. In correspondence he mentioned producing a work for himself, though he might have considering selling it at some later time, as he did with the *Sleeping Cupid;* after all, he apparently had been prepared to sell the *Battle.*

As for the *Madonna of the Steps,* its history is even less complete than that for the *Battle.* The first confirmable notice dates to shortly after Michelangelo's death, when his nephew and heir, Lionardo, presented the piece as a gift to Cosimo I de' Medici, since the duke of

Tuscany did not possess a single sculpture by the master. The small relief, which measures 26 by 18 inches, must have been in Michelangelo's Florentine workshop on Via Mozzo at the time of his death, but the absence of a firm provenance has occasionally given rise to doubts about the dating and even its authorship as a Michelangelo. A few modern critics would place it chronologically as much as fifteen years after he left the gardens, because of what are regarded as generic affinities to the *Sibyls* on the Sistine Chapel ceiling; but that line of thinking fails to account for the self-educative function of the relief, and especially the struggle Michelangelo had in formulating the proportions of the individual figures who appear in it and the uneasy scale among them.

While Michelangelo sought to master a complex narrative in the *Battle of the Centaurs* in high relief, he tried in the *Madonna of the Steps* to render a Madonna and Child with attending figures in the very low relief mode favored by Donatello, Desiderio da Settignano, and Antonio Rossellino. The technical challenge was considerable; he allowed himself two inches of material to construct a convincing physical reality. The huge seated Mary occupies the entire vertical space and the muscular Child is shown from behind as he suckles at his mother's breast. Both demonstrate that the aspiring sculptor had run into difficulties, although the work has undeniable appeal.

Madonna of the Steps.

The daring foreshortening of the Child, the high steps and banister on the left, with a youth holding a cloth behind the Virgin, and another figure on the other side in even lower relief, demonstrate problems Michelangelo was not able to unravel within such a shallow carving surface. These unresolved—and unresolvable—obstacles suggest once again that the *Madonna of the Steps* is an early effort. That it was carved in the years after the *Bacchus* and the *Pietà* is therefore impossible. Mary's head and feet are tiny in relation to her hands and the trunk of her body, while the boy on the stairs has proportions that would have been unthinkable for Michelangelo once he achieved more experience.

In the *Madonna of the Steps*, Michelangelo plunged into the delicate issues surrounding extremely shallow relief projection. He left untouched a segment about the size of a half dollar coin on the original block's front surface where the Child's head was carved, as a reminder to himself of his point of departure for the rest of the carving. The result was not perfect, but to pull it off at all must be regarded as a triumph. Perhaps in awareness of its inherent weakness, Michelangelo did not mention the *Madonna* to Condivi, although he must have felt some affection for it, as he had for the *Battle* relief, since it did not occur to him to destroy the *Madonna* as he had done with large numbers of drawings, clay models, and wax sketches.

Two distinct sets of issues have been constructed by critics and commentators when approaching the *Madonna of the Steps* and the *Battle* reliefs. One involves a search to isolate visual sources that Michelangelo is presumed to have dipped into as he was developing them, and the other concerns their presumed meaning, their iconography. For the *Madonna,* not only have the Donatellian origins been emphasized, but also the eventuality that Michelangelo called upon ancient gems to achieve the form of Mary's head, in profile. The unresolved spatial ambiguities have been put into context with Donatello's *Feast of Herod,* a marble relief Michelangelo must have seen in the Medici Palace. Still, these and other possible sources that may be brought up for one or another aspect of these reliefs are uninformative once Michelangelo's greater purpose is considered. The process of isolating apparent influences, especially for a genius like Michelangelo, becomes a misdirected hunt for the irrelevant.

Much the same may be said of the imposition of complex meaning in Michelangelo's presentation, at least at this very early moment in his career. The imagery represented in the two reliefs has been learnedly interpreted as looking forward to interpretations found in his mature work. For example, the combination of the large-scale seated Mary and the playful children behind and above her have been likened to the *Sibyls* from the Sistine Chapel, and, carrying this line another step, the Madonna has been described as "sibylline." Such readings load too much freight upon the tiny marble, which was, after all, a student work. The psychological implications that are imposed upon it are open to similar caveats. The notion, for example, that the Child represents Michelangelo's subconscious hunger to recall the happy days at his mother's (and wet nurse's) breast has often been put forward. Although the theme of a mother feeding her child is common, Michelangelo's rendering the Child with his face entirely hidden from the viewer is definitely unusual. Does it reveal the kind of infantile nostalgia suggested, or is it a brilliant way for the student to avoid the difficulties of presenting the head of the baby Jesus, or a combination? In later adaptations of the same theme, whether in three dimensions or in drawing, Michelangelo leaves much more latitude for showing the face of the Child.

Michelangelo's first full-size, in-the-round statue, the greatest challenge for a marble sculptor, was a *Hercules*. This figure was purchased by the Strozzi family for their palace in Florence; after remaining there for a time, it was sent off to France while Michelangelo was still alive. The details surrounding the commission of the work and its future history are vague and inconclusive. The *Hercules* is assumed to have also been "unfinished," as is suggested by indistinct engravings, and in any case by the middle of the eighteenth century it had completely vanished from its home in a French garden. This statue could have belonged, then, to the phase following the death of Lorenzo when Michelangelo "came back" to Piero di Lorenzo, in 1492/3–94, the time of the snowman, and when he also carved a wood *Crucifix,* before leaving for Bologna. In our present state of knowledge little more can be said of this still-lost *Hercules,* except that it served to complete his education as a sculptor and created a platform for greater artistic independence.

The painted wooden *Crucifix* is a more interesting story. Michelangelo, through Condivi, records that he produced a slightly under-life-size crucifix for the prior of Santo Spirito, and from later records it appears to have been in that Florentine

MICHELANGELO (?), *Hercules.* The *Hercules* was sent to France in the sixteenth century, but traces of the large sculpture have been lost. Recently, Italian scholar Alessandro Parronchi ran across photographs of this sculpture, which was in a private collection in the United States, and associated it with the missing work by Michelangelo.

church. Although there have been diverse candidates, the *Santo Spir-ito Crucifix* has remained unidentified (or was it destroyed by termites and neglect?). One thing is certain: the *Crucifix* was not strictly speaking a commission. Instead, it was Michelangelo's concrete expression of thanks to the prior for allowing him to conduct anatomies, that is, dissections, on corpses, at the Hospital of Santo Spirito. Despite the claimants, the *Santo Spirito Crucifix* should be regarded as lost, at least for now.

The few objects that Michelangelo carved in his early years at the Medici Gardens define not only his remarkable self-training but also his personal path to an original idiom. The expulsion of the Medici in November 1494 marked a turning point in Florentine history, in the history of the Medici family, and in Michelangelo's private history as well. When he left the city for the first time, he was still young and inexperienced as an artist and in life, but the change had been in-evitable ever since the death of his patron-father, Lorenzo de' Medici, two years earlier.

THE DEATH OF LORENZO

Michelangelo's idyllic life at the Medici Gardens, in fact, ended abruptly and unexpectedly when Lorenzo il Magnifico died on April 8, 1492. Three days before, on the 5th, strange signs and unusual oc-currences were observed in Florence as Lorenzo lay ill in the Medici villa at Careggi suffering excruciating stomach pains, his body riddled with gout, a hereditary disorder, and by muscular pains. That night a fearful storm enveloped the center of Florence and the people took it as a sign that il Magnifico's end was imminent. Bolts of lightning accompanied by hail struck one of the golden balls—the *palle*—of the Medici coat of arms on their house, while flashes of light ostensibly

originating from the hills above Fiesole in the direction of Caffaggiolo, location of the origins of the Medici, were seen hovering over
San Lorenzo, the Medici's family church, that night and the next
two. The multicolored Duomo with Brunelleschi's majestic *cupolone*
and the lantern were relentlessly hammered.

The storms alerted the entire city to the impending epochal
event, and Michelangelo must have been among the most apprehensive. According to a diary of the day, the disruptions began when
Lorenzo released a "spirit" that had been imprisoned for many years
in the ring that he invariably wore. Recognizing that his end was at
hand, Lorenzo had decided to set the spirit free. The intense force of
the liberation caused gigantic blocks of stone to crash down from the
cornice of the vast dome *(cupola)* and from the lantern of the Duomo,
plummeting to the pavement hundreds of feet below. Miraculously,
no one was killed. When Lorenzo was told that the lightning had
struck in the direction of his house on Via Larga, he was said to have
replied, "I am dead" *(Io sono morto)*.

There were other warnings of Lorenzo's impending death and
the ruin that would accompany it. At mass in the expansive Gothic-
style church of the Dominicans, Santa Maria Novella, a madwoman
began screaming that a raging bull with flaming horns was burning
the entire city. Marsilio Ficino saw ghostly giants battling in his garden, while two of the mascot lions of Florence fought each other to
death in a cage located, appropriately enough, on the Via dei Leoni
(Street of the Lions) behind the Palazzo Signoria. Reports also circulated of a flaming tower seen crashing to the ground.

Florentines would not have been overly surprised to learn that
Lorenzo possessed extraordinary powers. From the time of Cosimo
Pater Patriae onward, the Medici held the Three Kings *(I Tre Magi)* in
particular reverence. They were prominently illustrated in the chapel
of the Medici Palace, with Medici family likenesses incorporated
into their images, and besides, Cosimo's private cell at the monastery

of San Marco was frescoed with a vivid portrayal of the Magi, who were alternatively the three magicians. In a more recent depiction, Sandro Botticelli painted an exceptional *Adoration of the Magi* in which the kings were portrayed in the guise of Cosimo, Piero, and Lorenzo de' Medici, three generations of the family. The Magi came to Christ to offer the precious treasure of life: gold, frankincense, and myrrh (which Ficino said formed an excellent medication for the aged when properly combined, and which was tried on Lorenzo on his deathbed). The Medici-Magi connection had been formalized by Cosimo when he delayed the baptism of his grandson Lorenzo, the hope for the family's future, from January 1, 1449, until the 6th, the feast day of *I Tre Magi*.

The esoteric, magical flavor of Medici beliefs was not discussed openly, however, and even Michelangelo may have been surprised upon learning the circumstances surrounding the ring (three intersecting

BOTTICELLI, *Adoration of the Magi,* detail.

circles or rings were also a family device) and the other premonitions. More than anything else, he would have been frightened and saddened over the imminent death of his patron.

One of the physicians in charge of Lorenzo's care, Lazzaro of Pavia, prepared a potion of ground gems, but they failed to heal him. Another attending doctor, Pierleone Lioni of Spoleto, was so despondent over his failure to keep the forty-three-year-old leader of Florence alive that he threw himself into a well (or was he thrown?). After all, he had bragged about being able to cure the long-ailing Florentine, who had already lost feeling in his hands. These good doctors seemed oblivious to another incisive saying that Michelangelo could have recalled with resignation: "When the sickness is deathly, no doctor and no medication is of any use" *(A mal mortale, nè medico nè medicina vale)*.

A despondent Michelangelo may very well have accompanied the body as it was carried down the steep road from Careggi to San Marco, where Lorenzo was first laid out on April 9, which was a Monday. The funeral was held the next day at San Lorenzo, the arrangements turned over to the Confraternity of the *Tre Magi*. (Michelangelo's formal or "state" funeral would take place in the same church more than seventy years later, and would be conducted by his own "confraternity," the Academicians of Fine Arts.) We can expect that Michelangelo was present for Lorenzo's services, alongside Piero, Giuliano, Lucrezia, Maddalena, and Contessina. Giovanni, the cardinal, was not there, being then in Rome without time to return. Lamentations and praises for Lorenzo in life and in death came from every quarter of Europe, but the words would have been little consolation to Michelangelo. Barely seventeen, he must have appreciated the extent of his private loss. Yet "To deny the sounding of the church bells is useless" *(Quando la campana ha suonato, è inutile dir di no)*, as the Tuscan proverb went.

The funeral services were modest, in keeping with Medici practice, but not excessively modest either, because that would have been a presumption in reverse. Remarkably, no permanent tomb had been provided for il Magnifico before his death, perhaps because the time was insufficient for Lorenzo to have arranged for a fitting one, had he had a mind to do so at all. As fate would have it, decades later Michelangelo would have the opportunity to prepare his patron-father's final resting place among sculptures he had carved for other family members in the New Sacristy of San Lorenzo.

Lorenzo's death at the age of forty-three was a bitter blow for the Florentine republic. Through his prudence, reputation, and intelligence in everything honorable and excellent, to paraphrase the historian Guicciardini, the city had flourished marvelously with wealth and all those ornaments and advantages that usually accompany a long peace. The loss was made even harder because his death coincided with the passing of several other members of his circle. A few months later, Pope Innocent VIII (Cibò), with whom he was on excellent terms and whose son Franceschetto was married to Lorenzo's daughter Maddalena, died, leaving the way open for the ascension of Rodrigo Borgia as Pope Alexander VI, the raging bull of the madwoman's nightmarish vision at Santa Maria Novella. The Borgia emblem was the bull, and to multiply coincidences, Borgia's birthday was on the same date, January 1, as Lorenzo's.

The humanist Ermolao Barbaro died in the year after Lorenzo's death, during an outbreak of plague. Poliziano, heartbroken by the loss of his patron, died in September 1494, himself only forty, and in that same year the brilliant Giovanni Pico della Mirandola, only thirty-one, also died. This cluster of losses cannot but have affected Michelangelo. He was now without a mentor among the ruling Medici, and his own personal guide, Poliziano, was also gone.

II

Michelangelo and
His Father, Lodovico

▨▨▨

LEAVING *FLORENTIA BELLA*

THE ATTRACTIONS of one's own homeland are inevitably taken for granted. Only after separation, whether by choice or by circumstance, does anyone appreciate the character of the place he has been experiencing on a daily basis. Michelangelo was no different, and it was not until after October 1494 and the dream in which Lorenzo the Magnificent warned him of coming events in Florence that Michelangelo would have meditated about Florence, the city he had always taken for granted. Perhaps he recalled the old patriotic description, ascribed to the military hero Fazio degli Uberti, of Florence as the "flower of everything that is good" *(Firenze, fiore d'ogni ben)*.

The move from Florence must have been full of agitation for the nineteen-year-old. It separated him from his father, his four brothers, of whom he was fond, and an entire entourage of artists and intellectuals he had come to know at the Medici Gardens and in the Medici Palace. He was also separated from his friends, who were extremely important to him, as they would be throughout his life. More than that, he was leaving a much-loved place: its habits, customs, food and wines, and, even more drastic, its art, upon which he had been weaned.

Set in a river valley that stretches all the way to Pisa, Florence is surrounded by rolling hills, and at a greater distance, distinctive mountain ranges. Not far to the north, at Caffaggiolo, in the region where the Medici family originated, which in turn was not far from Giotto's birthplace, the mountains offered a natural buffer from invasion. As to climate, Florence's was far from ideal, though it was better than that of Bologna, where Michelangelo would soon spend a year. The city was oppressive in summer, and those who could passed the hot months in the countryside nearby. The winters could be biting, especially during *tramontana,* when icy winds whistled down from the Apennines and occasionally brought snow. It could get "cold as a cat's nose" *(Freddo come il naso d'un gatto),* as a popular Tuscan proverb put it.

Florentines, like the inhabitants of most other splendid cities in Renaissance Italy, held their own, with its approximately fifty thousand inhabitants, in the highest esteem. Florence was not only an ancient city with a long history of its own, but an independent political entity as well. Even smaller centers, such as Siena, Lucca, Ferrara, and Mantua, which managed to retain their independence despite greedy neighbors, engendered a deep pride and constantly competed with one another to build the most magnificent town hall, city walls, or cathedral.

The Florentine chronicler Benedetto Dei proudly claimed that his city had uninterruptedly maintained her independence for more than fifteen hundred years, since 72 B.C., and that she had never had a foreign ruler. Citizens like Michelangelo could have recited the commonly recognized seven blessings of his city. *Florentia bella* had full liberty; rich and well-dressed people; a river, the Arno, of sweet water with a mill in the middle; a *Signoria*—a government—over the city, and over nearby castles and surrounding lands; a university where Greek and mathematics were taught; twenty-three guilds representing the diverse arts; and finally, banks that provided services for the entire world.

Florentia bella was a circular city about five miles in diameter. It was without the encumbrances of a fortress and drawbridges but possessed eight mighty towers, constructed as part of the city walls and made of massive blocks of cut stone. Michelangelo's Florence had 108 wondrous churches, open in the mornings and evenings and all in good order; they were accommodated with cloisters, chapter houses, refectories, infirmaries, sacristies, libraries, and bell towers. Twenty-three distinguished palaces located within the city walls belonged to the leading families. *Florentia bella* had eighty-three silk manufactories, thirty-three large banks, sixty-six druggists, eighty-four woodcarvers' shops and *intarsia* studios; fifty-four stone-carving workshops, where decorative carving and building materials were prepared; and forty-four goldsmith and jewelry shops.

And there was more: fifty piazzas inside the city walls, where jousts or tournaments rich in pageantry regularly took place. Knights on horseback in full armor sought to knock their adversaries to the ground, an activity dear to the Medici, and there were dances, plays and representations, fencing, jumping contests, and celebrations *(tri-onfi)* with carts decorated by Florence's best artists. Fully 365 important family lines within the city—one for every day of the year—were counted; Michelangelo's, incidentally, was not among them. Florence was far and away the finest state that ever existed since it was founded. The city had been called a terrestrial paradise, as emperors and popes, kings and dukes, counts and princes, and the entire Christian and infidel worlds knew full well.

Having lost his mother when he was barely six, and his cultural father, Lorenzo the Magnificent, when he was seventeen, Michelangelo was now at nineteen in the process of losing his family, his homeland with its inviting surroundings, and the paintings and sculptures he knew so well. The second son of Lodovico di Leonardo Buonarroti Simoni was a presentable young man with a largish head, one might say disproportionately so, and a pronounced, square forehead. According to Condivi's description, his eyebrows were composed of a few bushy hairs; his pale, horn-colored eyes were enlivened by yellowish and bluish sparks; his lips were thin, the lower one somewhat fuller, so that in profile it seemed to project a little. His thick black hair, which was to recede prematurely at the forehead, was always disorderly. Besides large ears, his only other obvious visual defect was acquired: his broken nose. The artist was small of stature and slight of frame, yet wiry, with exceedingly strong, oversized hands.

Accompanied by two (unidentified) friends, Michelangelo first set out for Venice, a city with a well-respected and efficient republican government. The young Florentines must have marveled at the multidomed Church of San Marco, with its shimmering mosaics both inside and outside the building, the latter made even more brilliant by the flickering light from the sea. Perhaps they recalled the vast cycle of mosaics in Florence's Baptistery. Michelangelo and his companions had an opportunity, albeit superficial, to sample the artistic life of Venice, where Gentile Bellini and his brother Giovanni (known as Giambellino) dominated the painting scene. But the reason for Michelangelo's journey was not tourism or wanderlust: he was seeking safety and employment.

Unsuccessful in Venice, Michelangelo headed back south after only a few weeks, arriving in Bologna in early November 1494, just about the same time as the Medici abandoned Florence on November 9. Michelangelo found a patron there during the very days that French troops, with Charles VIII at their head, entered Florence, where they remained briefly. Ironically, Piero de' Medici, his brother Giuliano, and before long his other brother, Cardinal Giovanni, also made their way to Bologna, on the heels of a narrow escape from Florence. While Michelangelo stayed on in Bologna for a year after leaving Venice, Piero reversed his itinerary, shifting northward to Venice after a brief stay, although their paths must have crossed in Bologna from time to time.

Michelangelo's Bolognese experience turned out to be unexpectedly creative, expanding his artistic range by immersion in an unfamiliar culture. This happened while he was still young enough and in a frame of mind readily to ingest what appealed to him, even though he had barely finished his semi-official but unorthodox artistic education. The visual culture available to Michelangelo in "Bologna the learned" *(Bononia la docta)*, as it was called because of its ancient university, was quite distinct from that of *Florentia bella,* although by 1494, awareness of Tuscan innovations in architecture, painting, and sculpture had long since crossed the Apennines.

Michelangelo must have spent his first months absorbing the unfamiliar environment of Bologna, a city on the plains like Florence but otherwise quite different. Its character was defined by an endless series of covered arcades attached to the buildings, which provided the residents protection from the weather. Several very tall towers gave definition to the skyline, whereas in Florence, similar towers that had once existed were long since reduced in height for political reasons.

The mighty *Porta Magna,* the main portal of the Basilica of San Petronio, designed and decorated with sculptures by Michelangelo's predecessor, the Sienese Jacopo della Quercia, must have caught his attention. Jacopo was one of the contestants for the commission for bronze doors for the Florentine Baptistery in the famous competition of 1401 won by Ghiberti. The opinion was widely held in Florence and perpetuated by Vasari (incorrectly, to be sure) that Jacopo had also executed the influential sculpture on the north portal of the Florentine Duomo, the Porta della Mandorla. Jacopo's expressive figural

Jacopo della Quercia, *Creation of Eve,* c. 1430.

style, dominated by robust muscular nudes, would have been useful to Michelangelo in seeking to define his own artistic predilections, and he would recall Jacopo's treatment of Genesis scenes in Bologna when faced with similar ones in the Sistine Chapel years later.

Michelangelo found other sources of inspiration in Bologna, as well. He undoubtedly sensed an immediate compatibility with the Tuscan sculptural vocabulary of Nicola Pisano and his collaborators, including Arnolfo di Cambio, who had made a contribution to Bolognese art with the earliest sections of the Tomb of San Domenico. The majestic line of marble carvers had begun with Nicola Pisano and his talented son Giovanni in the 1250s in Lucca, Siena, Pisa, and Bologna more than two hundred years before. And Michelangelo was already familiar with the work of Arnolfo, whose sculpture back in Florence was displayed on the unfinished facade of the Duomo, a building Arnolfo actually designed. In other words, even if he sometimes felt out of place in Bologna socially as well as artistically, he was able to relate to the Tuscan tradition he found there, especially when it came to sculpture. Jacopo della Quercia's style occupied a central position in an illustrious chain for which Michelangelo's sculpture would constitute the final link.

As it happened, Niccolò dell'Arca, Bologna's leading sculptor, had died a few months before Michelangelo's arrival, leaving his masterpiece, the *Arca di San Domenico,* with empty slots for statuettes still to be executed. This marble monument, with a sarcophagus initiated by Nicola Pisano, was intended to provide a dignified home for the mortal remains of the founder of the Dominican order in the Bolognese church dedicated to him. Michelangelo's timing could hardly have been more fortuitous. The Bolognese had never been averse to hiring "foreigners" for their projects, since no native marble-carving tradition existed locally, even Niccolò dell'Arca was a foreigner. Michelangelo was commissioned by the authorities of San Domenico to produce three statuettes: *San Procolus; San Petronius;* and a somewhat larger *Candlestick Angel,* to match one done by Niccolò.

Niccolò dell'Arca's accomplished sculpture of the *Arca di San Domenico* reflected a spirit unlike anything Michelangelo had seen before. Very little about the origins of the mysterious Niccolò, who operated in terra cotta, wood, and marble, has come to light. He may have come from the Dalmatian coast across the Adriatic Sea, or from South Italy, perhaps from Bari in Apulia; as a developing artist,

Niccolò seems to have worked his way up the Italian peninsula from the south, via Naples and Tuscany. He must have been young when he arrived in Bologna, where he lived for thirty or more years, until his death in 1494. His reputation had not reached Florence, however, so his work was a true revelation for Michelangelo.

Niccolò had designed a sophisticated expansion to the *Arca di San Domenico,* begun by Nicola Pisano, which originally consisted of a large marble tomb standing on supporting figures with reliefs depicting events in the life of the saint. Niccolò added a curved marble cover for the tomb, as well as a tall central decorative element with an elegantly carved garland of fruits and leaves, and marble statuettes of saints in the upper areas of the monument. Niccolò was regarded as "bizarre" or "fantastic," much as Michelangelo would later refer to himself in a letter as being "like a common, poor and crazy man" *(come omo vile, povero e matto).* In the same letter the artist goes on to say that it serves to have mad people around, "as with onions, which change the taste of boring capons." In yet another letter, Michelangelo writes that the "craziness that they say I have does not harm anyone but myself," and he continues in ironic vein, "people are determined to speak badly of me and insult me: such is the prize of all good men." Niccolò, who turned out statuettes slowly year after year, clothed his figures in inventive, exotic garments and extravagant headgear and footwear, rendering them with a minuscule detail that may have been the source for his being considered bizarre.

To complete the cycle, Michelangelo had to harmonize his contribution with those statuettes already in place, and thus was required to study them intently. Niccolò's style, for which Michelangelo had no preparation, reveals a mediation between insistent realism in rendering detail (he was said to have carved natural-size flies in marble) and an appreciation of ideal poses and postures derived ultimately from Greek and Roman examples. Although Michelangelo did not wholly succeed in his collaboration and competition (it was a bit of both) with Niccolò, he managed to reflect the fiery intensity found in Niccolò's statuettes in his two standing saints, *Petronius* and *Procolus*. A similar intensity would later find its way into his marble *David*, begun in 1501 in Florence. Further, the measured balance that Niccolò dell'Arca achieved and passed on to Michelangelo is noticeable in a single work, Michelangelo's first unqualified masterpiece, the marble *Pietà* in Rome, begun in 1498. There the harmony between the ideal and the real parallels the balance that Niccolò achieved. Although the scale of the *Pietà* was beyond anything that Niccolò conceived in marble, the emotional impact and the precise, highly finished (and polished) surface of the sculpture are clear indications of Michelangelo's understanding of the language of his predecessor in Bologna.

Bolognese churches were full of paintings by the masters from nearby Ferrara, and Michelangelo also probably went there to see more of them. The innovations of this provincial "school" were among the discoveries Michelangelo made in that first year away from home. Traces of the dramatic expressionism of contemporary Ferrarese painting can be isolated in the Roman *Pietà*.

Undoubtedly, Michelangelo missed Florence during his Bolognese stay, and we can imagine that he sought out countrymen who happened to be in Bologna or were passing through, for company, as he was to do later on in Rome. Michelangelo's speech was easily distinguishable from the Bolognese style; indeed, a patron in Bologna asked him to read Dante aloud since his Florentine cadence was the same as Dante's. Michelangelo relished the banter and the witticisms of his Florentine compatriots; on the other hand, he was not blind to their shortcomings. He once wrote that he had "never dealt with a more ungrateful and arrogant people than the Florentines" *(che mai praticai gente più ingrate ne' più superbe che e' Fiorentini)*.

A fellow Florentine sculptor, Baccio da Montelupo, was active on a project in the same church as Michelangelo, San Domenico. He created four statues in terra cotta, a medium that was the specialty of his native town of Montelupo, not far from Florence. One can readily imagine that the two spent evenings exchanging the latest art gossip and analyzing every scrap of news from back home over a bottle of inferior (to a Tuscan) Bolognese wine. They must have been intrigued by the increasing power of the Dominican friar Savonarola, especially following the expulsion of the Medici. Beyond his artistic experiences, Michelangelo's year in Bologna was full of new relationships, possibly even amorous ones, judging by the sensuality of one of his early poems, sometimes dated to this period. After all, Bologna was famous for its agreeable women.

Michelangelo returned to Florence in the late autumn of 1495, once he had completed his assignment for the *Arca di San Domenico* and felt secure enough about his personal safety. The political climate at home had shifted decisively since he left the year before. The Medici were gone, their rule replaced by a republican regime, with Savonarola playing a major role. Michelangelo could hardly have predicted that only seven months later he would again pack his rucksack and leave Florence, this time for a five-year residency in Rome.

THE *BAMBINO* EPISODE

With his old patrons gone, upon returning to Florence Michelangelo went to live in his father's house. In the years following his own education, he was beginning to gain respect as a skilled, if still young, marble sculptor. His first days back were probably spent reviving family, social, and business ties; though the sons and daughters of Lorenzo were now gone from the city, their powerful cousins were not. Very quickly Michelangelo was befriended by Lorenzo di Pierfrancesco de' Medici, *il Popolano,* a republican, whom Michelangelo could have come to know earlier. This Lorenzo had been skeptical of his cousin Lorenzo il Magnifico's autocratic rule of the city and had actively opposed Lorenzo's son, Piero, helping to precipitate his downfall.

A good-natured but self-centered man, Lorenzo di Pierfrancesco was not considered to be very ethical (he was described as *"poco scrupoloso"*) when it came to matters of money. Despite their political differences, Lorenzo di Pierfrancesco and his older brother Giovanni di Pierfrancesco, were, after all, still Medici, and could trace their line back to Cosimo *Pater Patriae*'s brother Lorenzo; besides, they were very rich. Michelangelo's rapport with Lorenzo should be regarded as a consequence of his intimacy with il Magnifico, but Florence was different now, and Michelangelo too was different, a traveled sculptor, although still without major works to his credit.

Michelangelo produced a popular subject for Lorenzo di Pierfrancesco, a marble *Young St. John (San Giovannino)*, all traces of which have disappeared, although we might have expected it to reveal Niccolò dell'Arca's elegance. Also now lost is the statue of a nude *Cupid* modeled in the classical Roman manner. The strange circumstances surrounding this figure, which appears to have resulted from an odd collaboration with Lorenzo di Pierfrancesco, were to have repercussions for the artist, leading to unpleasant accusations of forgery (then, and ever since). It was also the main element in the chain of circumstances that prompted Michelangelo's move from Florence to Rome in the early summer of 1496, at the age of twenty-one.

On July 2, 1496, Michelangelo wrote a letter (his earliest extant) from Rome to Lorenzo di Pierfrancesco in which, curiously, he uses the pronoun "we." It begins:

> Magnificent Lorenzo, etc., merely to advise you that we arrived safe and sound last Saturday and immediately went to pay our respects to the Cardinal of San Giorgio and there I presented to him your letter. He appears to have received me with pleasure and wanted

me to look at certain figures, occupying me the entire day; on that day I did not give him your other letters, however. Then on Sunday, the Cardinal came to the new house and asked for me; I went to him and he asked me what I thought of the things I had seen. I told him what I thought and certainly I thought them very beautiful. Then the Cardinal asked me if I had the spirit to make some beautiful objects. I answered that I would not make such grand things, but he would see what I could do. We purchased a piece of marble for a life-size figure; and Monday I shall begin to work.

Doubtless, the first vision of Rome for any artist was an overwhelming experience; even more so for Michelangelo, a Renaissance sculptor who had not long before been studying antiquities and modern sculpture in the Medici Gardens. It is therefore surprising that not a hint of his personal reaction to the city and its monuments can be detected in this businesslike, impersonal letter. But throughout his life, Michelangelo almost never wrote about art as such, so that the omission in this letter of Roman impressions should not be given too much weight.

Lorenzo had furnished him with a letter of introduction to the powerful cardinal of San Giorgio, Raffaelle Riario, whom Michelangelo met at the cardinal's villa. There, Riario, who probably paid for Michelangelo's trip to Rome, proudly showed Michelangelo his collection of ancient sculptures. Like any collector, the cardinal was anxious to have a reaction to his treasures; the more effusive the better is the general rule in such cases. Michelangelo politely replied that the works were "very beautiful things," a cautious description given the circumstances, and the fact that he did not single out one or two pieces for praise must have signified an overall lack of enthusiasm for the collection. Evidently Michelangelo was unimpressed with what he had seen; indeed, throughout his life, he does not appear to have been unduly overwhelmed by the Greek and Roman carvings around him, with limited exceptions. Michelangelo never copied or slav-

ishly adhered to ancient models. He approached antiquity, if anything, in a spirit of competition rather than harmony, following several early explorations, including the *Cupid* and the *Bacchus.*

When the cardinal asked if Michelangelo could create something beautiful for him, a contest with the classical pieces in his collection was implicit. Straightway, marble was purchased, which was
destined to become the *Bacchus,* the over-life-size statue of the god
of wine he was to carve in the next few months. The finished carving ended up not in Cardinal Riario's collection but in that of the
Roman banker Jacopo Galli, though the details surrounding the
switch of patrons are not known. It is possible that although the payments came from Riario, the *Bacchus* may have been intended for
Galli all along, as Michelangelo was later to claim. Or it might have
been a gift by the cardinal to his banker (Galli was also Michelangelo's
banker). Nor can one rule out the possibility that Riario did not like
the work and let Galli have it. Michelangelo's interpretation of the
subject is far from sympathetic, for his *Bacchus* has lost control of his
uneasy movements, his eyes spin in his head, and his belly is swollen
with wine.

Regardless of who first asked him to make it—and from the evidence of the letter it must have been Riario—the *Bacchus* was
Michelangelo's first independent large-scale commission.

The second part of Michelangelo's letter to Lorenzo is even more
businesslike than the first: "Then this past Monday I presented your
other letters to Paolo Rucellai, who gave me the money I needed;
and the same thing happened with the letter to the Cavalcanti." Two
Florentine banking families, the Rucellai and the Cavalcanti, both had
Roman branches; apparently Lorenzo di Pierfrancesco had given
Michelangelo letters of credit so that he would have expense money
while getting established in Rome.

The final section of the letter raises an entirely different question,
once again involving Cardinal Riario. Michelangelo speaks of a

life-size marble statue of a baby *(bambino)* carved by Michelangelo in Florence immediately before coming to Rome. This was, at least overtly, the reason he had been called to Rome. He writes:

> Then I gave the letter to Baldassare [del Milanesi] and asked him for the *bambino,* and said that I would return his money to him. He responded very sharply and said that he would sooner smash it into a hundred pieces, that he had purchased the *bambino* and it was his and that he doubted that he had to give it up. Complaining a great deal about you [i.e., Lorenzo], he said that you had spoken badly of him. Now some of our Florentine friends are intervening to establish an agreement between us, but they haven't done anything [yet]. I am now hoping to do so through the Cardinal, a course of action suggested to me by Baldassarre Balducci. You will be informed of what happens. There is nothing else to say. My regards to you. May God protect you from harm.
> [signed] Michelagniolo [an alternative spelling of his name which he favored] in Rome.

Michelangelo's reference to the sculpture here as the *bambino* rather than the *cupido* or *cupidino* demonstrates a peculiar attitude toward his subject matter that remained constant throughout his career. Just as the *Battle* carved in the Medici Gardens was referred to simply as "battle" when offered for sale to the agent of the Gonzaga, and not some esoteric title like *Battle of the Centaurs,* he called this sculpture "the baby"—an elemental, generic label rather than "the sleeping Cupid," which we know from other evidence was the actual subject. Michelangelo also preferred the all-embracing identification of "giant" *(gigante)* for the *David,* revealing himself patently uninterested in designating or implying meaning. Of course this does not signify that he had no concern for meaning. His mode of expression was that of a sculptor, a maker, whose task it was to carve a child, a giant, a battle scene; if he instilled elaborate meaning into these works, one would hardly know it from his own references.

From the letter, it appears that Baldassarre del Milanesi, an art merchant of sorts, exploded. He would rather smash the statue into a hundred bits than return it, a reaction hardly motivated by aesthetic or critical considerations. Baldassarre had consummated a highly profitable deal, had purchased the sculpture fair and square, and he was not about to renounce it.

Further details surrounding the *bambino* episode can be fleshed out from other letters. Baldassarre del Milanesi had offered the carving to two other collectors, Ascanio Sforza of Milan and Isabella d'Este of Mantua. The piece is described when first mentioned as "either ancient or modern," and in a later letter, when the truth about its origins had become generally known, it was called simply "modern." Isabella, the most remarkable collector of her age, soon afterwards came into possession of this sculpture, which she received in Mantua as a present from the notorious Cesare Borgia, Pope Alexander VI's son. With what must be regarded as extraordinary critical insight, she commented that "the *cupid* for a modern work has no equal" *(el cupido per cosa moderna non ha paro)*. The prevailing snobbism among collectors of the time was clear enough: an ancient Roman work was treasured more than a contemporary one, notwithstanding intrinsic quality.

We learn from a written description derived from Michelangelo that the *bambino* was a sleeping God of Love, a slightly old-looking six-year-old going on seven *(Un Dio d'Amore d'età di sei anni in sette, a giacere in guisa d'uomo che dorme)*. After completing the work, if not during the very carving, Michelangelo had shown it to Lorenzo di Pierfrancesco, who thought it very fine. Then Lorenzo, at least according to Michelangelo's account, suggested that the sculptor prepare the *bambino* to appear like an antique, as if dug up from the earth. He intended to send it to Rome, where it would pass for a Roman (or Greek?) object and thus fetch a high price.

This falsification, if such is the correct term, has occasioned unfavorable commentary. Condivi, in a section based upon Michelangelo's remarkable memory *(tenacissima memoria),* lays the blame for the misrepresentation squarely on Lorenzo; but modern commentators have not been convinced. Lorenzo certainly had a role in the episode, confirmed by the fact that he wrote to Baldassarre about the matter and underscored as well by Baldassare's rancor toward him.

The *Cupid* had been sent to Rome, where the cardinal of San Giorgio purchased it as an antiquity for the tidy sum of 200 ducats, which was more than he would pay Michelangelo for the much larger *Bacchus.* The sale was handled by Baldassarre, who sent 30 ducats to Florence as Michelangelo's share—probably a fair price for a modern work of similar size. The extra 170 ducats was the added value for an antiquity. If the sculptor had duped the cardinal/purchaser, the agent, in turn, had duped Michelangelo (and Lorenzo di Pierfrancesco) when it came to the actual selling price. According to a contemporary report, upon learning of the sculpture's modernity, Cardinal Riario was so angry about having been taken in that he sent a representative to Florence to review the facts surrounding the *Cupid.* This man gained a certain intimacy with Michelangelo and become satisfied that Michelangelo had made the sculpture. Following his agent's report, the cardinal invited Michelangelo to Rome. In the meantime, Riario got his full 200 ducats back from Baldassarre.

Was there a moral lapse in Michelangelo's conduct in this episode of the *bambino,* dubbed by some a deception and by others a fake? Had the young Michelangelo slipped to the level of a common forger? After all, when Michelangelo was with Domenico Ghirlandaio, he had doctored his copy of Ghirlandaio's portrait by giving it an old patina. The artificial aging fooled Ghirlandaio, evidencing Michelangelo's skill, and it is possible that with the *Cupid,* his intention was the same. But since in this case there was a question of actually selling the object as an antique, one might fault Michelangelo's morals. Or, Michelangelo's actions could be seen as an attempt to belittle the widespread bias in favor of ancient art over contemporary work. In an environment in which an ancient object was held in higher regard than a modern one, and considering his age and his obscurity, Michelangelo's *bambino* should be understood not so much as an experiment in fakery but as a vivid demonstration of bravura by an ambitious twenty-year-old. Clearly he had no idea of the market value of a Roman antiquity anyway, for he had been originally satisfied with only 30 ducats.

The move to Rome was the end of a era for Michelangelo Buonarroti. Three years after Lorenzo's death, he was poised to make his way on his own by wit and by talent.

ROMA ETERNA E MAGNIFICA

Little did Michelangelo imagine during that June of 1496 that he would spend the larger part of the remainder of his long life in Rome, a city he would help reshape. *Florentia bella* would be exchanged for *Roma eterna e magnifica*—first for five years, later on for a decade, and finally for an uninterrupted thirty years following yet another interlude in Florence. Ironically enough, in terms of total years of residence, Michelangelo the Florentine should be regarded as Michelangelo the Roman, though never for a moment in his heart. During the last decades of his life in Rome, he fantasized about returning "home," a dream fulfilled only after death.

Giovanni Boccaccio's unflattering description of Rome in the *Decameron* could easily have been on Michelangelo's mind as he set out on short notice for Rome. In Boccaccio's pungent story, Abraham, a Jew from Paris who moves to Rome, discovers that at the

Roman court, from the highest to the lowest, "they all generally and most unworthily indulged in the sin of lechery, not only the natural way but sodomitically, without the slightest remorse or shame. And this to such an extent that the power of courtesans and boys was of considerable importance in obtaining favors. Moreover, they were openly gluttons, wine-bibbers, and drunkards, and afterwards lecherous, being like brute beasts, more servants of their bellies than of other senses." Abraham also saw that the Romans were "avaricious and grasping after money and that for money they bought and sold human, and even Christian blood, and also every sort of divine thing whether appertaining to the sacraments or to the benefices."

Lorenzo il Magnifico was equally uncomplimentary in a letter to his son, Giovanni, then still little more than a child, when as cardinal he was on the verge of taking up residence in Rome, a few years before Michelangelo's first migration. Il Magnifico warned Giovanni that the city was the "receptacle of all the evils imaginable, with no shortage of inciters and corrupters." Michelangelo, who never felt really comfortable in Rome even after half a lifetime there, seemed to share the opinions of his fellow Tuscans. His impressions of the city are manifest in the draft of a scathing sonnet that begins: "Here [in Rome] they make swords and helmets from chalices and the blood of Christ is sold by the bucketful, crosses and thorns become shields and blades, and even Christ is stripped of patience. Let him not come again to these places where his blood would shoot up to the stars; now in Rome his skin is being sold, and they have barred the way to every goodness."

St. Bernardino of Siena, preaching in Florence at the Buonarroti family's Church of Santa Croce, spoke of the trade in relics in much the same way in 1424. "The milk of a hundred cows," he said, "would not match the milk claimed as that of the Virgin Mary," and there are "so many pieces of wood of the true Cross of Jesus that putting them all together even six pairs of oxen would not be sufficient to drag them along."

Consider, for example, some of the relics that in Michelangelo's day were preserved in one church alone, San Giovanni in Laterano, said to have been built by Constantine the Great. A contemporary account lists the following accumulation: the head of St. Zachary; the head of St. Pancratius Martyr, from which blood issued for three continuous days when the church was burned down by heretics; relics of St. Mary Magdalene; a shoulder bone of St. Lawrence; a tooth of St. Peter; the chalice from which St. John the Evangelist drank poison at the command of the emperor but which did not harm him; the chain with which he was tied when led from Ephesus to Rome and one of his tunics which, when placed over three corpses, suddenly brought them back to life; some ashes and the hair shirt of St. John the Baptist; milk, hair, and clothing from the Virgin Mary; the shirt she made for Jesus; the cloth with which Jesus dried the feet of his disciples; the cane with which the head of Jesus was beaten; the red robe put on him by Pilate; wood from the Cross; the veil of Mary, which covered Jesus' genitals on the Cross; the shroud which was placed over his face in the tomb and some water and blood which issued from his side; the heads of Peter and Paul; the Rod of Aaron and of Moses; the table at which Jesus ate the Last Supper; and the stone slab on which the dice were thrown for the robes of Jesus. This is only a portion of the relics in a single church; multiplied by the number of relics elsewhere in Rome, it gives us an idea of the extent of a practice that Michelangelo discredited.

Still, though he seems to have been reluctant to admit it, perhaps because of his Florentine bias, Rome held infinite and matchless miracles for painters, sculptors, and architects. Like his predecessors, Michelangelo probably owned or at least consulted the *Marvels of the City of Rome (Mirabilia urbis Romae),* a manual for pilgrims that had gone through untold manuscript editions by the time Michelangelo made his first trip. As a sculptor, in addition to the classical sarcophagi that were scattered about, he must have been impressed by the *Dioscuri* on the Quirinal Hill (also known as the Hill of the Horses), the giant statues of horses and their tamers, handsome nudes later to be echoed, at least in scale and generic type, by his marble *David*. One legend had it that the monument was erected by the emperor Tiberius to commemorate two young men, Praxiteles and Phidias (the same names as the great Greek sculptors of the Golden Age), who were in the habit of going around Rome without clothes or possessions. Because they predicted the thoughts of the emperor, he awarded them the monument.

A large-scale bronze equestrian statue at the Lateran was thought by some to represent the emperor Constantine; others claimed, still according to the medieval account, that it was a squire who by heroics and wisdom saved the city, since the man is stretching out his right hand and sits upon his horse without a saddle. Today, it is believed that the bronze sculpture represents Marcus Aurelius; but beyond the subject, Michelangelo must have recognized its remarkable technical and artistic achievement. A decade later, he would struggle over a similar challenge when producing a twice-life-size cast bronze statue of Pope Julius for the facade of San Petronio in Bologna.

Could a sculptor of Michelangelo's learning have ignored the achievement attained in the carvings found on Trajan's Column in the center of Rome, not to mention so many illustrious ancient and medieval buildings? Michelangelo must have observed the Cancelleria, a Roman palazzo in the Renaissance style, as it was being constructed for his sometime patron, Cardinal Riario, although he might have preferred the clarity of the Palazzo Strozzi, the Palazzo Gondi, or the Medici Palace back home.

During those first years, as throughout his life, Michelangelo was an unrelenting worker; it is unlikely that he took much time out from his commissions for sightseeing. But friends from Florence like Giuliano da Sangallo must have shown him the significant landmarks, and it is recorded that Michelangelo admired the logical simplicity of the old St. Peter's, with its marvelous columns, lamenting its destruction a few years later to make room for the new basilica under the authority of the papal architect Donato Bramante. Once again, fate was to have its due: decades later Michelangelo would be responsible for redesigning and constructing the massive dome of the new building.

Shortly after Michelangelo settled in Rome, two of his brothers—his favorite, Buonarroto, and his oldest brother, Lionardo—came to visit him, possibly each more than once, proof of a family cohesion that was to become increasingly vital to Michelangelo.

During this first Roman interval, which lasted an unanticipatedly long time, the remarkable, all-encompassing cultural grip of Lorenzo de' Medici loosened its hold over Michelangelo. The artist's five years in Rome (1496–1501), at the ages of twenty-one to twenty-six, were an interregnum in his transformation from insecure neo-professional carver to self-confident, independent master. He devoted himself to establishing a reputation, which according to common wisdom was most effectively acquired away from home.

In Rome, each day was filled with intensive physical and mental activity; Michelangelo was wont to say that "one paints [but one can also substitute "sculpts"] with the brain and not with the hand." The objective proof of his hard work was two brilliant demonstration pieces: the *Bacchus,* pseudo-ancient in style and subject; and the *Pietà,* a commanding religious sculpture without rival in its genre. Both were in-the-round sculptures, universally regarded as belonging to the most demanding and prestigious category of stone carving, and each was rendered from a single stone, Michelangelo's self-imposed rule.

FATHER AND SON

Ironically, Michelangelo became more connected to his father and brothers when he moved away from them to Rome. Rediscovery of his immediate family, especially his father, filled the vacuum left by Lorenzo's death and the move out from Florence. With the passage of time, the attraction of il Magnifico's world was dissipating, although it never was wholly eradicated. In a shift of sympathy, Lorenzo's three sons, and his nephew Giulio, were supplanted in Michelangelo's life by the artist's own four brothers: Lionardo (born in 1473, two years before Michelangelo), Buonarroto (1477), Giovansimone (1479), and the baby, Sigismondo (1481), each one two years apart in age. And Lodovico effectively came to replace Lorenzo il Magnifico.

Although the external pretensions of the Buonarroti clan, even their petty mercantile aspirations and their disposition to acquire real estate, were a far cry from those of a young cardinal, a Milanese Sforza prince, or a Bentivoglio heir from Bologna, Michelangelo's familial attachments were natural since, after all, they were of his blood. As a well-known proverb says, "One selects his friends, but there is no choice when it comes to relatives" *(Amici a scelta, e parenti come sono)*. Without realizing it, Michelangelo was adjusting his social and intellectual orientation in a way that would affect the rest of his long life. Through need, or perhaps by default, he became the provider for his aging father and, when necessary, for his brothers and even their children. Another Tuscan proverb says: "First help your own, and then others if you can" *(Aiuta i tuoi, e gli altri se tu puoi)*.

In a particularly candid letter written in February 1500 from Florence, Lodovico expressed the hope of coming to Rome to visit his son for the Jubilee celebration organized by the Church for that year. Lodovico was responding to a recent letter in which Michelangelo had commented that his father seemed to be discontented or in bad humor (a sign of Michelangelo's attentiveness to his father's moods). Lodovico let his hair down in reply. "Yes," he wrote his second son, "you are quite right. While I have no complaints toward God, I have good reason to lament over my five children, all males. . . .

"Not a single one of you," he continued, unequivocally including Michelangelo, "is in a position to help me with so much as a glass of water, though I am now fifty-six years old." (Lodovico could not have known that another solid third of a century of life lay ahead of him.) "I have to pay for my keep," he continued, "and besides must cook for myself, sweep up, wash the pots and pans, bake bread, and in general I must think of everything; even when I have a headache, all I can do is scratch my balls [the Italian word is *le reni,* "kidneys"]. And if God were to take away my good health I would have to go to a hospice, for there is no one to look after me."

Lodovico's second wife, Lucrezia degli Ubaldini da Gagliano, had died three years before, leaving Lodovico alone. His lamentation must have struck his son to the heart. From Lodovico's perspective, Michelangelo had abandoned him, aged and alone, by leaving Florence four years before. His other sons were not helping much, to be sure. The oldest, Lionardo, named, as is customary, after his paternal grandfather, became a monk in the Dominican order, which greatly limited his actions. The other three, who lived in and around Florence, were disinclined to be swayed by their father's complaints, so the weight of Lodovico's mounting laments fell squarely upon the second son.

Meanwhile, a smoldering dispute between Michelangelo and his father surfaced in the very same letter: the nagging question of Michelangelo's occupation *(mestiere)* as marble carver. Lodovico acknowledged pleasure in having learned that Michelangelo had been the recipient of honors in Rome. But, he added pragmatically, and without much sensitivity for his sensitive son's feelings, "it would be far better indeed if there was financial gain. Of course, I esteem honor more, but the one and the other would be still better."

Like the good Tuscan he was, Lodovico went on: "I have long believed that the two contrary forces, honor and money, cannot exist together, but you have made them friends. Nonetheless, according to what you write, you are without money: one of my deepest misgivings, to be sure, is that you are in such bad straits."

At the close of the letter, Lodovico demonstrates a sensitivity not found elsewhere; he says that in this letter he has emptied himself out a bit. But "have patience," he asks of Michelangelo. "I am full of emotion and do not want anything from you, but I am concerned that you have been there [in Rome] such a long time and, according to what you write, you do not even have bread. If you were at your house [in Florence], perhaps you would have something and would not have to endure such exhaustion and undergo dangers. . . ."

The affection that Lodovico reveals at the end of this letter is confirmed by various touching little actions on both sides. When Michelangelo came to visit, among the old man's *ricordi* of June 20, 1517, we see that he purchased a couple of pepperonis and oranges for his son. And Michelangelo often reciprocated; when Lodovico was sick in 1526, Michelangelo sent him three capons and some candy. Again, Lodovico records a year later that Michelangelo had sent him "a pair of capons, three-quarters of a marzipan, a lot of candied almonds and anise."

Michelangelo did not return to Florence for another year after the first exchange of letters, which was part of a continuous stream. Although the *Pietà* was completed, he was awaiting final payment. Michelangelo was not always forthcoming over details when it came to his finances, so it is difficult to determine how much money he had at any given moment, though typically he tends to complain about being underpaid.

At the time the letter in question was written, Michelangelo was not yet spectacularly successful financially, but he soon would be. Still, he had been earning regularly, beginning with the *Bacchus* and then the *Pietà,* a condition that cannot be claimed for his four brothers. With guilt as his principal weapon, Lodovico skillfully manipulated his sculptor son's emotions. Lodovico must have understood Michelangelo's vulnerability. From time to time, when he was touched too close to the heart, an exasperated Michelangelo would beg Lodovico not to write any more.

The old man was not without initiative; much later, when he was over seventy years old, he took on a bureaucratic post at San Cassiano, a rural hill town about fifteen miles from Florence. Nevertheless, in varying circumstances, Michelangelo provided for Lodovico, although he was rarely available to bring the old man his glass of water or to console a headache. In time, Michelangelo began to look after his entire family: his father, brothers, a nephew and a niece; and when, in 1509, a dispute erupted between Lodovico and Giovansimone, an infuriated Michelangelo invited his father to stay with him in Rome.

Lodovico's lingering disapproval of Michelangelo's profession was virtually impossible to overcome. Being a sculptor was bad enough, honors apart, but Michelangelo was not even earning much money from that essentially demeaning activity, or so it seemed to his father. The source of disagreement festered: whatever Michelangelo accomplished, whatever successes came his way and however devoted a son he was, his efforts failed to satisfy the single individual in the entire world he most passionately vied to impress—Lodovico Buonarroti.

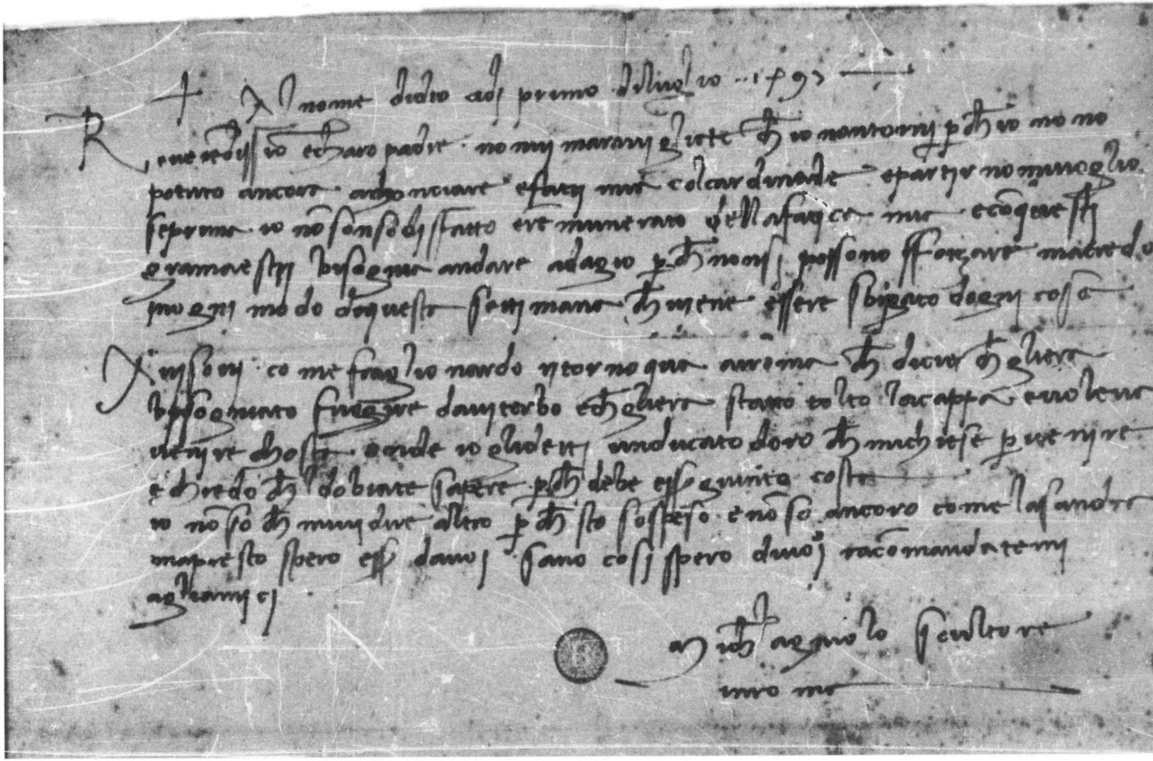

MICHELANGELO, letter to his father, 1497.

MICHELANGELO'S BROTHERS

The bonds between Michelangelo, his father, and his brothers were strengthened during his first five years in Rome. In 1497, Michelangelo wrote his father to the effect that he was working for Cardinal Riario and would not leave until he was paid in full for the *Bacchus*. He used the identical rationalization for staying in Rome while awaiting final payment for the *Pietà*. He mentions a visit from his oldest brother, Lionardo, who came to Rome from Viterbo, an ancient hill town about fifty miles north. We must assume that Lionardo, a known Savonarola supporter, had to flee Viterbo, then a stronghold of the Borgia pope, who was Savonarola's enemy. Since Lionardo was penniless, Michelangelo presented him with a single gold ducat, sufficient for the trip home to Tuscany. In a switch from the natural order of things, the younger brother was helping the older.

The rapport between the Buonarroti brothers is confirmed by another letter to Lodovico in the same year, in which Michelangelo mentions that his brother Buonarroto was in Rome for a visit. Michelangelo paid for his lodgings at an inn where "he will lack for nothing," explaining apologetically to their father that he could not personally host Buonarroto "because I am not residing in my own house." He may have been staying in some rooms supplied to him by Cardinal Riario. Meanwhile, between the two letters, on July 9, 1497, Lodovico's second wife, Lucrezia Ubaldini, died. But we have no hint whatsoever of Michelangelo's reaction, and his stepmother's name never occurs in his correspondence.

Did Lodovico actually make the trip to attend the Jubilee that he had mentioned in his letter of February 1500? Evidence is lacking, but since there is no confirmation, we might assume that he did not. Therefore, only after Michelangelo reestablished himself in Florence in 1501 was there occasion to cement the direct relationship with Lodovico and his brothers. As with other families, relations sometimes suffered inharmonious chapters when Michelangelo or one of the others lost patience. In a particularly gray mood, Michelangelo was once quoted by a family friend as saying, "I realize that I have neither father nor brothers nor anyone in the world who is devoted to me," language all too similar to that used by his father.

Yet Michelangelo demonstrated his affection and loyalty constantly. As late as 1521, he wrote to Lodovico that "I am certain that never since the day I was born until today was there ever in my soul the impulse to do anything either trivial or grand that was against you, and all the difficulties I have undergone I always did for your love." In this letter, the middle-aged Michelangelo, who in his own repeated rhetoric believed himself already "old," poignantly pleads for appreciation from his father. In another, somewhat earlier statement of his love (from 1509), Michelangelo avowed that he would rather be poor and have a father than to have all the money in the world without one. That there was a good deal of pain in the relationship between father and son might have reminded Michelangelo of the popular adage, "Family relations are like shoes, the closer [narrower] they are, the more they hurt" *(Parenti sono come scarpe, più sono stretti più fanno male)*.

Back in 1497, when Michelangelo was in Rome, Lodovico ran into problems with a debt he had incurred with a merchant named Consiglio d'Antonio Cisti, his brother-in-law—husband of his sister Brigida, of whom, incidentally, nothing is known. Michelangelo advised his father to compromise in order to settle, and even to "pay a little extra if necessary." And if Lodovico could not come up with the money, Michelangelo, then twenty-two and not exactly swimming in cash, would come up with it if at all possible, even if it meant that he would have to "sell himself as a slave" *(s'io dovessi vendermi per istiavo)* to do so. Lodovico, obviously relieved, triumphantly annotated the letter that Michelangelo would pay the debt.

Michelangelo often had trouble communicating with his father. A touching statement is tucked between the lines of a letter an exasperated son wrote in June 1523: "I do not know any longer what you want of me." He seems to be pleading, as he had done before and would do again. We can imagine his thought: "I've done everything possible to please you; I am the most famous artist in the world; I have purchased property for the benefit of the entire family; I have sacrificed my own life and the possibility of having a family of my own to look after you, Lodovico, and your sons, my brothers. I have worked night and day and undergone hardships of every description with no end in sight. But when all is said and done, I still do not know what [more] you wish of me." Through all this, Michelangelo's commanding impulse remained constant: his mission, the work.

Michelangelo also sought approval from his patron-father, Julius II. In a poem directed to the pope, he complains: "I am and long have been your faithful servant. I gave myself to you like rays of the sun; but . . . the more I exert myself, the less you like me." If we take his words at face value, the uncontrolled yearning for affection and appreciation from his elders seems such a dominant trait that it could be considered a flaw in Michelangelo's makeup. But if we recognize Michelangelo's use of rhetoric, the lamentations become part of a posture that presumably offered him solace. Sometimes his words are particularly poignant, as in the June 1523 letter in which Michelangelo says to Lodovico, "If my very existence troubles you, you have found the way to shelter yourself. Scream . . . and tell me whatever you wish, but do not write me anymore because you are not letting me work. . . ."

FRATE GIROLAMO SAVONAROLA

In his days in the Medici Gardens, Michelangelo had to be aware that across the piazza, in the Convent of San Marco, lived and practiced Florence's most notorious resident, Frate Girolamo Savonarola. The precise nature of Michelangelo's relationship with this man, and with his ideas, has been the subject of much speculation. There are those who would deny any significant exchange, while others consider Savonarola's ideas an inherent ingredient in Michelangelo's thinking; after all, he had a strong impact upon a whole generation. Savonarola was the most dynamic personality in Florence during the time Michelangelo was growing up, more so than il Magnifico. He had a fundamental effect on the political and religious life of the city, even long after he was burned to death in 1498.

ANONYMOUS, *Portrait of Savonarola.* Bookplate from *Oracolo della renovatione della chiesa* (Venice, 1543).

Michelangelo's first awareness and contact with the frate in Florence occurred before his Roman stay, yet the experience of that fiery preacher really belongs to a later phase in his life, when Michelangelo had the time and the distance to contemplate the frate's teaching. The artist had left Florence well before the upheavals and the "martyrdom" of Savonarola. But his friends and family members were in contact with the frate, and Michelangelo was probably well informed of what was transpiring.

Michelangelo must have been impressed with the entourage of cowled Dominicans in their black and white habits moving swiftly in and out of the convent, accompanying the frate to his sermons and public appearances at San Lorenzo and the Duomo. Even after half a century, Michelangelo vividly recalled the frate's powerful voice *(restandogli ancor nella mente la memoria della sua viva voce),* which drew a larger congregation than any other clergyman, including the popular St. Bernardino in his heyday. Savonarola, who grew up in Ferrara, was from an educated Paduan family of moderate means. He openly declared that he had been sent by God to announce that the Church was to be renewed, which would come about with terrible tribulations in Italy. Florence must suffer a devastating scourging, he said, but because the city was chosen by God as the site from which great events would be prophesied, Florence, where Savonarola preached, would be spared.

A man of dark complexion and medium height, Savonarola was regarded as having a sanguineous and bilious temperament, as well as being very high-strung. Gleaming dark gray eyes flashed out from beneath thick black brows, especially when he preached. He had an aquiline nose and a large mouth, which often revealed an attitude of stubborn fixedness; occasionally, however, his thick lips broke out in a benevolent smile.

Trained in philosophy and theology, Savonarola, once described as "the Socrates of Ferrara," began preaching in Lorenzo's time. Although Savonarola's predictions did not please il Magnifico, Lorenzo tolerated and perhaps even respected the frate, whom he recognized as a saintly man. According to credible reports that circulated in the city during those turbulent days, Lorenzo called Savonarola to his side when he was at death's door in April 1492. Poliziano, who was an eyewitness, says that Savonarola admonished the dying Lorenzo to hold on to the faith. As the frate was about to leave, Lorenzo said to him, "Give me your blessing, father, before you go," and he joined Savonarola in prayer. Yet, according to another account from the frate's followers, even at such a crucial moment, the two could not come to an understanding about liberty for Florence. When Savonarola asked Lorenzo to yield in favor of popular rule, Lorenzo shrugged his shoulders and did not speak; then Savonarola departed without giving him absolution.

After Lorenzo's death, which Savonarola had predicted as accurately as he did his own violent end, the frate conspicuously increased his public activity and his undisguised anti-Medici and anti-papal posture. As his prophecies became increasingly graphic, he acquired an increasingly large following, while his reputation as a holy man and prophet was strengthened. Some of the most learned persons in Florence attended his sermons, including the brilliant Giovanni Pico della Mirandola. Artists came to hear him: Sandro Botticelli, one of the few painters from the older generation whom Michelangelo admired; Verrocchio's pupil, Lorenzo di Credi; the architect Simone del Pollaiuolo, known as il Cronaca; several of the Della Robbia, those skilled sculptors of colored terra cotta; not to mention Savonarola's fellow Dominican, Fra Bartolommeo della Porta, a first-class painter of Michelangelo's generation.

Michelangelo's information about Savonarola's activities would have been indirect after 1494 when he left the city, except for the interval between Bologna and Rome when he was back in Florence. By coincidence, however, Michelangelo was employed by the Dominicans in Bologna for the Arca of their patron at the very same convent that had been Savonarola's home years before he turned up in Florence.

Michelangelo returned from Bologna to Florence early in 1496, and it was then that the voice of the preacher was imprinted on his memory. He was undoubtedly among the excited listeners on February 17, 1496, when Savonarola preached in the Duomo despite papal threats of excommunication. Public opinion held it to have been the most momentous day of the frate's life—his "eyes flashing like burning coals."

When Michelangelo left for Rome in June, he lost track of Savonarola. By the time he returned five years later, the frate was long since dead. But the artist stayed informed through his Florentine network in Rome, and through letters, even though his Florentine correspondents were guarded in their written reports, while Michelangelo was his usual closed-mouthed self. "Never leave anything written" *(Mai iscritti)* was a motto he seemed to live by when it came to potentially controversial questions, such as his opinion about Savonarola or the Medici. And he constantly admonished his father to do the same. Michelangelo was so successful in concealing his private views that no one has ever been quite sure where he stood in the controversy over the frate, although it is known from Condivi that his careful and attentive study of the Old as well as the New Testaments included interpretations by Savonarola.

Michelangelo probably was fascinated by accounts of the burning of the vanities, instigated by Savonarola. Public spectacles like this were not new, although Savonarola's were far and away the most widely attended. In February 1497 at Carnival time, almost a year after the last occasion Michelangelo heard Savonarola, bands of children with their hooded guides, followers of the frate, combed the city for anything that was styled as "vanities" or "anathemas." Savonarola's supporters collected gambling implements, dice, cards, indelicate costumes, and masks, as well as "indecent" paintings and books. A beautiful marble image of the baby Jesus kept at San Lorenzo, which had been carved by a favorite of Cosimo *Pater Patriae,* Desiderio da Settignano, was carried at the head of a procession that moved toward the Piazza della Signoria, where a seven-story pyre was constructed on the colorful ceramic pavement. At the agreed signal, torches were put to the 60-foot-high pyramid while the bells of the Palazzo Signoria echoed through the narrow cobblestone streets. The vanities were swept up in flames on the very spot where Savonarola himself would later be consumed by a similar blaze.

Savonarola continued to speak out openly, claiming that the events he prophesied came directly from God. He asserted that the city would be freed from tyranny, referring of course to the Medici, and would be ruled instead by a popular republican government, like that of Venice. Ironically, for a brief time after the expulsion of Piero in 1494, Savonarola was, in effect, the ruler of the city. His painful end

ANONYMOUS, *Savonarola Preaching.* Bookplate from the *Compendio di revelatione* (Florence, 1495).

came soon enough, as animosity intensified between his partisans, among whom one must number the young Michelangelo, and his enemies.

Savonarola predicted that Florence would regain Pisa, which it had recently lost, and that the city would become more powerful and more glorious than ever before. Still, opposition mounted from both inside and outside Florence. From Rome, Pope Alexander VI (Borgia), who had succeeded Innocent VIII, expressed a particular loathing for Savonarola's preachings about the renovation of the Church. The Venetians and the Milanese hated Savonarola, whom they saw as favoring the French and Charles VIII's plans for controlling Italy. Devotees of other religious orders, especially the Franciscans, vigorously opposed the frate, possibly out of jealousy for his power and popularity. Since he vigorously preached against sodomy and other "vices," licentious living, and gambling, he incurred the wrath of yet another faction within the city, known as the "angry ones" *(arrabbiati)*. Among those who were disposed to see his downfall was Michelangelo's own patron, Lorenzo di Pierfrancesco de' Medici.

Bartolommeo della Rocca, known as Cocles, was a chiromancer and physiognomer from Bologna, as well as an astrologer and an interpreter of dreams. His negative opinion of Savonarola was adduced from his slanty eyes, which signified a hot, envious, and deceptive individual, "a great deceiver and seducer of the people, defrauder of defrauders." Cocles's judgment was based entirely on physical appearance: "small pointed head, eyes longitudinally shaped, aquiline nose, thick lips, and the livid, ashen color of the face, the oblique neck." An indication of Savonarola's enormous body heat was that he could not endure to wear undergarments, or any covering on his head. For the Bolognese mystic, the friar's baldness indicated dryness in the brain. At the same time, Savonarola was described as being very hairy all over his body. Finally, Cocles warned, "Beware of pseudo-prophets thus complexioned."

Botticelli's brother, Simone Filipepi, left a favorable impression of Girolamo Savonarola: "To observe him when not in the pulpit, he seemed like a little lamb [*agnellino*], as indeed he was, full of humility and charity . . . but in the pulpit he seemed larger than his normal stature, revealing a lively and virile spirit . . . without fear of any living man, just as the ancient prophets and martyrs were."

Various intrigues were brewing over the direction of the Florentine government and the division of power. Besides, Piero de' Medici, supported by the Franciscans (who were the natural competitors of the Dominicans), sought with unrelenting determination to resurrect his former role. In June 1497, the pope excommunicated the prophet, accusing the frate of preaching heresies and of disobedience for having refused to appear before him when summoned. Savonarola did stop preaching for a time as a consequence of the papal order, but early the following year he began public preaching at the Duomo once more. In these months, the Florentine government was in general disarray due to a new system of electing officials, and talk persisted of forming a government with Lorenzo di Pierfrancesco de' Medici and his brother Giovanni.

As the Jubilee Year, 1500, approached, the stage was set for the downfall of the frate. Through trickery and ingenuity, in a staged trial by fire with the Franciscans, he was taken to the pyre and burned in the very Piazza della Signoria where the vanities had been ignited. But first he was tortured, so that he would make a confession. He died—some said a martyr's death—on May 23, 1498, just before Michelangelo was commissioned to create his Roman *Pietà*. One has to wonder whether the news of Savonarola's fiery demise affected Michelangelo's conception of the work, with its intense spirituality.

The sculpture, commissioned by a French cardinal, was an enormous challenge because Michelangelo had to include two fully grown, nearly life-size figures within a single marble block, and to establish a convincing emotional but also a formal rapport between them. He came up with a brilliant solution: two sets of proportions, one for the body of Mary—large, robust, and powerful enough to visually support the weight of her thirty-three-year-old son—and the second for the head of Mary, small in relation to the scale of her body, and for the whole figure of the dead Christ. Artistic treatment of the theme of the *Pietà*, which was by no means original to Michelangelo, had always suffered from the inherent disparity of size, but Michelangelo successfully resolved the problem in such a way that his shift of proportions is hardly noticeable.

The enmity between Lorenzo il Magnifico and Savonarola must have disturbed Michelangelo, as both men had meant much to him in different ways. Lorenzo had a far stronger impact on the evolution of his art, but many continue to believe that Savonarola's ideas were on Michelangelo's mind as he plotted out the Sistine Chapel ceiling and other religious works, not to mention his poetry. Proof of some kind of connection between Michelangelo and Savonarola is revealed in passing in a letter written by Michelangelo's assistant and friend, the Ferrarese Piero d'Argenta, to Michelangelo's brother, Buonarroto, while the artist was in the quarries of Carrara getting marble. (In fact, this letter until recently was thought to have been written by Michelangelo, using his assistant's name for the sake of secrecy.) Pietro reminds Buonarotto to send Fra Girolamo (Savonarola) his regards *(rachomandarmi a fra Girolamo)*. As we have seen, Michelangelo was always cautious about any public display of his relationships or allegiances; not so Piero d'Argenta. Buonarroto and Piero, two people very close to the sculptor, were undeniably in contact with Savonarola: Michelangelo probably was too; but *mai iscritti*. The work that is closest in time to Savonarola is, of course, the *Pietà*, where the apparent ages of Jesus and Mary—the latter appears unusually young—were a source of contemporary controversy. A French member of the cardinal's entourage who ordered the work questioned Mary's age:

where could she appear so young with a thirty-three-year-old son? Michelangelo, quick to react to the criticism, was said to have given a response worthy of Savonarola: "in Paradise, that is where."

VICTORIOUS AT HOME

Michelangelo returned to Florence in 1501, no longer a struggling young sculptor but one of recognized achievement. By then his

LEONARDO DA VINCI, detail of a map of Tuscany showing the Arno River, c. 1503–04. • The area that is reproduced here lies directly to the west of Florence and includes Leonardo's home town of Vinci, as well as Lamporecchio, the place where Michelangelo's friend the poet Francesco Berni was born. Lastra a Signa, the river port where the marbles were shipped from Pisa on their way to Florence, is also shown.

memories of the Medici Gardens and the Medici Palace may have dimmed. But there was still to be one final incident. On December 28, 1503, Piero de' Medici drowned in the Gargliano River in southern Italy during a battle. This was the tragic end of Piero's unfortunate campaign to return triumphant to Florence. Although buried in Montecassino, it was several decades before an appropriate tomb for him was provided by Francesco da Sangallo, the son of his mentor Giuliano, who was selected to execute the monument, presumably on Michelangelo's recommendation. A few months before Piero's death,

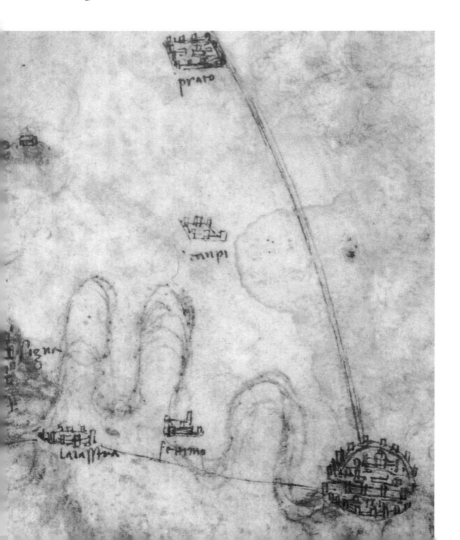

his cousin Lorenzo di Pierfrancesco de' Medici died, some said of the dreaded syphilis. Once these two men had disappeared from Michelangelo's life, the world of the Buonarroti Simoni took first place.

During his five years in Rome, Michelangelo had captured the attention of the papal court, had produced the *Pietà* for a French cardinal, and had executed the *Bacchus* for Cardinal Raffaello Riario, nephew of Sixtus IV and cousin of the man who would become pope as Julius II; besides, he had been patronized and befriended by Jacopo Galli, a leading Roman banker. All things considered, Michelangelo had to have been pleased with himself upon arriving back home around mid-March, just in time for the New Year, which was celebrated on March 25, the feast day of the Annunciation in Florence in those days. He had every right to be proud. On the practical side, at twenty-six he had accumulated substantial credits in the Balducci bank from his two sculptures and he was considered the premier marble carver in Rome.

Yet Michelangelo must have realized that the real test of his career would be in Florence, for, after all, Florentines were far more discerning than Romans when it came to art (and everything else for that matter, in Michelangelo's opinion). They were known as merciless faultfinders, so their approval would signify genuine accomplishment. For Michelangelo, success would be sweetest in the shadow of Brunelleschi's massive cupola, where, to be sure, he was happiest. He had been homesick in Rome, hungry for contact with his father, brothers, and friends. He must have missed the coarse, crusty, saltless bread, the salty ham, Trebbiano wine, early green pears, the marzipan that his father would treat him to now and again, the narrow, bustling streets, Ghiberti's *Gates of Paradise,* Donatello's *St. George* set in a niche at Orsanmichele, the Arno with its fine bridges, and the cool hills called Monte Morello on the Bologna road overlooking the Arno Valley.

The next challenge was to make his mark at home in order to

win new commissions. He sought, besides, the respect of established artists, painters, and sculptors who already had achieved rank and reputation, while at the same time he kept a watchful eye on the younger ones who were emerging. Sandro Botticelli, whose art, with the exception of his delicate illustrations for Dante's *Divine Comedy,* probably did not attract him, but whom he respected, was at the top of Michelangelo's list. They also shared the admiration of Lorenzo di Pierfrancesco, who patronized them both. Generous old Cosimo Rosselli was still painting in his stiff, outmoded manner, while his best pupil, Piero, took on his master's name, "di Cosimo"—a strange chap, though learned and witty, he painted mainly panel pictures of puzzling erudition on the primitive history of mankind, besides more traditional altarpieces.

RUSTICHI, **drawing of Florence Duomo,** c. 1440.

Michelangelo did not worry much about the opinion of the urbane Filippino Lippi, son of the frate Filippo. Filippino had trouble with the human figure, treating it schematically, without bones or muscles. Although Filippino was regularly awarded the best fresco commissions in Florence and Rome, we can assume that Michelangelo judged his style as overly decorative. Besides, could Michelangelo ever have forgiven Filippino for adjusting and completing Masaccio's unfinished Brancacci Chapel frescoes a half a century after they were begun? These were the same frescoes that Michelangelo had studied so attentively in his youth, the works for which he suffered a broken nose.

Michelangelo would have sought to prove himself to Pietro Perugino, the painter from Umbria, who had an active *bottega* in Florence, and to Lorenzo di Credi, pupil of the sculptor-painter Andrea del Verrocchio.

The news surely reached Michelangelo that another Verrocchio pupil, Leonardo di ser Piero, from Vinci on the edge of the sprawling, low Montalbano, had returned to Florence after nearly twenty years in Milan. The talk of Leonardo's presence in Florence may have stirred Michelangelo's competitive streak. Although we must presume that word of Michelangelo's Roman achievements reached Florence, he had to prove his worth as an artist all over again, firsthand. None of the painters and sculptors in Florence, even Giuliano da Sangallo, had a clear notion of Michelangelo's capacities.

Fully prepared by skill, technique, and artistry to flex his muscles, Michelangelo was entering into a new phase in his personal as well as artistic life. He had passed the learning stage, with all its excitement, when everything was fresh and inspiring, and when he drank in the past, whether the tradition of his immediate predecessors or their more distant heritage, from Greece and Rome. Now he itched to take on all comers. Like an alert pugilist, Michelangelo was at the height of his powers: lean, lithe, and agile. While he continued to expand his visual vocabulary with a vast repertoire of forms and images, the moment had come, at age twenty-six, to spar with the greatest artists of the past and present.

It is fitting, then, that the object that best represents this new phase, the marble *David,* should reflect metaphorically his state of mind and his moment in time. To vie with giants, the artist produced one of his own, and in so doing, became one himself. This transformation had to take place in Florence: his *David,* located at the main entrance of the governmental headquarters, the Palazzo Signoria, would become the symbol of his city as it has become the symbol of Michelangelo's art.

Michelangelo's reentry into Florence, which turned out to be not as permanent as he might have preferred, was thus essential for his personal evolution and for his mission. He was aware of babble in the workshops to the effect that the huge marble block he had eyed throughout his adolescence, which lay in a courtyard at the side of the Duomo, was to be carved. A lucky sculptor would win the commission—or perhaps an unlucky one, considering the inherent difficulty of the assignment. Some believed that the block, which had been attacked by several sculptors a generation before in efforts to carve from it a *David,* was ruined. There were rumors that the mythic Leonardo entertained ambitions to carve the *David,* although he was not a sculptor and would have botched the job as he had the gigantic horse he had begun in Milan. Probably also hoping for a chance would have been the talented sculptors Benedetto da Maiano and Baccio da Montelupo, as well as Andrea Sansovino. All the more reason for Michelangelo to hasten back to Florence and put in his claim for the block.

The Gonfaloniere of Justice, Piero Soderini, who was appointed to this office as chief administrator of Florence for life *(a vita)* in 1502, was among Michelangelo's most devoted supporters. The circumstances and precisely when Soderini, who has been described as a colorless model of an "anti-prince," took notice of the sculptor have not been determined. We do know, however, that Soderini held Michelangelo in the highest regard and that their relationship lasted nearly twenty years, until Soderini's death in 1519. Soderini was at the pinnacle of anti-Medici politics and effectively in charge of the

Florentine government a few years after Piero de' Medici's enforced departure. Since Soderini was allied with the *Popolani,* or pro–republican branch of the Medici, and since Lorenzo di Pierfrancesco was close to Michelangelo, it is likely that Michelangelo met Soderini before he left for Rome, through the good graces of Lorenzo di Pierfrancesco.

Within a few months after his return to Florence in 1501, Michelangelo had obtained three sculpture commissions directly or indirectly attributable to Soderini's influence: statuettes for the Pic–colomini Altar in Siena's Cathedral; a bronze "copy" or adaptation of Donatello's *David* for a French patron specifically arranged by Soderini; and the marble *David.* Additionally, Michelangelo was awarded the commission to execute twelve marble *Apostles* for the in–terior of the Duomo, a demanding project that was never actually car–ried out (he began just one figure). But it was the *David* that was to catapult him into the highest ranks of sculptors.

THE GIANT: *DAVID*

The chronicle of the marble *David* predates Michelangelo's involve–ment by nearly forty years. Back in 1463, the directors of cathedral works *(Operai del Duomo)* had awarded the sculptor Agostino di Duccio, perhaps even with indications from his by then very elderly master, Donatello, a commission to carve a *David* of extensive dimensions to be placed on the Duomo, possibly on one of the but–tresses. Agostino abandoned the project, and a few years later another sculptor, Antonio Rossellino, had a fling at it: both of them, proba–bly overwhelmed by the sheer size of the block, over fourteen feet in

MICHELANGELO, **drawing for the bronze** *David,* **c. 1504.**

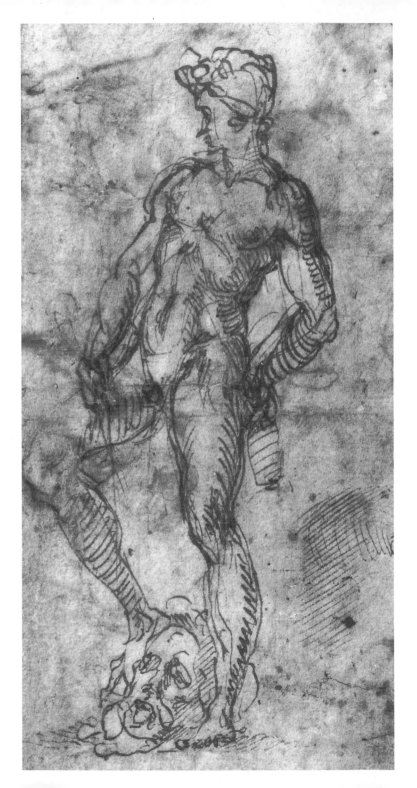

height, and the expansive scale required, gave up. The partially carved marble block was left all but forgotten until the beginning of the new century, when attention was drawn to it again.

On July 2, 1501, the directors of the Duomo and of the Wool Guild *(Arte della Lana),* who had a supervisory role over the Duomo, held deliberations and decided that "that figure called *David,* poorly roughed out and carved [*male abbozzata e scolpita*]" should be finished. Six weeks later, Michelangelo was awarded the commission, one that was to consolidate his position in Florence as the *Pietà* had done in Rome. Even though the block belonged to the Cathedral and the church administration had actually assigned the work to Michelangelo, the Signoria had an embracing interest as well. To be sure, there is some mystery about all this, for it would be surprising that the commission was handed out and the image was carved before a site was agreed upon by the commissioners as well as by the sculptor.

RAPHAEL, study after
Michelangelo's *David,* c. 1505.

Michelangelo first constructed a brick wall around the working area and a roof above it, so that he could proceed unobserved and undisturbed. In early September 1501, he appears to have begun carving by ceremoniously knocking off a node of marble on the figure's chest *(uno vel duobus dictibus scarpelli substulisset quoddam nodum quem habebat in pectore).* He proceeded with gusto, and by the end of February 1502, the *David* was described in a document as "semifinished" *(semifactus)*, meaning that it already must have had its over-all shape and appearance. According to the contract, he had only two years in which to finish the *David*, so Michelangelo continued to work effectively during the following months. It must have been very far along by June 23, 1503, when it was given a public viewing on the eve of the feast day celebrating St. John the Baptist. Since John is Florence's patron saint, the statue—which Michelangelo inevitably referred to as *the giant (il gigante)*, never as *David*—had acquired a pa-triotic aura. In the following months the work of surface refinement was finished, so that by the end of 1503 the *David* was close to com-pletion.

The most remarkable meeting of Renaissance artists ever recorded, and arguably the most extraordinary encounter of its kind in history, occurred on January 25, 1504, when some two dozen painters, sculptors, artisans, and architects were convened to take up the question of the appropriate location for Michelangelo's all but fin-ished marble *David*. This kind of consultive assembly (known in Florence as a *practica*) represented a sophisticated vehicle by which the government obtained advice, but was not obligated to accept it; in fact, no vote as such was taken. The opinions vented were signifi-cantly varied, making the implicit recommendations thoroughly in-conclusive. Nevertheless, the symbolic impact of the meeting has to have been formidable because the prestige of the participants was un-equaled.

History is surely indebted to the priest who transcribed verbatim the participants' statements. They are preceded by a preamble:

> . . . the officials of the Duomo, seeing that the statue, that is, the *David*, is almost finished, and being desirous of placing it in a suit-able and commodious place, one that is secure and solid, as Michelangelo, the master of the aforesaid *giant*, has requested, and the directors of the Wool Guild, desirous of putting into effect these wishes, decided to call a meeting of selected masters, men and

architects, whose names appear in the common language [i.e., Italian, not Latin], along with what they said, word for word.

Clearly, as he was concluding his assignment, Michelangelo sought assurances that the placement would prevent vandalism, which it did not.

The names of the participants (Michelangelo himself was conspicuously absent) are a Who's Who of Florentine art and allow for unprecedented insights into the world in which Michelangelo operated. The artists involved reveal themselves as insightful, intelligent, practical, and direct.

The opening speaker, Francesco di Lorenzo Filarete, was the First Herald of the Signoria, a state official whose competence pertained mainly to civic, ceremonial questions; his recommendations deserve particular attention. The First Herald spoke with authority and perhaps with a knowledge of what may have been decided in secret before the meeting, very possibly between high government officials and the sculptor.

Two sites could support the weight of the *giant,* the Herald observed. One was the area next to the entrance of the Palazzo Signoria, where Donatello's *Judith and Holofernes* had recently been placed, and the other was in the middle of the courtyard of the Palazzo Signoria, then occupied by another *David* by Donatello. These bronzes had belonged to the Medici, having been transferred from their palace on the Via Larga to the Palazzo Signoria after the expulsion of the family ten years before, an action that sought to redefine Donatello's sculptures as public, republican images rather than private Medici ones.

The Herald, whose suggestions set the tone of the entire meeting, explains that "The first statue [the *Judith*] is a mortifying symbol anyway; nor is it appropriate for us [i.e., Florentines], who have as an insignia the cross and the lily, to have a woman kill a man." The logic employed here is shabby: the story of Judith, who beheads the Assyrian general Holofernes to save her people, is from the Old Testament Apocrypha (and is in fact a theme that Michelangelo was to paint on the Sistine Chapel ceiling several years later). Since the Herald's explanation rang hollow, probably even to himself, he found it necessary immediately to offer a more credible argument for the gathering.

"The statue of *Judith*," he went on, "was placed at the Palazzo [Signoria] under an astrologically negative sign, and after it was put there, things have gone from bad to worse and we have lost Pisa." Since the placement of the *Judith* on the *ringhiera*, the low wall in front of the Palazzo beside the main portal, was the first location mentioned by the Herald, who was the most "official" speaker at the meeting, it must have been the one favored by the government.

The Herald offered an alternative. They could place Michelangelo's *David* "Where [Donatello's] *David* now stands," in the inner courtyard of the Palazzo, a location which he justified because Donatello's statue "is imperfect and besides its back leg is ridiculous." This negative aesthetic claim, which probably can be ascribed to Michelangelo, is not readily confirmed visually. Rather, it seems like an excuse. The First Herald's arguments demonstrate the extent to which the government was willing to go, even to deprecate the valued Donatello sculptures, in order to get Michelangelo's *gigante* where they wanted it. The real text, as revealed here, is that the government wanted the new *David* to be placed either on the parapet outside the Palazzo Signoria or in the courtyard of the same building. The current inhabitants of those locations therefore had to be disqualified.

The next speaker, the woodworker Francesco Monciatto, waxed philosophical, saying commonsensically that "everything that is made is made for a purpose." The statue was made to be placed on one of the pilasters of the church, where he thought it would look good. Yet he did not insist upon the location, adding that either the Duomo or the Palazzo would be acceptable.

Cosimo Rosselli, the much-beloved painter and teacher, also advocated both general locations, the Palazzo and the Duomo, but he preferred the latter, where he would place the *David* on the right side of the church. Rosselli then raised a new issue: what kind of base, which he sees as necessarily high, should the sculpture have? Michelangelo and his sponsors, whoever they really were, had postponed a decision about the base until the more fundamental decision of the permanent location was taken. Like the previous speaker, Rosselli seems not to have been privy to any secret deals, and was evidently oblivious to the political implications of the statue and its placement.

Sandro Botticelli underscored Rosselli's opinion, also opting for the side of the Duomo, to be matched by a figure of *Judith*. "There it would rest well and there I would place it," he

DONATELLO, *Judith and Holofernes*, 1450s.

said, overtly rejecting the notion that *Judith and Holofernes* was an inappropriate theme; after all, Botticelli himself had painted it.

The next speaker, Giuliano da Sangallo, demonstrated a more acute sensitivity to political realities when he said that "yes, he would have it in the same place as Botticelli recommended but . . . considering the imperfect state of the marble, which is tender and 'cooked,' and because it has been in the open air, it might not last." This line of argument, hinted at by the Herald, had not been taken up earlier, though for Sangallo it became fundamental. All things considered, he maintained that it would be much better to place the work in the Loggia dei Lanzi, a vast three-arched structure open on two sides, which stands at right angles to the Palazzo Signoria. The statue could appear either in the middle, so that people could walk around it, or in the center of the right bay, close to the back wall, with a black niche behind. In the Loggia, the statue would be protected from the elements. The notion of isolating the white *David* with a black niche was in itself a revolutionary proposal. Besides, the placement on the back wall would have eliminated the possibility of viewing the statue from different angles, but especially from behind. In his conclusion, Giuliano argued again that leaving the statue in the open air around the Duomo would cause it quickly to disintegrate. The question of the Loggia, which would be repeated often by later speakers, was not raised by the Herald. But since Giuliano was Michelangelo's friend, presumably his alternatives were acceptable to the sculptor, or at least not objectionable to him.

The legend of the imperfect, not to say ruined, block has become an integral part of *David* lore, and was stressed by both Condivi and Vasari, who based their comments upon Michelangelo's point of view. The implication is that if the block is recognized as having been abused *before* Michelangelo was assigned to carve it, his achievement with the *David* would have to be regarded as an even greater miracle than it is recognized to be. On the other hand, one should distinguish between the mutilation of the marble by earlier sculptors and the possible damage to the block provoked by exposure to the elements. The claim of Giuliano, which will be repeated, that the work would disintegrate if left in the open air seems like a trumped-up argument without solid support, as history would prove, for the statue in fact withstood the elements although it stood out-of-doors for four hundred years.

The opinion of the next speaker, the Second Herald, nephew of the First Herald, should also be regarded as echoing the official government line. He too considered only the Loggia. Like Giuliano, the reason given for this covered location was that the work must be under protection because of its poor condition. Two alternative positions inside the Loggia were put forward: the central bay, which the Second Herald immediately rejected as interfering with ceremonies normally held there; and the bay nearest to the Palazzo's main doorway, his preference.

The goldsmith Andrea, known as il Riccio, an artist of reputation, agreed with the Second Herald, but added an unexpected consideration. If it were placed in the Loggia, passersby could go and look at the statue ("the thing," *tal cosa,* is his exact phrase) and not have the statue seem to look at them. Ascribing a human quality to the work is implicit in his observation. As for the main point at issue, the state officials and their supporters, including the next speaker, the famous clockmaker Lorenzo della Volpaia, were in general agreement, as were the two who followed, the painters Biagio and Bernardo di Marco.

There must have been a rustle of anticipation when the bearded Leonardo da Vinci's turn came to speak. He had given no thought whatsoever to putting it on or near the Duomo, as his brief remarks record: "I support the opinion that it should be in the Loggia where Giuliano advocated, on the little wall where the seatbacks [*spalliere*] are attached to the wall, with an appropriate ornamentation, in such a way as not to upset the ceremonies held there."

After Leonardo, the jeweler Salvestro made a new suggestion. "I think," he said, "that the man who made the statue should be the one to name the best place." Salvestro himself believed that an area of the Palazzo was to be preferred, but "the person who has made it, notwithstanding what I said, knows the best place, better than anyone else, because of the character of the figure." Filippino Lippi agreed, saying that the sculptor should choose, "since he must have contemplated for a long time where he wished it to be placed."

The weaver Galliena referred specifically to the work's beauty, the only speaker to do so. "Seeing the quality of the statue," he would place it in the most public spot possible, where the Lion, symbol of the city, is located, on the wall in front of the Palazzo Signoria. The speaker proceeded to raise the question of a fitting base for the statue. As for the seated Lion (the well-known *Marzocco*, yet another work by Donatello), an essential image for the piazza since it was the symbol of Florence, Galliena suggested that it should be placed at the side of the palace's main portal. As it turned out, Galliena's proposal was prophetic, only the objects were reversed, with Michelangelo's *David* going beside the portal rather than the Lion. This location was seconded by someone who had been close to Michelangelo in his youth, Davide Ghirlandaio, who along with his brothers Domenico (who had since died) and Benedetto supervised Michelangelo in their shop. If there had been any rancor between them, it did not crop up in Davide's unambivalent statement.

Another person who belonged to Michelangelo's circle, Antonio da Sangallo, rejected the idea that the *David* should go where the Lion was because the weakened marble would not survive the elements, thus following his brother Giuliano's line of argument. Placement in the Loggia dei Lanzi was revived in the discussion. As an alternative— sliding over the question of the danger from weathering—Antonio also proposed a location on the street, but in this case the passersby would have difficulty seeing it, he concluded. A few months later,

Antonio would help in the risky task of moving the *David* from the workshop at the Duomo to the Piazza Signoria. He also had a hand in designing the base.

A goldsmith named Michelangelo (who was, incidentally, the father of Baccio Bandinelli, Michelangelo's sculptor-rival in the next decades), with political correctness praised all the speakers, but especially Giuliano da Sangallo. His first choice was to place the *giant* in the Loggia as proposed by Giuliano. If the solution was disagreeable, then the work should be housed in the middle of the Hall of the Great Council *(Sala del Maggior Consiglio),* the main hall of government, an engaging new alternative. Little did he know that in a few months Michelangelo and Leonardo da Vinci would be projecting vast mural projects for the same room.

Giovanni Piffero, another official of the government whose assignment had to do with public ceremonies (and who was the father of Benvenuto Cellini, the most famous sculptor and goldsmith of the next generation), supported Giuliano's proposal, provided that the statue would be visible in its entirety. A man close to Gonfaloniere Piero Soderini, he had in mind the question of how the sculpture should be properly viewed: as he thought, one must be able to move around it; this, beyond such factors as the size, the space, the walls, and the roof. Giovanni Piffero introduced a curious suspicion. If located out in the open, some nasty person might do the statue harm. That is, for some unexplained reason, the *David* might become the target of vandalism (this was, as we know, a concern of Michelangelo's, and such a possibility supports the suspicion that there was a political aura surrounding the *David* that could have made it offensive to some). In his considered statement, Giovanni noted that he would rather see the work in the courtyard of the Palazzo, as the First Herald had proposed; such a placement would give profound comfort to "the author," since the statue would be both protected and in a dignified place. His remarks show considerable diffidence and respect for Michelangelo.

The medalist and carver of gems Giovanni Corniole took a different tack. He was at first inclined to put the *David* where the Lion stood, but admitted that he had not considered the fact that the marble was tender and could be ruined by water and the cold; with that in mind, he supported placement in the Loggia, as advocated by Giuliano da Sangallo.

The priest's direct transcription ends with Piero di Cosimo, who also opted for placement in the Loggia, especially "if the man who made it should be in agreement, for he knows best how it should be." The others who spoke, also masters of the highest caliber, alluded to positions already expressed, so the scribe considered it unnecessary to report their words. Among those whose names occur but who were not explicitly quoted were Andrea della Robbia, heir to the famous workshop of colored terra cottas; Attavante the miniaturist; Michelangelo's oldest friend, the painter Francesco Granacci; the architect Simone del Pollaiuolo, known as il Cronaca; Pietro Perugino, then the most sought after painter in Italy; Lorenzo di Credi, a pupil of Verrocchio's along with Leonardo da Vinci; and the sculptor Giovan Francesco Rustici, a frequenter of the Medici Gardens with Michelangelo, who had a close working association with Leonardo da Vinci. The name of the accomplished sculptor Andrea da Sansovino was raised, but he was in Genoa at the time.

The *David* was finally placed where the First Herald advocated, on the *ringhiera,* flanking the main doorway of the Palazzo Signoria, in place of Donatello's *Judith and Holofernes.* This was probably the intention of the city fathers from the very beginning, once they assumed control over the statue, and the creating artist must have been in agreement. Such a conclusion seems inevitable, implying that the meeting of "experts" was something of a formality, or worse, a sham, conducted to defuse any possible opposition before it could materialize.

The meeting certainly helped Michelangelo's reputation, since all of the participants, from Leonardo, who had made a thumbnail sketch of the *David,* perhaps in anticipation of the meeting, to influential sculptors like Rustici and Giuliano da Sangallo, to Florence's finest painters, Filippino Lippi, Botticelli, Perugino (the teacher of Raphael, who soon would become Michelangelo's most serious competition as a painter), were assembled specifically to contemplate his master-

LEONARDO DA VINCI, drawing of Michelangelo's *David,* 1504.

piece. Michelangelo was not merely the talk of the town but the focus of the artistic community's attention.

Behind the secrecy, unquestionably political thinking had a role at the meeting. The Medicis' return constituted a very real threat. Although for the moment enfeebled, the Medici faction remained intent on their ambitions to unseat the government, which were fulfilled eight years later. Unlike the elegant and sensual adolescent of Donatello's bronze *David,* Michelangelo's *David* is older, more determined, and stronger, a much larger man. His intense gaze expresses vigilance; his increased physical strength, the ability and determination to defend the republic. This was not the victorious Old Testament hero—giant killer with the severed head of Goliath at his feet. Michelangelo's *David* has yet to confront Goliath. The enemy is present only potentially, although the inevitability of David's victory is made clear, all of which served as a material warning to real and potential enemies inside and outside the city, but especially the Medici. The patriot *David* underscored the city's determination to remain free.

Michelangelo had shifted his figure's meaning from the conventional "Victorious David" to a hero only potentially victorious; in so doing, he reversed the roles of David and Goliath. His statue, consequently, cannot be interpreted as a lesson in moral conduct, in which good triumphs over evil, as is found in Donatello's *David,* or his *Judith* for that matter. Instead, Michelangelo recast the juvenile David into David-Giant, thereby eliminating all traces of Goliath: the spectator must imagine Goliath somewhere off in the distance. The David-Giant marks off his territory and warns the invisible Goliath-Giant to stay away.

Practical considerations could have affected Michelangelo's unusual interpretation, for there does not seem to have been sufficient stone in the block as it had been handed over to him to carve the head of Goliath. It would have to have been correspondingly larger in scale than David. Michelangelo could have added a separate stone, of course, but that choice would have run contrary to his working methods, which he had solidified in the *Bacchus* and the *Pietà,* both carved from single blocks.

Small wonder that Michelangelo took pains to explain to his principal biographers, neither of whom was a sculptor, the enormous difficulties he had to face in order to get anything at all out of the abused block. For one thing, he proved himself capable of reclassifying a figure with overwhelmingly religious connotations, intended for an exterior architectural location, into a powerful secular image with strong civic connotations. We do not know for certain whether the block was really "ruined" or not. Even relatively slight interventions by previous sculptors imposed such restrictions on any new carver that most sculptors would have been discouraged from accepting the challenge in the first place.

There is solid evidence that the republican message of the *David* standing beside the main doorway of the Palazzo Signoria mirrored Michelangelo's political inclinations, although he was, as usual, cautious in articulating them.

The ruthless Sack of Prato in 1512 led to the return of the Medici in Florence, and with the ascension to the papacy of Giovanni de' Medici as Leo X in the following year, governmental authority was put into the hands of the new pope's brother, Giuliano. Florence's republican phase came to an end. The Medici reinstalled their coats of arms, the easily distinguished gilt balls, throughout the city, but they did not remove Michelangelo's *David* from its much-pondered location guarding the door of the palace, in spite of its republican overtones. Instead, they redefined the Palazzo Signoria altogether, changing its function and changing its name from Palazzo Signoria to Palazzo Vecchio, "old" palace. The *David's* political charge had been effectively defused, although its power as a sculptural image never diminished. The delicate state of the marble claimed by Giuliano da Sangallo and others at the meeting turned out to be a false issue. It was simply not true. The statue remained outside for four centuries without serious deterioration, until it was taken indoors and a copy put in its place a hundred years ago.

The *David* confirmed the high opinion that Piero Soderini, the *Gonfaloniere a vita,* held of Michelangelo's talents. More than once Piero describes Michelangelo's art in glowing terms, maintaining it has no equal in Italy or the world. But was stubborn old Lodovico Buonarroti finally mollified? Recognizing that all the artists in the city were talking about the statue and its maker, considering the prestige of its final placement, and its remarkable appearance, were Lodovico's doubts about his son's choice of career at last erased?

THE *DONI TONDO*

With the *David,* Michelangelo had conquered the Florentines, and he was even singled out in Pomponius Gauricus's treatise of 1504 *On Sculpture* as a sculptor and, surprisingly, as a painter too *(etiam pictor).* There is very little evidence of any painting he did during the fifteen years after he left the Ghirlandaio studio, but at the time of the *David,* he created an important painting for the merchant Angelo di Francesco Doni. Probably painted in 1504 and 1505, it was in the form of a *tondo,* or circular picture, with a richly carved wood frame.

Doni, a year younger than Michelangelo, lived and worked in the area around the Badia, in the same Santa Croce quarter as the Buonarroti. The two men had probably known each other since childhood. The well-to-do Doni family ran a shop out of their home and Angelo had acquired over time several other shops which he rented out, increasing his wealth. In the years while Michelangelo was away, Angelo built himself a fine city house. Though not a full-fledged palazzo, it was the town house of a gentleman, with numerous bedrooms and sitting rooms, a loggia, and a chapel. Here Angelo had taken his new bride, Maddalena of the prestigious Strozzi family, following the celebration of the marriage in January 1504. Maddalena, the plain sixteen-year-old daughter of Giovanni di Marcello Strozzi, brought a substantial dowry. Her physical appearance is documented by Raphael's portrait, executed after the marriage, along with a matching portrait of Angelo Doni. She is shown wearing a huge pearl dangling from her neck.

According to an anecdote that has a ring of truth, after the *tondo* was completed, the shrewd Doni sought to cut the originally agreed-upon price. Adamant, Michelangelo responded by asking for and ultimately obtaining double the original amount; even Piero Soderini was brought into the dispute. The carving on the frame, in which Michelangelo may have had a hand, includes the coats of arms of the Strozzi family buried within intricate decoration and five busts. The picture is rather large for the genre, with a vertical diameter of 41 inches and a horizontal diameter of 37 inches, so that the *tondo* is not absolutely round. Michelangelo chose to represent the Holy Family, a fairly uncommon subject; one may suppose that he suggested it for the private chapel of the Donis' home.

The figure of Mary, who is seated on the ground in front of a parapet, establishes the focus of the composition. Behind her, Joseph seems to be sitting on the parapet, supporting the Child balanced on Mary's raised right arm. She moves her left arm and hand in the direction of the Child, as she turns with uplifted head and eyes to look in his direction, although it is impossible physically for her actually to see Christ. These three figures are tightly bound together, as if chiseled from a single stone mass; indeed, they are more like a sculpture than a painted image, as the circular movement of their arms and hands accentuates the implicit central "block."

The presence of five male nudes in the background is perplex-

Head from frame of *Doni Tondo.*

MICHELANGELO, *Doni Tondo,* c. 1505.

ing: they are sometimes identified as men preparing for baptism, since John the Baptist is also to be seen on the right behind the parapet. Or, conversely, the nudes have been regarded as representing angels. This possibility is especially engaging because in such an interpretation they would refer to Angelo Doni, whose first name, of course, means "Angel."

Another puzzling aspect of the painting, which includes a bit of landscape in the background, is the area where the five young men are seen. While not totally clear, there appears to be a semicircular foundation for a structure that could be either a classical ruin or the beginnings of a new building, perhaps a baptistery. This identification would once again be consistent with the presence of John the Baptist, and reflects the Donis' devotion to the saint, whose name they gave to their first son.

The *Doni Tondo,* as it is called, is the only non-controversially attributed panel picture by the master. Executed in the more traditional medium of tempera rather than oil, it might well be regarded as an example of a *desco da parto,* that is, a birth plate, which had the talismatic quality of wishing for a birth.

The theme of family is central to any interpretation of the *Doni Tondo,* but here the old father, the younger mother, and the child coincide with Michelangelo's rediscovery of his own family in those years. The unique features of the work, in which Michelangelo deviates from tradition, offer personal, unconsciously private insights. The emphasis on family was to become an increasingly fertile concept for the artist. There might even be an openly autobiographical element, since Michelangelo, one of five brothers, depicted five "angels" and the same number of heads on the frame. And he, like his patron, was an angelo, too. The benevolent Joseph could refer to Lodovico Buonarroti, who played such an encompassing part in Michelangelo's life, especially now in his twenties. But such highly speculative suggestions remain just that and are not essential for approaching this brilliant if somewhat cold painting.

As evidence of his new primacy in the Florentine art world, Michelangelo was commissioned to paint a large wall mural illustrating the *Battle of Cascina* for the main hall of the Palazzo Signoria. He never actually began the painting phase of the commission, but he did prepare a huge cartoon. The commission was the most prestigious the Florentine state could offer, and he shared it with Leonardo da Vinci, who was to paint its companion, the *Battle of Anghiari*. But whereas Leonardo had a solid record as a painter, having recently completed the *Last Supper* in Milan, Michelangelo thus far had shown no proof of his skills as a painter except for the *Doni Tondo*.

III

Michelangelo and
Pope Julius II

▨▨▨

THE *DAVID* WAS BROUGHT OUT of the workshop at midnight on May 14, 1504, to begin its five hundred-yard journey from the Duomo down narrow streets to the Piazza Signoria. For its displacement a wall had to be broken, since the *David* was too large to be removed through the door. Earlier in the night the statue had been pelted with stones by unknown persons, so it was guarded as a precaution. For the move, the *David* was placed upright, suspended by ropes in a specially designed rig so that it would not touch the ground. The *gigante* made its entrance in the piazza at high noon on May 18. Clearly, astrological calculations were taken for its departure from the Duomo and its arrival in the town square.

Once the *David* was placed on public view, Michelangelo—who was soon back in Rome—became recognized as the finest marble sculptor in Italy, perhaps in the entire world. Already known in Rome for the *Bacchus* and the *Pietà*, his reputation exploded with the *David*, because of its huge size, the ingenuity Michelangelo exhibited in salvaging a partially carved block, and the statue's highly visible place-ment in front of the government headquarters.

Not surprisingly, in the fall of 1504, hardly a year after his elec-tion, Pope Julius II was eager to obtain the services of such a com-manding artist. Perhaps the pope was encouraged by Giuliano da Sangallo, who was a friend of Julius as well as his personal architect. Whatever the circumstances, Julius allocated to Michelangelo a sub-stantial travel advance to come to Rome. He left in March 1505, with his Florentine assignments unfinished, including the preparations to create an imposing mural from the cartoon of the *Battle of Cascina* for the Sala del Maggior Consiglio in the Palazzo Signoria. Gonfaloniere Soderini was undoubtedly reluctant to allow Michelangelo to leave the city and interrupt activity on the project, just as he was when Leonardo, who had begun the painting stage of the matching mural for the same room, had to leave Florence for renewed service in Milan. Probably Soderini was helpless in view of the powerful de-mands for his artists. Neither Michelangelo nor Leonardo da Vinci ever fulfilled their obligation in what would have been the most spectacular artistic confrontation of the Renaissance. Soderini espe-cially lamented Leonardo's behavior to his patrons in Milan, because the artist had received a good deal of money without doing very much, according to the Gonfaloniere.

After his success in Florence, Michelangelo's reaction to return-ing to Rome must have been quite different from his first trip, four years before. No longer a stranger, he was well acquainted with life there, and instead of being patronized by a cardinal like Riario, pow-erful though he was, Michelangelo was to work for the pope. He ti-died up his affairs in Florence and moved to Rome, where he opened a bank account toward the end of March 1505. From 1505 to 1513, when his patron Pope Julius II died, Michelangelo entered a new phase that would be dominated by his relationship with the pope. Prolonged separation would again place a strain upon his family relations, since he inevitably lost direct, day-to-day touch with his father, brothers, and friends in Florence.

MICHELANGELO'S SEXUALITY

Michelangelo's return to Rome raises knotty questions about the artist's private life. Did he succumb to the temptations Boccaccio and Lorenzo il Magnifico had described on his second Roman stay, if not during the first one, or earlier still, in Florence? As with his political and religious convictions, Michelangelo was extremely secretive, never bragging about his sexual exploits as Benvenuto Cellini did. Reviewing all the evidence, it is most likely that his sexual experiences, whether hetero- or homosexual, were minimal—and possibly even nonexistent.

Starting from what he had learned and heard in the Medici household, Michelangelo might have regarded sexual abstinence as a highly desirable option. The Neoplatonist Marsilio Ficino, who as we have seen had been a dominant personality in the Medici court since Cosimo's day, in a treatise dedicated to il Magnifico argued that coitus was the most monstrous enemy of the scholar, especially if the scholar proceeded beyond his strength. Sexual intercourse drains the spirit, he said, and more subtly, it weakens the brain, interferes with proper digestion, and ruins the heart. Ficino often reiterated that no evil could be worse for one's powers of invention and imagination, a conclusion that must have struck Michelangelo close to home.

Ficino would remind those in the Medici household that Hippocrates considered sexual intercourse a disorder, like epilepsy. Ficino's observation that the ancients held the Muses and Minerva to be virgins seems to have been confirmed by the budding sculptor, who, when he carved the *Pietà,* his first grand religious work, portrayed a very young-looking Virgin Mary holding the dead Jesus on her lap. After the unveiling, many criticized the statue because of Mary's youthful appearance, since by then she had a thirty-three-year-old son. In a conversation with Condivi a half century later, Michelangelo said, "Don't you know that chaste women remain much fresher than unchaste ones? How much more so for a virgin who never entertained the slightest desire that would change her body?" He seemed to apply the same principle to himself. At age seventy-five, Michelangelo asserted that, aside from kidney stones, which had caused him considerable distress, "I am now almost as I was when I was thirty years old" *(Io del resto della persona son quasi com'ero di trenta anni)*. The implication is clear enough: his mode of life, including sexual abstinence, had ensured his youthfulness and general well-being over the decades as it had preserved Mary's.

Savonarola could have been an instructive model for Michelangelo on the question of sexuality. The frate struggled to cope with nagging guilt over physical desire, "the hot carnality of libidinous thought" *(el calore carnale della libidene),* which had propelled him when young to seek the affections of a Ferrarese lady, Laudomia Strozzi. After her rejection, his suffering ego helped lead him to the religious life. For Savonarola as for Michelangelo, the temptations could have been immense.

The Dominican frate, who had tamed his heterosexual desire, adamantly decried homosexuality and recognized that Florence surpassed even Rome as the "sodomitic city." Florence's reputation as a center of homosexuality was so notorious that homosexual intercourse was dubbed "to florentinize" by the Germans of the day. Savonarola's condemnation of sodomy reverberated throughout the city, and during his heyday prosecutions were more common and fines were greater. Upon hearing of his death, one Florentine magistrate observed gleefully, "Thank God, now we can return to our sodomy."

Savonarola's stance on sodomy and other issues prompted vitriolic reactions even after his death, when his memory continued to be debased. Simone Filipepi, brother of Sandro Botticelli, both of whom had been followers of the frate, reports in his *Cronaca:*

> One morning when I, the writer of this chronicle, was going to San Marco, after the brothers had been given permission to reopen the church as usual after it had been officially closed, I found that the night before, some nasty fellows had attached a dead ass, still with its skin on, to the knocker on the door, suspended with a rope. The thing stank to high heaven because the beast had been dead for many days and they had punched many holes in the belly, so that an awful stench came out, which infected the entire piazza.

In the same place, Simone recounts the tale of a certain Pacchierotto, who habitually spoke very unfavorably of the frate: ". . . it happened that he, Pacchierotto, was arrested for being a sodomite, and under torture, he confessed to the most unheard of and most extraordinary aberrations, as well as certain thefts . . . he was imprisoned with the sodomites, thieves and cursers, after having been lashed. In prison he was greeted with joy."

Yet another story recorded by Simone that circulated in the city—one with which Michelangelo was very likely familiar—was even more grotesque. A dishonest cleric wrote to Savonarola's enemies in the Florentine government while Savonarola was in prison (suggestively nicknamed "the little hotel," *Alberghettino*), shortly before his execution, and said that Frate Girolamo Savonarola was, of all things, a hermaphrodite: "he is both male and female, and . . . would make use of one or the other gender [for his pleasure], whichever happened to turn up."

The Signoria ordered that verification of this terrible accusation be conducted, sending an official, Giovanni di Gianozzo Mannetti, with a companion to the frate in prison. After Giovanni explained why he had come, Savonarola answered, "I cannot be persuaded that either the Signoria or you yourself wish to come to me with such an enormous charge and treat a poor servant of God in such a manner." Then he warned, "Therefore be most careful what you are doing not to me but to God, who would take it ill; such a dishonest thing could reflect back on the Signoria, on the city and on you." The official was not swayed and insisted that he must obey orders, urging Savonarola to "have patience."

Savonarola, recognizing that he was under their control, begged the official that he at least be content to do the task by himself and as honestly as possible. Giovanni agreed and sent away his companion. Then he took a candle, lit it, searched and with his right hand touched those parts of Savonarola's body that he wanted to. Not much time passed before God revealed his justice; Giovanni, then Gonfaloniere, became dangerously ill at that very instant. Extending his right hand, he exclaimed: "This hand, this hand," and crying out, he died a miserable death. Shortly thereafter his companion also died, without warning or illness.

The theme of sodomy surrounds another story connected with Savonarola about a storekeeper and pursemaker. We learn that a roguish fellow nicknamed Scheggia ("Splinter," the same nickname as Masaccio's brother) had a reputation as a sodomite. After the frate's death, his shop was always full of ribaldries, and when followers of Savonarola passed by, they were bombarded with insults. On the eve of St. John the Baptist's feast day, June 24, when every storekeeper in Florence made his shop as attractive as he could, Scheggia put a large, lively bird out front. (A bird can readily refer to the penis, probably the intention here.) He dressed it in the black and white outfit of the order of San Domenico and placed upon its head a lighted candle with a large notice saying, THIS IS THE TRUE LIGHT, one of Savonarola's favorite phrases.

One night not long after, the story goes on, Scheggia and many of his group became very drunk under the vault behind the Church of San Tommaso, near the Old Market. They left the place to go and hold religious services at their guild's hall, as was customary. When Scheggia's turn came to go up to the lectern, he became quite sick, and after vomiting out some of the wine, his companions carried him home. Scheggia got worse and a priest was called, but before the priest could arrive, Scheggia, the sodomite, died without the final sacrament. This, the writer concluded, was the irony of the "true light"— and the result of making fun of Savonarola.

With the examples of Savonarola and Ficino, sexual abstinence must have loomed as a desirable ideal for Michelangelo. In his biography, Condivi said that the artist exercised "continence" in sexual intercourse, a statement that there is no reason to doubt. In fact, some years after its publication in 1553, Michelangelo in a conversation that was recorded reiterated the value of abstinence; he is quoted as saying, "I have always practiced it. If you wish to prolong your life, restrain yourself as much as you can...." A similar viewpoint is affirmed in *Fiore di Virtù (Flower of Virtue),* a popular book of aphorisms, which Michelangelo could have owned. We know that Leonardo da Vinci, as well as a fellow Florentine sculptor, Benedetto da Maiano, both had copies. One aphorism reads: "He who fails to control his libido lies with beasts." The same theme is echoed decades later by Michelangelo's Florentine follower, Jacopo Pontormo, in his diary, which was devoted to digestive disorders.

Another factor could have kept Michelangelo from exploring his sexuality. He seems to have shared a widely diffused fear of women. We know that the fable of the viper left a strong impression on Leonardo da Vinci, who recorded in his notebooks the following description from a medieval bestiary: "Viper: during sexual intercourse she opens her mouth and when it is over she grits her teeth and kills her husband; then the children in her body grow, and choking her throat, kill their mother."

148 · THREE WORLDS OF MICHELANGELO

In addition to his desire to concentrate on his mission, his art, and his devotion to the needs of his father and brothers, Michelangelo may have avoided starting a family out of distaste for the sexual act; after all, women were commonly thought to be more lustful than men. Once again we can call upon Leonardo, who wrote that "The sexual act and the members which are operative in it are so repulsive that were it not for the beautiful faces and the ornaments of those involved and their controlled dispositions, nature would lose the human species."

Michelangelo also might have been wary of sexual encounters for a more practical reason. At the time of his youth, a violent new affliction, syphilis, had been spreading throughout Italy. It was popularly known as the *morbus gallicus,* the "French disease" (the French, for their part, called it the "Neapolitan disease"), and the ugly, painful, odiferous sores were termed "French abscesses" *(bolle franciose).* The origins of the sickness were traced to Christopher Columbus's expeditions in the New World. But whereas the West Indian Islands, where the disease came from, had abundant natural cures, these remedies were not understood or not available to the Europeans, especially the doctors in Spain, where the disease first seems to have been brought ashore.

In the years when the French armies occupied Naples (1492–1503), many of the soldiers contracted the horrible affliction, which they carried throughout Italy rapidly *(cum summa celeritate).* It appears that Florence was first hit with an outbreak in 1496. Ghastly boils, which often became incurable sores, broke out all over the body, accompanied by intense pains in the joints and nerves. Since doctors had no cure, men and women of all ages died or were hideously deformed by the disease. Duke Lorenzo, son of Piero the Unfortunate and grandson of il Magnifico, and the man for whose memory Michelangelo designed a tomb in the New Sacristy in San Lorenzo, died wretchedly of the "French disease" two decades later. His wife, ironically a French princess, followed him to the grave soon after. Michelangelo's most powerful patron, Julius II, was said to have been afflicted with the dishonorable disease as well.

The outbreak of syphilis was predicted by the astrological conjunction of Jupiter and Saturn in November 1484, according to one reading, or a conjunction of Saturn and Mars in Pisces in January 1496, in another; whatever the cause, and however it might have been predicted, the disease was very much on the common mind. The Bolognese astrologer Nifo, whom Michelangelo could have run across personally and who was patronized later by Giovanni de' Medici after he had become pope, predicted cataclysms as the outcome of such conjunctions. Like those relegated to Dante's *Inferno* without prejudice for rank or station, the *morbus gallicus* affected kings and pontiffs, friars and burghers, rich and poor. Michelangelo's conduct, like that of other thoughtful young people, must have been affected by an awareness of this looming danger, which was almost always transmitted through sexual intercourse.

As for homosexual activity, it was regulated by stringent laws everywhere in Italy. For the fifteenth-century preacher St. Bernardino of Siena, the practice, which he describes as a "custom" in all of Tuscany, was compared to the action of "pigs." Punishment varied slightly from place to place and over time, but it usually included a combination of heavy fines, imprisonment, and the pillory *(gogna),* which was located near the column of Florence's Mercato Vecchio; total or partial castration after repeated violations; and in extreme cases such as the brutal rape of a boy, death. One Savonarola sympathizer produced an elaborate series of proposals, which included significant fines, prison, and the removal of one or both testicles of perpetrators who were three-time offenders. The legal registers as well as the diaries of Florentine and Venetian contemporaries are full of accounts of dreadful punishments for sodomy.

Savonarola preached against sodomy, which he regarded as a sure road to eternal damnation, so besides the fear of earthly punishment, Michelangelo would also have feared for his soul, had he a mind or inclination to engage in such practices in the first instance. Earlier in the century, the Dominican theologian St. Antoninus (†1451), who was Savonarola's predecessor at San Marco, listed homosexuality among crimes against nature, including sodomy between both men and women when conducted "outside of the natural place where children are made." Actually, the legal distinctions of the day were quite refined, and differences were drawn between the punishment of passive and active participants. Under any circumstances, the risks were considerable.

A precise measure of Michelangelo's sexual experience during his long life will always remain impossible. There are only hints, which are difficult to corroborate. We do not know, for example, whether he had a relationship with a woman named Caterina in Bologna, for whom a vague echo may survive in a sensual poem, "How joyful is the garland . . . ," and we do not know whether encounters with studio boys occurred. Did he have feelings for any of Lorenzo il Magnifico's daughters? Contessina, three years his junior, probably knew him well from their time together at the palazzo on Via Larga, but she was promised to Piero Ridolfi. Lucrezia, the oldest, was already married to Jacopo Salviati by the time Michelangelo came to the Medici Gardens, and Maddalena was also married by then. Luigia, the youngest, was betrothed at age eleven, before she could have met Michelangelo. But more likely, Michelangelo, shy and inexperienced, was oblivious to the young women in the Medici household.

The skimpy evidence that survives suggests that Michelangelo— whether through disinclination, restraint, shyness, conviction, or fear—held his libido in check and that he had few, if any, sexual experiences.

The widely repeated contention that Michelangelo was a homosexual, closet or otherwise, that is, a participant in the Florentine vice, is without solid historical support. His own responses to accusations of this type, which were already circulating during his lifetime, are convincing and are in harmony with his character and religious convictions, as far as we know them. He readily admitted to Platonic relations with men. According to Condivi, Michelangelo loved the beauty of the human body and knew it extremely well, as he unequivocally demonstrates in his art. Some people, Condivi goes on, cannot distinguish love of beauty from "dishonest and lustful" love, leading them to think and speak ill of Michelangelo, but they failed to recognize that the handsome young Alcibiades was loved deeply but chastely *(castissimamente)* by Socrates, whom he regarded like a father. Later in life, Michelangelo spoke frequently of love, but it was exclusively of the Platonic variety, Condivi continues.

The biographer goes on to testify, here speaking for himself and not for Michelangelo, that he never heard phrases uttered from the mouth of Michelangelo that were not completely proper *(parole onestissime);* and more, what he said had the force of extinguishing uncontrolled desires among the young. Besides, "obscene thoughts never issued from him." We come to recognize, and here is the basic point for Condivi, that Michelangelo not only loved human beauty but all beautiful things—a beautiful horse or dog, a handsome landscape, a tree, a magnificent mountain, a beautiful forest: in fact, he admired with deep reverence *(ammirandole con maraviglioso affetto)* "everything and every beautiful place." His admiration for the human body— and especially but not exclusively the male body—was therefore part of his larger world view. He was oriented toward the visual because he was, above all, a sculptor and a painter.

In his own defense against charges of homosexual behavior that had arisen because of his appreciation of the nude male body, Michelangelo vividly queried (through Condivi), "Whose judgment would be so barbarous as not to appreciate that the foot of a man is more noble than his boot, and his skin more noble than that of a sheep, with which he is dressed?" He also knew the body scientifically. Like Leonardo, he trained himself while still a young artist with stomach-turning "anatomies," which included human dissections. He performed them in Florence at Santo Spirito; and much later, he conducted one at the Hospital of Santa Maria Nuova in Florence (in 1518), perhaps to refresh himself.

The fact that he admired and rendered marvelous images of young men cannot be used as evidence of latent or real homosexuality, nor, for that matter, can the masculation of his woman subjects. We are dealing here with aesthetic choices, ones that may have had an experiential foundation: Michelangelo did not use female models and never drew a nude woman from life, basing his renderings on males, usually his studio boys, as was customary; relying upon ancient and modern sculptural prototypes; or alternatively, creating types from his imagination.

Throughout his correspondence, as well as the letters directed to or about him by his family, friends, and colleagues, Michelangelo never hinted, even obliquely, at marrying. (The same was true for Leonardo da Vinci, Botticelli, and Raphael, none of whom married. Raphael, in response to the prompting of his uncles, claimed to merit a dowry worthy of a prince before he would take the fatal step, but the occasion never presented itself.) Our best picture of Michelangelo's thoughts about marriage is the information that can be gleaned from the series of letters Michelangelo wrote to his nephew Lionardo about the young man's agonizing, drawn-out search for a wife, which lasted from 1546 until 1553. Michelangelo is full of advice and counsel about how to select the appropriate wife and is disposed to help find an acceptable candidate any way he can, although being in Rome while looking for a Florentine wife was something of a handicap. Michelangelo insisted that Lionardo must have a decent and ade-

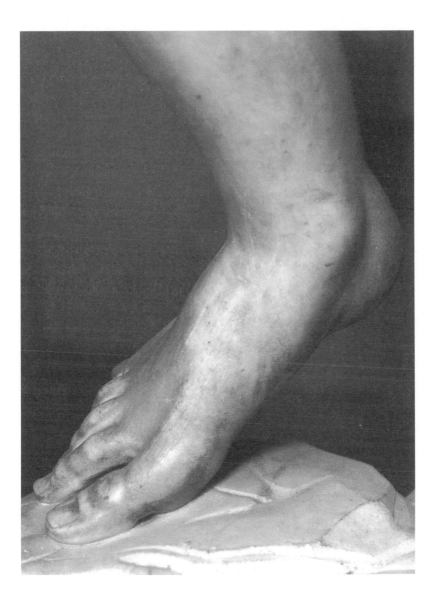

MICHELANGELO, *Bacchus,* 1496–97, detail of foot.

quate dwelling to sustain a proper marriage, and he urged his nephew that the house should be in their family's quarter of the city, Santa Croce.

The evidence surrounding Michelangelo's sexuality with respect to either men or women (or both men and women, for that matter) is sketchy to say the least. What does result from the facts as we know them is that he controlled his sexual activities, wherever his inclinations may have turned. Whether secretly a practicing homosexual, which seems quite dubious, or a devoted heterosexual, also a doubtful situation, he kept close reins upon the carnal aspects of his life. More than anything, he is best understood as having sought abstinence. Besides the pressures already indicated, both cultural and moral, his control of sexual appetite was accomplished by his absolute devotion to his mission and to an obedience to the role he had assigned himself, which was to conduct a moral life.

POPE JULIUS II

Michelangelo's association with Julius II began less than a year after Julius was elected pope on November 1, 1503. Even at the height of the Renaissance, dates and times were still taken very seriously, and Julius postponed his coronation twenty-six days on the advice of astrologers. The new pope was born Giuliano della Rovere, from the Ligurian town of Savona, which lies on the coast northwest of Genoa. The della Rovere family had become influential from the papacy, but his grandfather Leonardo was a peasant from a village outside of town. Leonardo had many children, one of whom, a son named Francesco, would give rise to an influential clan whose imprint on Italy and the papacy during the last third of the fifteenth

century and the early decades of the sixteenth century was without
equal. Francesco, who was raised by Franciscans, became a theological scholar and the General of the Order before becoming pope in
1471. He took the name Sixtus IV and became the main instrument
in establishing the power of the della Rovere. Among his early acts
as pope was to make his brother's son, Giuliano della Rovere, a cardinal.

Sixtus IV was a potent model for his nephew Julius. He was a significant patron of the arts in Rome as pope, but his most impressive
effort was the building of the Sistine Chapel, a robust and austere
structure whose name derives from *Sixtus, Sisto, Sistine.* For the decoration of the chapel, Sixtus had the good sense to summon the best
masters of his day, including Perugino, Botticelli, Signorelli, Cosimo
Rosselli, Domenico Ghirlandaio, and Piero di Cosimo. He also hired
the ingenious painter Melozzo da Forlì, who rendered Sixtus's portrait along with that of Julius. Sixtus's bronze tomb was created by the
leading practitioner of the medium, the Florentine Antonio del Pollaiuolo.

With such an illustrious example set by his uncle, it is hardly
surprising that Julius sought to leave his imprint on Rome. If anything, he outdistanced Sixtus, turning to architects and artists like
Bramante, Giuliano da Sangallo, Raphael, and, of course, Michelangelo Buonarroti. And he began the most ambitious project of his
day: the building of the new St. Peter's.

Julius's physical appearance is known from portraits and representations on coins and medals, the most famous of which is Raphael's
painting of the regally seated pope. Besides, Raphael included the
pope's likeness in several frescoes he painted for the Vatican rooms. A
man of medium height, well proportioned except for a short, thick
neck, Julius had a round face, full cheeks, a rosy complexion, and
fine, large eyes. Toward the end of his life, he let his beard grow in the

Greek manner *(bar-batus more Greco),* contrary to tradition since popes were always cleanshaven until then.

People feared and hated Julius, but they respected him and his fiery impetuosity lent him dignity. Under Julius's patronage Michelangelo conducted his most prestigious commissions as a painter, as well as a sculptor, and he created works of stunning accomplishment: the ceiling of the Sistine Chapel and the individual statues for the Julius Tomb. These statues include the so-called *Bound* and

After MICHELANGELO, project for the Julius Tomb, c. 1505.

the *Dying Slaves* (now treasures of the Louvre), and the seated *Moses,* which was already celebrated while Michelangelo was still alive and is today part of the truncated Julius Tomb in the Roman Church of San Pietro in Vincoli. With its fiery demeanor, the *Moses* is frequently

regarded as a touch-stone of *terribilità* in Michelangelo's art. The image of *Moses* has been regarded with justification as an oblique portrait of Julius himself.

THE JULIUS TOMB

After what must have been a brief interval during which Michelangelo prepared project drawings and presumably had discussions, the pope ordered him to execute his tomb. In April 1505, the contract for the tomb was drawn up—for either 10,000 or 10,500 ducats. The massive monument was conceived as an imposing structure, to be placed within the fabric of St. Peter's, and Michelangelo set out immediately for Carrara to procure the marble for the forty figures—an unheard of number—he had envisaged for the tomb.

Michelangelo spent more than half a year uncomfortably in the infertile mountains on the edge of the Apennines near the Tyrrhenian Sea. Undoubtedly, it would have been easier to purchase stone from the middlemen located amid the comforts of Pisa or Florence rather than going to the quarries, but for Michelangelo the first step was essential, of utmost consequence for the process of creation. This process can be reconstructed as follows: First, he formed an idea of the figure he was to make in his mind, with or without the aid of a drawing or clay model; then he combed the marble quarries to find a block from which he could carve the figure in the pose he had invented. The variables were nearly infinite: not only the nature of the pose but the size of each figure varied, depending upon the planned position within the monument and the position from which it was to be seen.

For Michelangelo, the selection of the block was an essential step in the creative process and one that could not be delegated to assistants or marble sellers. While in the Carrara Mountains, Michelangelo had a fantasy (recorded through Condivi) triggered by a mountain on the shore. He was consumed with desire to carve a colossus that could be seen by sailors and navigators from a great distance, and this fantasy or daydream induced him to prepare models, which have long since disappeared. Still later in life, Michelangelo added a comment to the effect that the colossus idea was a "madness" that came to him because of his age. Whatever the circumstances, several observations are pertinent. Michelangelo obviously was in a charged mental state as he prepared to initiate the most elaborate tomb of modern times. However assured he might have felt with the *David* prominently on display, he must have had moments of doubt when, isolated on the barren hills above Carrara, he wondered if he was capable of producing something as vast as the Julius Tomb. In his fantasy, he sought consolation from the sculptors of antiquity: his *David-Gigante* would appear like a dwarf beside the imaginary Colossus.

The relationship with Pope Julius was severely tested when

Michelangelo returned to Rome from Carrara early in 1506. Whatever cordiality and mutual understanding had evolved over plans for the tomb a year before was disrupted just as the exhilarating, much-anticipated task of carving the statues was about to become a reality.

Both the pope and Michelangelo were regarded graphically by contemporaries and by history as *terribile*—a term that referred to a person whose actions and demeanor generated terror in others. Although their close ties were ruptured only once in their eight years of association (1505–13), according to conventional wisdom they acted with *terribilità* in their relations with one another. Was Julius really the *papa terribile* that history has made him out to be? And was Michelangelo Buonarroti the pope's temperamental counterpart?

TERRIBILITÀ

There is solid confirmation in contemporary accounts about Julius: Venetian diplomats described the pope's "excessive irascibility," reporting that "he does not have the patience to listen calmly to what they have to say and to take men as they are." But their commentary helps verify Michelangelo's claim of mutual affection between himself and Julius: " . . . nevertheless, one who knows how to handle him, and who has given him trust, always will find him the best disposed person in the world." Julius's *terribilità* was also attested to by agents of the ruling Gonzaga of Mantua, by the theologian Egidius of Viterbo, and by Julius's master of ceremonies, the Blognese Paris di Grassis.

A "terrible" nature implied an ability to surmount impossible odds; Julius was perceived as a fulminating deity, who made all in his presence tremble. Contemporaries claimed that even his painted portrait had the effect of making the viewer shudder. The bearded por-

RAPHAEL, *Portrait of Julius II,* c. 1510–11, detail of head.

trait that Raphael had painted for the Roman Church of Santa Maria del Popolo was regarded as particularly powerful. In the painting, he is shown as the "old one" *(il vecchione),* deep in thought, his left hand clasped to the arm of the grand chair. His deepset eyes are lively, his nose abundant but not pointed, and his determined mouth with its tightly closed lips revealing, more than any other aspect, a volcanic spirit that could explode at any moment. A similar quality has been noted in certain figures found on the Sistine Chapel ceiling, in particular, God the Father in the Creation scenes. But no one has attributed to portraits or sculptured busts representing Michelangelo powers like those thought to be inherent in Raphael's portrait of Julius.

One example that illustrates the supposed *terribilità* of both Julius and Michelangelo concerns the artist's precipitous flight from Rome in April 1506. According to Michelangelo, after a shipment of marble for Julius's tomb had arrived from Carrara, he sought payment from the pope, really a reimbursement for the money already laid out for shipment, the unloading of the stone, and presumably something for himself in the bargain. Michelangelo went to the Vatican every day for an entire week. Each morning he waited without success to be received.

On Friday, a guard finally told him: "Pardon me, I have been ordered not to let you enter."

On that particular morning, the cardinal of Lucca happened to be present and overheard the guard's statement. He shouted at the man: "You must appreciate who this man is!" The prelate, Galeotto Franciotti della Rovere, had considerable authority since he was the son of the pope's sister, Lucchina—i.e., the pope's very own nephew, who was made cardinal shortly after his uncle became pope.

The guard responded, "Of course I know who he is, but I am obliged to carry out the orders of my patrons and not question them."

Only at this point did Michelangelo speak out, for he had never before been refused entry. In a reply that is frequently considered worthy of an unreconstructed *terribile,* Michelangelo said, "Tell the Pope that, from henceforth, if he wants me, he should search elsewhere and not in Rome."

Michelangelo went straight to his house, told his two servants to sell his furniture, and departed for Florence the following morning. After twenty hours of uninterrupted travel (according to Michelangelo's recollection), by which time he arrived at Poggibonsi, a small town to the north of Siena, five papal couriers caught up with the perturbed artist in order to escort him back to the Vatican. But despite their threats, he refused to return, claiming asylum from papal authority because he was by then in Florentine territory. The couri-

MICHELANGELO, studies for the *Slaves* for the Julius Tomb, 1513.

ers then handed him a letter from Julius, which Michelangelo paraphrased as follows: "The person who sees this letter must return immediately to Rome, under penalty of disgrace if he refuses." The pope's *terribilità* must have gotten the better of him, for he was so furious that he did not even address Michelangelo by name.

Michelangelo responded to the papal couriers, saying that he was "not disposed to return; and from his good and loyal service he did not deserve such a change in the Pope's behavior, to be thrown out of his presence like some lout; and since His Holiness no longer wished to proceed with the production of the tomb, he [Michelangelo] was no longer obligated to him; nor does he wish to be obligated to others." These are strong words, but they do not establish Michelangelo as a certified *terribile,* despite his sudden withdrawal

from Rome. Is it not more accurate to regard him as the victim of another's uncontrolled temper?

Other details help explain Michelangelo's flight from Rome. A week before, on Holy Saturday, Michelangelo had overheard a conversation that took place at the dinner table in the Vatican with a jeweler and the pope's master of ceremonies present. Julius unequivocally announced that "he did not want to spend one single penny more on either small or large stones." Hearing this, the sculptor must have realized that the pope's enthusiasm for the tomb project had cooled. Before leaving the company, an apprehensive Michelangelo asked the pope for money to pay expenses he had incurred for the marble. The pope told him to come on Monday, which he did and then every day until the Friday on which he was bluntly refused admission and thrown out. Michelangelo interpreted this as confirmation of his suspicion that the pope had had a change of heart over the tomb and he felt deep despair *(gran disperazione)*.

Michelangelo reviewed the details of this incident in the draft of a letter intended for Giovan Francesco Fattucci in 1523. In it he recalled: "At this time, Pope Julius changed his opinion and no longer wanted to make the tomb; and not realizing it, and going to him to request the money, I was thrown out of the place. . . ."

With these circumstances in mind, what should we make of Michelangelo's hasty departure? He believed that he had devised the most ambitious tomb the Christian world would ever see, claiming in a letter sent to Giuliano da Sangallo on May 2, 1506 (which he asked be shown to the pope!), that if the tomb were made, there would be nothing like it in the world. For eight exhausting and lonely months in the quarries of Carrara he had strained to obtain the required marble. When the stone finally arrived, and his struggles seemed to be over, Michelangelo was led to believe (correctly) that the project would be abandoned, plunging him into the depths of disappointment.

Michelangelo relates with an air of mystery in this letter to Giuliano da Sangallo that, in Rome, his life was in danger. He provided no details, but in the following months when negotiations were under way between Pope Julius and the Florentine Signoria for Michelangelo's return to papal service, the artist continuously insisted upon guarantees of his personal safety. Whether the danger was actual or imagined, there is no question about Michelangelo's pervasive anxiety at the time. In his flight from Rome, he had acted not as an unbridled *terribile* ready to do battle, but as a cautious, sensitive person worried about his security and his career. After all, Michelangelo was witnessing the cancellation of his most ambitious work to that point, a serious threat to his earnings, and the frustration of his mission.

Piero Soderini, Michelangelo's friend and patron in the Florentine government, recognized that Michelangelo had been frightened *(impaurito)* by the entire affair. In a letter to his brother, Soderini captures the flavor of other aspects of the artist's character as well. "Michelangelo," he wrote, "is an excellent young man and in his own art unsurpassed in Italy, perhaps in the universe. We cannot recommend him too highly: his nature is such that with good words and kindness, if these are given him, he will do everything. One has only to show him love and treat him kindly and he will perform things that will make the whole world wonder."

In the autumn of 1506 Michelangelo had set out for Bologna to ask the pope's forgiveness for his precipitous departure from Rome without papal authorization. In other words, six months after the pope had all but physically removed Michelangelo from the Vatican Palace, a reluctantly repentant Michelangelo sought his pardon. At the meeting (as reported by Condivi) with the pope in Bologna, the city Julius had recaptured in the name of the papacy, the sculptor explained that his reason for leaving was not bad faith but disappointment over the pope's rejection of him. Julius remained silent during the interview, still seething at the young artist's disobedience, but the Florentine cardinal Francesco Soderini, who was also bishop of Volterra, intervened to cut the tension. He sought to support Michelangelo, as he had been instructed to do by his brother, Florence's Gonfaloniere.

The cardinal interjected, "Your Highness, pay no attention to Michelangelo's error because he erred out of ignorance. Painters, after all, are universally ignorant in matters outside of their art."

Indignantly, the pope snapped: "What you say is outrageous and I myself would never pronounce such a thing. You are the ignorant one and disgraceful too, not he. Get out of my sight!"

When the unfortunate cardinal balked at leaving, the pope's servants threw him out, much as Michelangelo had been expelled from the pope's quarters, the very incident that had triggered the controversy. (Michelangelo had interpreted this as being "thrown out" because he normally had free access to the pope.) But then the pope, having vented his uncontrollable anger *(collera sborrata)* at Soderini, pardoned Michelangelo straightaway. A vivid example of Julius's *terribilità*.

Following the outburst, Julius commissioned Michelangelo to produce a twice-life-size statue in bronze, since he was not entirely satisfied with the stucco one he had ordered from a local sculptor. Michelangelo hardly relished the assignment, because casting was not his "art" (he said the same thing time and time again about painting), but he was in no position to refuse, and besides, the fee for the statue was 3,000 ducats, according to Soderini. He began work on the wax model at once, being extremely anxious to finish the figure as soon as possible so that he could leave Bologna, which he found unbearable by then. More than a year after the rapprochement, on a late Friday evening at the end of January 1507, while Michelangelo was working on the statue, the pope came to visit him. Michelangelo confessed to his patron that he was not sure how the left hand should be represented. Michelangelo suggested putting a book there, but the pope replied: "What do you mean, a book? Better a sword, for I know nothing of letters."

Julius meant that he was a general and a warrior, indeed, a furious battler. In the same conversation, which lasted about half an hour, the pope asked Michelangelo whether the right arm was offering a benediction or a malediction, and the sculptor's skillfully chosen answer was neither. Michelangelo explained that he conceived the gesture as one of warning to the rebellious Bolognese whom the pope had conquered—an explanation that Julius surely would have relished. Michelangelo was overjoyed at the pope's visit and the pope's evident approval of the image as it was coming along. Writing to his brother Buonarroto, Michelangelo confided: "I hope to recapture Julius's good graces."

Julius's fierce temper was more than once heaped squarely upon Michelangelo. Several years after the Bologna encounter, while Michelangelo was struggling to fresco the vault of the Sistine Chapel, the pope again revealed his vehement nature *(natura veemente)* as well as his deep-seated impatience. He insisted that the portion of the ceiling that had already been painted be uncovered for public viewing. The pope had his way, as might be expected. Then, while Michelangelo was executing the second half, the pope's impatience to see the cycle completed increased, and he insisted on being told exactly when the work would be finished. The artist, annoyed at the pressure, responded, "When I can." Such a vague and apparently impertinent retort, though quite typical of artists of all times, triggered the *terribile* Julius to respond: "You want me to have you thrown down from the scaffolding!" Michelangelo knew enough to concede.

What about the other side of the coin? Was Michelangelo an inveterate *terribile,* too? To answer this question, we must distinguish between Michelangelo's nature, his persona, on the one hand, and qualities that can be inferred from his sculpted and painted images on the other. An artist's temperament and the temperament of his pictorial creations, his artistic "style," are two very different matters that are often inappropriately confused.

Consider Raphael, Michelangelo's younger contemporary, universally regarded as being as "gracious" as his visual representations. The characterization is at best a simplification. Raphael was exceptionally competitive and ambitious. Still an unknown in his early twenties, he sought in vain to replace Leonardo and Michelangelo in the commission for the murals in the main hall of Florence's Palazzo Signoria. Later, Raphael made himself available to replace Michelangelo to paint the second half of the Sistine Chapel ceiling, after the dramatic unveiling of the first half. Raphael even hoped to become a cardinal, an ambition hardly in keeping with his background.

As for Michelangelo's images, some of them are indeed *terribile*. Fiery qualities, intensity, a raging self-confidence infuse his marble *David,* the *Moses,* and the painted renderings of God the Father on the Sistine Chapel ceiling. Observers have singled out this awe-inspiring power in their assessment of another major pictorial masterpiece, the massive *Last Judgment* fresco, with its determined, aloof Judging Christ. Even if these images are properly regarded as *terribili,* the question remains: as a person and in his daily actions, was Michelangelo a *terribile?*

Michelangelo was, to be sure, sometimes regarded as personally *terribile* during his lifetime. One of the earliest anecdotes preserved is of his fight with the sculptor Torrigiani during their days at the Medici Gardens. Michelangelo's conduct in this incident has inaccurately been labeled as *terribile;* in actual fact, he was the victim of someone else's anger, that is, he was the object of Torrigiani's *terribilità.* That he may have provoked his adversary is another matter. Giovanni Paolo Lomazzo, a late contemporary of Michelangelo's and a writer on art, proposed that Michelangelo's symbol should be the dragon because of his *terribilità;* Lodovico Dolce in his dialogue on painting has one of his speakers (Pietro Aretino) refer to Michelangelo's *terribilità.* Yet this reputation is surely undeserved.

A portion of the artist's reputation for *terribilità* may have derived from Michelangelo's sometimes angry comments in letters to family members. During the summer of 1509, when he was totally immersed in the physically and intellectually draining frescoes for the Sistine Chapel, Michelangelo learned that his brother Giovansimone had threatened and mistreated their father. Michelangelo fumed in a letter to the offending brother, offering a proverb: "He who does a good turn to a good man makes him a better man; he who does a good turn to a lout makes him worse" *(Si dice che chi fa bene al buono, el fa diventare migliore, e al tristo, diventa peggiore).* Michelangelo pointed out that he had helped Giovansimone and the entire family live well and peacefully, but Giovansimone continued his abusive conduct. He proceeded, "Now I am certain that you are not my brother because if you were, you would not threaten my father; instead, you are a beast, and I will treat you like a beast. Remember that a person who threatens or hits his own father risks his life." Indeed, Michelangelo would surely show Giovansimone a thing or two, and break down his brother's arrogant pride *(superbia),* were he to come to Florence. Although one could interpret such threats as evidence of *terribilità,* in the larger context in which a father laments to one son of being physically mistreated by another, Michelangelo's language seems comprehensible, even justified. Besides, his rage was limited to the written word.

Money was a common source of friction between Michelangelo, his brothers, and his father. In one instance, Michelangelo discovered that Lodovico had withdrawn funds from his Florentine account without permission. Michelangelo was furious at this, as he was in other situations when he thought he was being mistreated by his family. Understandably, Michelangelo was keen to defend his hard-earned wealth, even from his family, and when one considers that he supported the entire menage for decades with the proceeds of what he conceived as excessive physical sacrifice, his anger is surely justifiable.

Pope Leo X, in conversation with a trusted friend of Michelangelo's, Sebastiano del Piombo, raised the issue of Michelangelo's presumed *terribilità,* observing that "one can do nothing with him." Sebastiano, a Venetian who had settled in Rome where he attached himself to Michelangelo, was a talented but lazy painter who considered himself Raphael's equal. His reference, which is to Michelangelo's nature rather than his art, requires interpretation. Leo X, Lorenzo il Magnifico's son, and Michelangelo were almost the identical age and presumably became acquainted at Lorenzo's table decades before. The pope's reaction to Michelangelo probably had its roots in their past competition for Lorenzo's affection. But Leo's cousin Giulio, both as cardinal and later as Pope Clement VII, dealt successfully with Michelangelo, so it is likely that the personal chemistry between Michelangelo and Leo was askew, while it was in harmony with Clement.

Sebastiano passed on to Michelangelo Leo X's remarks and his reply, in which he told Leo that "Michelangelo's *terribilità* harmed no one," and that he "appeared to be *terribile* out of respect for the importance of the great work he has to accomplish." In a later letter, Sebastiano, having thought about the matter, must have realized that his first comment on this touchy subject might not have been satisfactory to Michelangelo. He explained further: "Of your *terribilità* of which I am told, for my part I do not consider you *terribile,* and if I have not written to you about the matter, do not wonder at it, because you do not seem *terribile* except in art. . . ."

Michelangelo was in fact a far more agreeable person than critics have sometimes made him out to be. At different times and on different projects he had a large number of assistants and collaborators, with whom on the whole he maintained cordial relations. In the 1520s, when he was busy at work at the Church of San Lorenzo, in particular the *Medici Tombs* in the New Sacristy, he got along surprisingly well with his immediate staff, marble suppliers, and shippers. More impressive is the sheer number of friends he kept throughout his lifetime. Sebastiano del Piombo was a friend from the 1510s until Sebastiano's death in 1547. Michelangelo's friendship with Francesco Granacci lasted more than thirty years, and spilled over into the entire Buonarroti Simoni clan. It was Granacci who set Michelangelo on the path of becoming an artist. The two left Ghirlandaio's workshop together, as far as we can reconstruct the situation, both moving on to the Medici Gardens. When Michelangelo thought he needed help for the painting of the Sistine Chapel ceiling, he turned to Granacci to round up qualified assistants, and when he needed a special blue pigment from Florence, he alerted Granacci. In Condivi's biography, Granacci is treated more like an older brother than a friend: " . . . among those most intimate was one Francesco Granacci, a pupil of Domenico Ghirlandaio, who seeing the inclination and heightened desire of Michelangelo, decided to assist and constantly encouraged him. He helped by supplying drawings [for copying] or bringing him to the shop of the master, or bringing him to look at pictures, from which he might profit."

Michelangelo repaid Granacci, who lived in the same neighborhood as the Buonarroti, by securing him a place in history. He was acknowledged as opening the way for the greatest artist of his age. Michelangelo also helped Granacci materially by arranging employment and occasionally supplying a drawing upon which he could base a painting. This generosity on Michelangelo's part was not reserved for Granacci; he was to offer similar drawings to pupils and even a Roman barber who thought himself a painter.

Another early friendship was with the much older sculptor-turned-architect Giuliano da Sangallo, who may have had some as yet undetermined role in Michelangelo's training as a marble carver. He was Michelangelo's sponsor with Pope Julius and acted as intermediary during their famous dispute. The head of the influential Sangallo clique in Rome, Giuliano also resolved a problem that troubled Michelangelo while painting the Sistine ceiling. A disfiguring mold began to grow on the section depicting the *Flood* soon after it was painted, and Giuliano came up with a technical solution to eliminate the mold.

Michelangelo proved to be a dependable friend, one who could and did maintain relationships for decades. Jacopo Galli was one of his most loyal patrons in Rome, clear evidence that Michelangelo could win the confidence even of hardheaded bankers, and we should not forget the politician Piero Soderini. The point is that while the intensity of his figural representations was sometimes *terribile,* on a private level Michelangelo's own temperament was a gentle and compassionate one. At the end of a letter to his father, the second one that is preserved, from Rome, he says longingly, "but soon, I hope to be with you all . . . healthy as I trust you are. *Send my regards to my friends"* (italics added). Among Michelangelo's five hundred odd extant letters, in fact, variations on the words "friend" and "friendship" *(amicho, amici, amicissimo, amicitia, amicizia, amico)* occur 110 times, and on "love" *(amor, amorevole, amore)* 67, while "enemy" or "enemies" *(nemico, nemici)* occurs but thrice.

THE *LAOCOÖN*

In early January 1506, Michelangelo was back in Rome awaiting the arrival of the marble from Carrara for the Julius Tomb. Idle time, of which he had a good deal, was passed at the home of Giuliano da Sangallo, and on January 14, Michelangelo was party to a remarkable event, as we learn from a letter written six decades later by Giuliano's son, Francesco da Sangallo. Francesco, then just a child, remembered that on that day, a statuary group was unearthed in a vineyard near Santa Maria Maggiore in Rome. The pope, informed of the discovery, sent a servant to Giuliano da Sangallo asking him to have a look.

Michelangelo went along, too. Giuliano, a respected enthusiast of antique art, immediately recognized the *Laocoön* mentioned by Pliny. And so did Michelangelo. The excavation was expanded so that the entire work, which consisted of three figures, could be liberated. After seeing the work, Giuliano, Francesco, and Michelangelo returned home to eat and discuss antiquities together.

The *Laocoön* came to light near the so-called Baths or Palace of Titus, where Pliny had said it was, though one should be a bit skeptical of the exact date that Francesco gives, because a half century had passed between the event and his letter describing it. The excavation could not have taken place in a single day, anyway, for the labor of extracting the statue would have required many days or even weeks, after which Sangallo and Michelangelo made the identification. Acting upon their advice, Julius acquired the *Laocoön*—which depicted an old Trojan priest and his two sons—on March 23, 1506. By July 1, it was located in the newly created sculpture court in the Belvedere Palace in the Vatican, where it immediately became the object of ad-

Laocoön detail, head.

miration. By then, Michelangelo had already made his withdrawal to Florence.

We do not know exactly what Michelangelo was doing during those approximately three months between his return from Carrara in January and the arrival of the marble in early April, besides hanging around Giuliano da Sangallo's house, until that tumultuous week of April 13 when he left Rome for Florence in a huff. A sliver of evidence can be brought into reconstructing events early in 1506. On January 26, less than two weeks after the unearthing of the *Laocoön*, Michelangelo redeemed marble from the bankers' heirs he had left with his Roman patron, Jacopo Galli, except for two pieces that had been sold by them—ironically, to Pietro Torrigiani—for 8 florins. Thus, shortly after viewing the famous classical *Laocoön* for the first time, Michelangelo had quality marble and ample time to carve. Did he produce a figure or two for his own pleasure that has gone unrecorded?

Along with the *Torso Belvedere*—a mighty, over-life-size marble torso of a male figure carved in the first century B.C., which was located in the Colonna Palace at the time—the *Laocoön* could not have failed to impress Michelangelo. He must have reflected on the figures of the strained, muscular old Laocoön and his two lithe sons, although not a trace in the guise of a drawing, much less a written reference or, for that matter, a sculpture, has turned up. Writing to his brother Buonarroto on January 31, 1506, Michelangelo requested that certain drawings be sent to him from Florence. He urged his brother to take extreme caution so that "not a single sheet" would be lost or damaged by water during the trip, and he also asked Buonarroto to arrange to have a small marble sculpture, known as the *Bruges Madonna,* brought to his house (in Florence). As evidence of Michelangelo's secretiveness in these matters, he admonished Buonarroto not to let anyone see it.

MICHELANGELO, study for the *Bruges Madonna,* 1504.

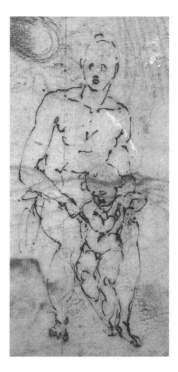

Once in Florence, he was continuously urged by local leaders to make his peace with Julius by going to Bologna and asking pardon, which he finally conceded to do a half year later, as we have seen. He stayed in Bologna for almost a year and a half, until he finished the gigantic bronze statue of the pope early in 1508. This assignment caused Michelangelo considerable grief, because he had casting problems and difficulties with assistants. The sculpture survived a mere four years: on December 30, 1511, an anti-papal mob pulled down the image of Julius II from its niche on the facade of San Petronio and destroyed it.

The period of imposed penitence in Bologna caused Michelangelo discomfort, but his creation of the bronze statue served to heal the rift between the artist and the pope, who had him come to Rome almost immediately after a brief interlude in Florence. Michelangelo constantly hoped that sooner or later he would be allowed to execute his projected Julius Tomb, but now another impediment was thrown in his path: the decoration of the Sistine Chapel ceiling.

THE CEILING OF THE SISTINE CHAPEL

Two intense years had lapsed between the time the marble arrived in Rome for the Julius Tomb in April 1506 and the commission to paint in the Sistine Chapel, although the idea had already been floated in the Vatican and Michelangelo definitely knew of the plan. Piero Rosselli, his friend—who was to become an active collaborator on the ceiling by constructing the scaffolding and preparing the surface for painting—was party to one of the pope's discussions on the subject in early May 1506. In a letter dated May 10, exactly two years to the day before Michelangelo officially entered into the agreement to paint the ceiling, Piero sent details to the artist, then self-exiled in Florence, of what had been discussed in the papal apartments.

Rosselli's letter, the authenticity of which cannot be doubted, confirms Michelangelo's concerns about the people close to Julius. Simply speaking, Michelangelo's reading of the politics within the papal court was quite correct. The letter also reveals the kind of remarkable loyalty that Michelangelo inspired among his friends. Rosselli's sister was married to Simone del Pollaiuolo, a Savonarolean partisan and an influential architect in Florence with close ties to Michelangelo; and both men should be regarded as pertaining to what might be called Michelangelo's Florentine circle. Addressing Michelangelo as "Dearest practically brother," Rosselli provides fascinating snippets of the exchange between the pope and his architect, Donato Bramante, together with Rosselli's interpolations.

According to Rosselli, Julius had confidently announced after dinner on the previous Saturday night that "Tomorrow morning Giuliano da Sangallo is going to Florence and he will bring Michelangelo back, to paint the ceiling of the Sistine Chapel."

Bramante interjected, "Holy Father, nothing will come of the project. I know Michelangelo quite well; he has told me time and time again that he does not want to attend to the chapel although you want him to do so." At this point, Rosselli reminds Michelangelo that as he (Rosselli) knew all too well, "you wanted to attend to the [Julius] Tomb and not to the painting."

"Holy Father," Bramante continued, "I do not think Michelangelo has the stuff in him to paint the chapel anyway, because he has never done much with figure painting, and besides, the figures are high up in the vault and require foreshortening, which is a far different matter than painting at ground level."

The pope revealed both concern and optimism: "If Michelangelo does not come, he is making a mistake with me, but I am confident he will return in any case."

At this point Rosselli intervened after a reference to Bramante's nastiness, relating what he told the pope, which was "what I believe you, Michelangelo, would have done if the situation has been reversed."

"Holy Father," Rosselli said to the pope with indignation, "Bramante never spoke with Michelangelo, and as for what he has said up to now, were it true, I wish you would cut off my head. In any event, Michelangelo will return as your Holiness wishes."

"Here," Roselli concluded his letter, "the matter ended."

Despite a certain obscurity in the language of the letter—Rosselli was unschooled—the recorded conversation proves that around the time of Michelangelo's impetuous departure from Rome, the pope had it in his head to redirect Michelangelo's energy from the tomb project and have him paint the ceiling of the Sistine Chapel. According to Rosselli, the idea did not originate with Bramante, as is later claimed, but from the pope or an associate of his such as Cardinal Francesco Alidosi, the pope's confidant and papal legate of Bologna, who drew up the agreement in 1508.

Michelangelo has been considered paranoid about his perceived "enemies" in Julius's Rome. No doubt, there were voices speaking against Michelangelo's interest resounding in the corridors of the Vatican Palace; he was badmouthed at the highest levels. Donato Bramante, the architect of St. Peter's who had trained as a painter, was a principal, most formidable adversary. When Michelangelo left Rome in April 1506, he must have sensed that the pope had been convinced to drop the projected tomb, and Rosselli's letter less than a month later would have confirmed Michelangelo's suspicions that there was a conspiracy against him or at least against the tomb project. Talk circulated that it was bad luck to construct one's tomb while still alive, and the projected expenses were considerable.

Michelangelo, for his part, did not hide his antagonism toward Bramante. He was to complain a few years later about how the architect was mercilessly tearing down the thousand-year-old columns of the old St. Peter's to make room for his new building, and that he had designed a faulty rope support from which Michelangelo was supposed to paint the Sistine Chapel ceiling. Small wonder that Michelangelo was reluctant to return to Rome with Giuliano da Sangallo, or with anyone else. Months of negotiations and assurances were required to arrange for Michelangelo to meet the pope in Bologna. Ironically, Bramante was probably there at the same time, designing the grand stairwell of the town hall of Bologna for the pope.

Michelangelo had no more experience in fresco painting on May 10, 1508, when he began the Sistine Chapel ceiling, than on May 10, 1506, when Bramante had raised devastating doubts. His only first-hand familiarity with such work took place in the Ghirlandaio *bottega* in the late 1480s. He had never dealt with radical foreshortenings, the challenge that lay at the core of Bramante's stated reservations. The *Doni Tondo* was painted in tempera on panel, while the *Battle of Cascina* never got beyond the cartoon stage; besides, neither had pre-

Engraving of the Sistine Chapel before Michelangelo's ceiling, late 1800s (Reconstruction).

sented the kind of demands he would face on the ceiling in Rome. Michelangelo worried that "painting was not my art," as he told everyone who asked, and he soon discovered that *buon,* or pure, fresco was a tricky medium, requiring that fluid, muddy-looking pigments mixed with limewater be applied to a fresh, wet, plaster surface.

Michelangelo returned to Rome toward the end of March 1508 to begin painting the ceiling. He sent word to Granacci in Florence that he required experienced hands to help him, and perhaps more than that, to teach Michelangelo the technical skills of fresco. At this stage, Michelangelo seems to have been hoping that by constituting a team, he could rush through the job in order to quickly reactivate the Julius Tomb. We know from drawings that his first intentions were conventional and simple, with the twelve *Apostles* and little more by way of figural representations.

The chapel had been built by Pope Sixtus IV, Julius II's uncle, who had made him a cardinal and whose memory Julius held in high esteem. Since Sixtus managed to complete only a portion of his chapel's decoration before he died, Julius must have felt an obligation to complete the scheme by providing the chapel with an appropriate ceiling, as soon as he was able to do so.

Almost immediately, Michelangelo and the pope concluded that the rudimentary first plan was not worthy of the older frescoes on the side walls by Botticelli, Perugino, Signorelli, Ghirlandaio, and others; much less the intrinsic importance of the place. At that point Michelangelo forged a much more ambitious plan, which was the one executed. After a few months of ineffectual collaboration with perhaps as many as six painters, Michelangelo dismissed them all and went about the painting of the ceiling pretty much on his own.

The Sistine Chapel ceiling is one of those awesome human efforts that tends to defy total analysis. To compound this difficulty of interpretation, no contemporary evidence offering insight into Michelangelo's and Julius's intentions survives. Michelangelo never wrote about the project specifically, either out of purposeful secretiveness or such nonchalance that it never occurred to the artist that clues would be priceless nuggets to later commentators. Julius appears to have been either discreet or removed.

As with other masters of the time, an habitual question raised is whether Michelangelo worked out the meaning of the whole—the iconography—on his own, or whether he had the aid of a learned theologian, or someone available for extended explanations. Surely there was no lack of qualified individuals among the Vatican prelates and theologians. But in contrast with most other painters and sculptors of the time, Michelangelo had received unique intellectual preparation at the Medici Gardens, at the Medici Palace, and by his own independent efforts. Still, even if he was better prepared than most of his contemporaries to develop an iconographic program, he probably also availed himself of suggestions from others. On the other hand, the final decisions must have been his.

From the planning stage to its completion, and even in the centuries that followed, every facet surrounding the chapel's ceiling fresco is complicated by hearsay, myth, fantasy, contradictory reports, and outright speculation. Unraveling the pictorial contents of the ceiling decoration detail by detail and ferreting out assumed layers of meanings is an almost insurmountable task. Considering the broad range of complex and diverse subjects Michelangelo painted here, certain crucial choices offer an unparalleled access into the artist's mind. The choices are especially revealing in instances where he was required to invent a new representation, theme, or combination—situations, that is, in which there were no precedents. In these cases, we should be particularly alert for revelations that depend most directly upon his vision, without the interference of tradition.

The Sistine decoration is remarkable in Michelangelo's art because so much of it is entirely new, regardless of the biblical and theological requirements. Whenever choices were thrown open, Michelangelo was forced to interpret them on his own. One of the challenges, therefore, that the Sistine Chapel ceiling presents is to single out precisely those areas where his personal interpretation is most readily revealed.

An overview of the frescoes, which were finished after more than four years, in early October 1512, is necessary to place the mammoth undertaking in the context of his patron's temperament and his own. A description of exactly what one sees upon looking up with the head sharply tilted is illuminating. Beginning near the top of the

Overleaf: Full view (looking toward the altar) of the Sistine Chapel ceiling, with the names of the scenes superimposed.

walls of the long, narrow building, "lunettes" contain sixteen representations (two of which were sacrificed to give way to Michelangelo's own *Last Judgment,* painted twenty-five years later on the altar
wall). These are unique compositions, really tableaux, with several
adults and inevitably children, who turn out to be the "heroes" of the
individual scenes.

Michelangelo began frescoing the ceiling with the chronologically most recent events as they occur in the Old Testament; he then
moved down the vault to the earliest events, an essential factor considering the shifts in pictorial style found on the ceiling. The Noah
scenes were painted first (when he had technical problems with the
preparation of the surface), the *Separation of Light and Darkness* last.
Changes between the two and those in between, therefore, may be attributed to the thematic requirements of each subject, but also to stylistic considerations. After all, four years separated Michelangelo's first
applications from his last ones, and stylistic shifts can be assumed. At
the start, Michelangelo was uneasy with the demanding technique of
true *(buon)* fresco, but over time, he grew technically more venture-
some, employing the brush freely and relying to a greater extent
upon thin washes, glue-painting, and other *secco* applications.

Collectively, the sixteen lunettes form part of the *Ancestors of
Christ* theme, which spreads onto the curved ceiling itself with eight
triangular scenes (*vele* or veils) along the long sides of the chapel, to
bring a total of twenty-four units or generations. Beyond serving as
the structural base for the imitation marble superstructure which
Michelangelo invented to calibrate an overall system, the *Ancestors* occupy a rather shadowy zone in the plan.

Interspersed among the *Ancestors* on the ceiling and on the two
short walls are the Prophets and Sibyls: twelve seated figures, male and
female, old and young, heroic massive *Seers (Veggenti).* These are the
individuals who in one way or another predicted or signified Christ's
coming: seven Prophets from the Old Testament and five Sibyls from

traditional classical literature, who had long before been co-opted into the Christian legend. Reading clockwise and beginning at the entrance wall, directly opposite the site where Michelangelo would paint the *Last Judgment,* is *Zachariah.* Like all the other *Seers,* he sits on a massive marble throne, beneath which stand a number of painted (not marble) children—*putti*—sometimes male, and, quite remarkable for their rarity, sometimes female. Each holds a plaque which bears the name of the individual seated above. (The ones on the short sides of the chapel have given way to new representations.) The inscription-holding putti *(putti reggitarga)* make up part of Michelan-

After Michelangelo, copy of Michelangelo's Sistine Chapel ceiling. Detail: *Lunette with Ancestors of Christ,* c. 1530.

gelo's exploration of an ever present subtext on the ceiling, that of children. The insertion of nameplates must signify that the *Seers* were not readily identifiable without them even to a sophisticated Roman audience. The *Ancestors,* whom Michelangelo composed as family units consisting of a mother, father, and a child or two, included similar written identifications of the male line, surely for the same reason. Conversely, the Genesis stories and the other narratives from the Old Testament that cover the ceiling would have been more familiar and hence did not require explanation.

The thrones themselves contain paired nude putti painted to look like marble in relief. These forty-eight children form subjects in harmonious poses that dignify the upper portions of the enthroned

MICHELANGELO, composition sketch for the Sistine Chapel ceiling, 1508.

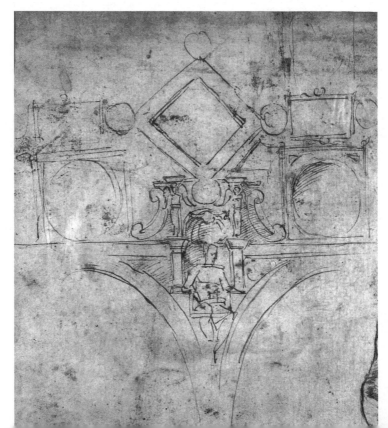

figures. The *Seers* are all deeply engaged in texts, either from scrolls or books, with the exception of *Jeremiah* and *Jonah,* who are communicating directly with God. Jonah is, of course, a conventional prefiguration for Christ, since Jonah too rose from the dead, after three days in the belly of the whale.

In addition to the marble putti, twenty-four assistants, mainly children, of the Prophets and Sibyls, are flesh-colored. Among the children on the entire ceiling, then, several age categories can be isolated: those in the *Ancestor* scenes are perhaps three years old, the plaque supporters perhaps eight or nine, and the assistants about eleven or twelve, although the apparent ages are not always distinguishable (and there are several adults in the last group). The marble putti, who are lively and often shown in dance poses, are about three or four years old. But more important than determining the exact ages of the children, which can only be approximate anyway, is the very fact of their presence in such extensive numbers and the variety of types and poses they represent.

The Prophets and Sibyls, reading clockwise, are: *Zachariah,* the *Delphic Sibyl, Isaiah,* the *Cumaean Sibyl, Daniel,* the *Libyan Sibyl,* and *Jonah,* and then across to the other side of the ceiling, *Jeremiah,* the *Persian Sibyl, Ezekiel,* the *Erythrean Sibyl,* and finally *Joel.* These twelve potent, inspirational *Seers* are located on decisively curved surfaces, which made them especially challenging for Michelangelo to paint. An unprecedented collection of majestic figures, they increase in size and scale as one moves toward *Jonah* and the altar, spilling out and exploding from their confining niches. Their number, twelve, is rich in connotations. It corresponds to that of the Apostles, which was to have been the main figurative element when Michelangelo and Julius first began to consider the decoration, as well as to the tribes of Israel, the months of the year, the houses of the horoscope, the number of Evangelists multiplied by the Trinity, and so on.

The noble, straightforward, and intelligible hand gestures of the

Seers vary from one to another, offering a handbook for this aspect of communication. Colorful attire, such as the yellow drape on *Daniel's* knee, or the bright yet earthy reds, pale blues, and violets on the simplified garments of others, is typical. Several of the *Seers* are bareheaded, others have small caps, and still others sport elaborate headdresses. They are all fully clothed, though with strong indications of their physicality underneath. Some have flowing hair or fine beards, while *Zachariah* is "as bald as the rear end of monkeys," according to the Florentine saying.

Located between the *Seers* and the *Ancestors* are twelve pairs of mostly male, rather thinly painted nudes, treated as imitation bronzes. Set in precarious, angular spaces separated by goat skulls with twisted horns, their meaning is obscure, but an underlying strategy of duplication can be detected since each member of the pair is the reverse of the other. Michelangelo must have reused the same cartoon or preparatory design but turned it over, a procedure he occasionally employed elsewhere on the ceiling. These bronze nudes, who move lazily within their constricted, spiky spaces, project an aura of pure sensuality as they visually link the cornice of the central trellislike structure with the *Ancestors*. As adult nudes, they are echoed thematically and expanded in the inner zone by the presence of larger paintings of nudes. These painted male nudes are the famous *Ignudi,* interspersed alternately among the narrative scenes of the central area. Indeed, the nude as a coherent motif has a total of forty-four representations on the ceiling, not including the children and the nudes found within the various narrative scenes.

Four vast curved triangular or pendentive spaces at the corners of the ceiling—larger than any of the others—operate to permit a smooth transition from the flat walls to the curved surface of the vaulted ceiling itself. These surfaces were especially awkward or at least demanding for painting narratives, requiring a control of foreshortening that Bramante for one did not believe Michelangelo could manage. The pendentives with their subjects can best be understood when taken together as a unified or at least an interconnected cluster of narratives.

Once again, reading clockwise from the prophet *Zachariah,* Michelangelo situated *Judith and Holofernes,* and across to the altar wall the *Brazen Serpent,* and the *Punishment of Haman* on the other wall, while back across to the entrance wall he frescoed *David and Goliath.* The *David* and *Judith* scenes, therefore, are on the entrance side and the other two on the altar side. The events are paired, with the victories of the Israelites at the entrance; both, significantly, depicting decapitation of enemies. The triumph of the Cross can be read into the pair on the altar wall, for the brazened serpent is on a cross and Haman is appended to one, although in the biblical account he was hung at the gallows. Michelangelo must have envisaged that an actual cross would be physically present at the altar table, so he had no pressing need to represent it. Still, the *Punishment of*

MICHELANGELO, **studies for three** *Ignudi,* c. 1508.

Haman would have reminded the faithful present in the chapel of the Crucifixion.

Michelangelo gave a programmatic role to his *Ignudi,* all but one seated (in distinction to the reclining bronze ones on the zone beneath), by having them support garlands of leaves and gigantic acorns. The nudes function like angels and, in fact, probably should be regarded as such, as should the nude men in the background of the *Doni Tondo* and as one finds in the *Last Judgment,* with its even more massive young men floating on the upper reaches of the altar wall. The identity of the *Ignudi* as angels is best explained when seen along with all the other "angels" on the ceiling: the marble relief "putti" who support the cornice, the slightly older painted assistants to the *Seers,* perhaps the bronze reclining nudes, and the hosts of angels representing different ages who assist God in the *Creation of Adam,* where the whole repertoire may be found.

The marvelously athletic *Ignudi* either struggle and tug at their burden or seem utterly relaxed. As if forgotten by the artist, the motif of the swags disappears near midway, only to reappear at the end of the cycle nearest the altar, where the acorns gain a particular dominance. The *Ignudi* act and react in pairs down the length of the chapel, turning and twisting to break any semblance of monotony, but their visual role is mainly to frame the five "small" narratives. (One of the *Ignudi* from the first section has almost completely disappeared due to damage from an explosion.) The *Ignudi* are also crowning devices for the *Seers* since they sit upon squarish marble blocks that, in turn, rest upon the cornice, with the paired putti acting like caryatids from ancient Greece supporting the architecture. Their dual function reinforces the two directions from which to approach the ceiling cycle: segmented, compartment by compartment with histories, *Seers, Ignudi,* Medallions; or lengthwise down the nave, bay by bay.

The pictorial conviction of Michelangelo's *Nudes,* their powerful presence as physical beings, as well as their sheer youthful beauty, accentuates the illusionistic authenticity of the entire Sistine Chapel ceiling, within the context of Renaissance artistic objectives. Painting, which is flat, is successful to the extent that it appears like sculpture, that is, to the degree it has a three-dimensional effect. Here the artist accepts the challenge of nature, comes to grips with it head on, and comes up victorious.

Beyond the meaning (or meanings) of the fresco as a totality, the significance of individual parts to the whole or to each other, and the personal implications for Michelangelo and for his patron, the Sistine Chapel ceiling is a decorative mask for the vault itself, presenting a world that delights and inspires. For his work to be seen and contemplated—surely the embracing imperative for any creator—Michelangelo had to seduce the viewer, a requirement accomplished both by introducing engaging devices familiar to the craft and also by inventing new ones, such as violent foreshortening and the gigantic *Ignudi*. Once the viewer has been so engaged, the complexities of form and meaning that require a more immediate rapport can be confronted.

Supported by ribbons or strips of cloth entwined in their frames and attached to the pedestals of some of the *Ignudi,* the ten Medallions were painted to appear like circular relief sculptures, probably to represent gilt bronze, though a few were not finished. Their subjects have never been convincingly decoded, nor has their precise place in the larger program; do they refer to the stories nearby, as one can readily believe along with Condivi, or do they have an independent coherence, possibly representing the Ten Commandments? Formally, their circularity is repeated in several of the Genesis narratives, particularly the depiction of the Sun and the Moon, and in the swirling movement of draperies, especially those of God. Besides, a glittering effect seems to have been intended for them, had the pope allowed Michelangelo time to apply the final treatment, especially for the medals and the bronze nudes.

The central unit of the vault, established visually by the marble

MICHELANGELO, detail of God the Father from *Creation of Adam,* 1508–12.

cornice and subdivided by ten bands of white marble, constitutes the structural skeleton for the decoration, and contains the core meaning of the program, subjects taken from Genesis, rendered in alternatively "large" and "small" panels. Michelangelo painted the *Separation of Light and Darkness* nearest the altar (alongside *Jonah*). In terms of proportions, the cycle begins as it will end, with a "small" scene with sufficient space for four *Ignudi* and two Medallions. Next, the *Creation of the Sun and Moon,* a "large" or "full" scene, occupies all by itself the entire space of the second bay. Also in distinction to the first scene, besides the change in size, God appears twice in the second, the *Creation of the Sun and Moon:* shown frontally and from behind, as if we are witnessing the passage of time in the heavens.

In the third bay, the *Separation of the Land and the Waters* (also called *God Blessing the Earth*), Michelangelo conceived the entire representation, the image of God and the whirl of clouds, in a state of transformation: undeterminable, swirling, billowing masses gradually metamorphosing into tangible shapes while God gesticulates as He prepares to create human life. Although not specifically shown, He must be generating the animals, for Michelangelo left out this essential incident normally represented in Genesis cycles.

The fourth bay shows the *Creation of Adam,* and the fifth the *Cre-*

ation of Eve, but the image of God continues its transformation. Psychologically, in the first scene Michelangelo depicts a remote, indistinct God. In the second, God becomes a fear-engendering presence, that is, he is *terribile.* Then in the third, the *Separation,* He appears as a more benign presence, while in the fourth, the unforgettable *Creation of Adam,* Michelangelo portrays an intense yet understanding God, even allowing Him a faint smile. Finally, in the fifth bay, the *Creation of Eve,* an older, hoary human God, whose beard has grown much longer, is introduced. His large body seems exhausted but He emanates an air of satisfaction; He is God as *paterfamilias.* These "God scenes" read all together constitute a coherent grouping in which God is both protagonist and hero.

The next two scenes—the sixth, showing the *Fall of Adam and Eve and the Expulsion from Paradise,* and the seventh, *Cain and Abel Offering*—according to Condivi's reading as it is regarded here, although commonly today called the *Sacrifice of Noah*—are best understood as referring to Adam and Eve and their immediate family and the consequences of the Fall. The expulsion of the first parents from Paradise caused hardships in eking out a life and raising their children, Cain and Abel. The final two representations are Noah scenes; the eighth is the incomparable *Flood,* undoubtedly Michelangelo's finest narration and the single work that best reveals his humanity; and the ninth and last is the *Drunkenness of Noah.*

Conventional wisdom divides these centrally located nine scenes into three subgroups of three each: three "God Creating" panels; three depicting "Adam and Eve"; and three with Noah as the defining personality. This tripartite system suggested a Trinitarian overlay to the program, an interpretation that is not unsuitable; nor do the early sources hint at this or any other interpretation for that matter. Besides, no particular advantage derives from rigidly insisting upon the three-three-three arrangement. The alternative interpretation, with the first five narratives devoted to God's direct intervention as a unit, has the advantage of common sense and visual confirmation.

Bays six and seven, as proposed here, are "Adam and Eve" scenes where, that is, the first children appear without God, and the final pair, in bays eight and nine, are "Noah" ones. What results is a system of five and four, the four composed of two closely related units of two.

Harmony and balance require a slight modification of the five-plus-four arrangement, however. To establish a more tectonic pattern, one consistent with Renaissance habits, the middle scene, the fifth, which illustrates the *Creation of Eve,* is best apprehended as pivotal and independent. It pertains to the small-sized format scenes, like the first and the last, and is not a truly "God scene" because, although God is present, He stands on the ground and is "on Earth," in the same environment as the sleeping Adam, as Eve emerges from his side. But neither is the *Creation of Eve* strictly speaking an "Adam and Eve" scene, for unlike the others, Eve here is not fully present simply because she has yet to be completely created.

Just as the treatment of God undergoes a gradual transformation both pictorially and psychologically along the length of the ceiling, the humans also grow and change. In the Noah scenes, the actors are more naturalistic than those in the Adam and Eve scenes: the figures are tactile, sculptural masses that occupy a convincing space within a palpable atmosphere. The *Cain and Abel Offering* (which was heavily repainted during the middle of the sixteenth century due to physical damage to the fresco and is therefore the least authentic of the nine narratives) betrays the same realistic tendency. On the other hand, the figures of the *Fall and Expulsion,* though solid, are, if anything, more symbolic than those in the Noah ones, and in this respect at least, are more consistent with the figures in the *Creation of Eve.* They are pictorially closer to the surface and the sensation of distant space has been severely impaired.

The four "God scenes" constituted the unit of the ceiling closest to the altar and therefore the most sacred area in the chapel. Here along with God are those representations which imply the Crucifix-

ion in the pendentives and the Resurrection with Jonah, the prototype of Jesus, who is awarded the most prominent position on the
ceiling and is the largest of all the figures. The second unit consists of
the *Creation of Eve,* a separate entity in the very center all by itself. Eve
is a common prototype of Mary, who is termed the second Eve just
as Christ is the second Adam. Mary *is* the Church. Yet Mary is
nowhere specifically represented in the frescoes, except as embodied
in Eve, despite the fact that the chapel was dedicated to Mary (of the
Assumption). There are, of course, Marian analogies among the *Ancestors,* in the guise of mother and child. The third unit, with the final
four representations, can be interpreted as "Family" scenes, those of
Adam and Eve and of Noah. As a group, these scenes are the most
"modern" and temporally closest to contemporary viewers, sharing
the condition of the viewers down below, and the painter, for that
matter. They reflect man's fate in chronological time, forming an opposite to the eternal time encapsulated in the first unit.

The proper division of the ceiling's central bank of histories is,
then, four+one+four. When this pattern is considered, multiples of
four can be seen to have a decisive role on the entire ceiling: twenty-
four *Ancestors*/generations, divided into subsets of sixteen and eight;
sixteen bronze *Nudes;* forty-eight marble putti; twelve *Seers;* twenty-
four assistants to the *Seers;* twenty *Ignudi;* and four pendentives. There
are ten Medallions. Thematically, these could also break down as
four+four+half of four (i.e., two). Occasionally, there may be a slight
divergence between the actual numbers and the implied numbers, as
with the number of assistants. But the number 4 is truly the essential
key to Michelangelo's ceiling, and refers to the number of the Evangelists, the winds, and the sides of a square, which along with the circle were regarded at the time as having special status because of their
perfection.

To recapitulate: In the conventional groupings of three sets of
three scenes, we have the following breakdown:

GOD SCENES: *Separation of Light and Darkness*
Creation of the Sun and Moon
Separation of the Land and the Waters

ADAM AND EVE *Creation of Adam*
SCENES: *Creation of Eve*
Fall of Adam and Eve and the Expulsion from Paradise

NOAH *Sacrifice of Noah*
SCENES: *The Flood*
Drunkenness of Noah

The revised arrangement of four–one–four scenes goes as follows:

GOD SCENES: *Separation of Light and Darkness*
Creation of the Sun and Moon
Separation of the Land and the Waters
Creation of Adam

INTERIM SCENE: *Creation of Eve*

FAMILY SCENES: *Fall of Adam and Eve and the Expulsion from Paradise*
Cain and Abel Offering [Sacrifice of Noah]
The Flood
Drunkenness of Noah

The ceiling decoration stresses family as a constant theme: the family of Adam, including Cain and Abel; and the family of Noah in the Ark and especially his sons Ham, Japheth, and Shem. The *Ancestors of Christ* in fully twenty-four separate compartments also stress family. In fact, they constitute as a group the most expansive treatment of the subject in Renaissance art, and contain implicit references to the Holy Family (the subject of Michelangelo's *Doni Tondo*). Michelangelo gives the children special attention, emphasizing their role in the chain that leads to the coming of Christ.

The prolific and sympathetic treatment of parents and children found on the ceiling is crucial to the artist's overall interpretation, as are the nudes. Although he incised only the names of the male ancestors who denote the generations on the plaques, Michelangelo gives the mothers and the children preferential treatment pictorially over the adult men. In the process, he often pinpoints poignant relationships between a mother and her child. So, if Mary is not present on the Sistine ceiling, the Madonna and Child theme often appears.

Did this unprecedented concentration on family and on the interaction between mother and child reflect Michelangelo's nostalgia for his own lost mother, for his family and his childhood? In a poem praising the simple country life of a couple similar to those he must have known in Settignano, Michelangelo says: "Envy has no place here / pride of its own self is devoured / . . . their most valued treasure is a plow / . . . shovels and hoes are their golden vessels."

The singularity of his devotion to family on the ceiling was confirmed later in the artist's life. He took a strong interest in the welfare of his only niece, Francesca, the daughter of Buonarroto, who had been named after her paternal grandmother, that is, Michelangelo's mother. Michelangelo paid for her education in the Convent of San Giovanni Evangelista a Boldrone and provided her with a handsome dowry. Francesca's brother Lionardo was Michelangelo's only nephew, his universal heir and sole hope for the Buonarroti family line; Lionardo became almost a son to the artist, who raised him after Buonarroto died.

Michelangelo, already over seventy when he helped Lionardo find a suitable mate, advocated that the most pressing qualities in a wife are the "goodness" of the young woman, her health, and that she belong to a noble family, though not rich, so that Lionardo would not be subject to the pretensions and whims of "certain" women. Besides, as the uncle observed pitilessly, "you Lionardo are not the sort of person who is worthy of the most beautiful woman of Florence.

Rather," he wrote authoritatively as if from experience (which he did not have), "you need someone who is not ashamed, when there is need, to wash the pots and pans and look after things in the house." Subsequently, after Lionardo had set up a family, Michelangelo recalled how he was hardly surprised over the death of a baby girl, because the Buonarroti family seemed to have difficulty in perpetuating itself.

Michelangelo's devotion to the concept of family in his own life and in the larger thematic outline of the Sistine ceiling is readily decoded in his interpretation of the *Flood*. Here heroic, unselfish efforts of mankind are enacted: men saving their wives, women their children, fathers their sons; old people rescuing the young. The *Flood,* Michelangelo's most panoramic representation, has suggestions of landscape, water, and other natural phenomena—such as a bolt of lightning smashing a tree trunk—as well as common household objects like chairs and jars, which are hard to find elsewhere in his art. Furthermore, the *Flood* is the most populated scene on the ceiling, making the example especially poignant. Implicit in the various incidents here shown is Michelangelo's humanity, his view of man's earthly lot, which is only hinted at in the constrained format of the lunettes.

Like the other eight central scenes, but unlike the four pendentives and the *Seers,* the *Flood* panel is oriented so that the viewer—the presiding priest in the chapel (the Pope), for example—is assumed to be looking up from the direction of the altar. In this panel, Michelangelo operated within a rectangular space twice as wide as it was tall, in a proportion of two to one. Compositionally, a reasonably high horizon is broken by an outcropping of rock, which signifies the tip of a mountain and hence offers an indication of the awesome height that the waters have already reached. On this tiny island, desperate people have devised a rudimentary tentlike haven from flood, wind, and, presumably, rain: men, women, and children huddle together as a person is fished out of the water, while another half-drowned young man is consoled following his recovery from the swirling waters.

The barren sliver of high ground on the left, with one wind-blown tree, is a point of salvation that the multitude seek with all their wit and energy. But we know, and so does Michelangelo, that their efforts are in vain. One old, uncharacteristically nude woman lies exhausted on the ground, while another woman struggles with one child in her arms and a second clutching her leg. She appears like a personification of Charity, which was rendered in this way for centuries and would have been familiar to contemporary viewers. Slightly lower down the hill, a determined, powerful man carries his terrified young wife to temporary safety; and still further down, people struggle to preserve a few possessions, even putting them on their heads in hope of hanging on to humble household objects as refugees have done for centuries, a universal image of great clarity. Monumental nude men energetically seek to stay alive in a tublike boat floating near the center of the picture, not far from the outcropping where the tent has been raised.

Of all the separate incidents within the *Flood,* the most touching, and the one that reveals Michelangelo's feelings most deeply, is the smallest. A bald man within the tent, who, incidentally, looks like the Prophet Zachariah, calls attention to two nude grown men, one older and one younger. The older is supporting the younger man, presumably his son, who appears to be recovering from near drowning or exhaustion. They are presented in a poignant paraphrase of constant struggle. The weight of the young man inspires an almost Herculean effort by the father, as he stands with his legs planted far apart for extra leverage. His action expresses deep affection, and mirrors representations of Christ being lovingly lowered from the Cross. This should be regarded as a visual illustration of Michelangelo's love for his own father and his never-ending longing for affection and support, so poignantly revealed in his letters.

The motif of salvation, effectively the main lesson of the *Flood,* is symbolized by Noah's Ark on the horizon. This palacelike structure, not altogether dissimilar in appearance to the Sistine Chapel itself, is immense when one takes into account the assumed distance

from the front plane of the painting. Here Noah and his family have been gathered, along with two of each of all the beasts and the fowls of the earth.

They alone will be saved, leaving all the courageous individuals that populate the rest of the picture to be swept away all

MICHELANGELO, *The Flood,*
1508–12. Above, detail.

too soon by the rising waters. Metaphorically, the Ark has long stood for the Holy Church. Thus, salvation is interpreted to come only through the Church and, implicitly, its vicar on earth, the pope. If this aspect is conventional, Michelangelo's depiction of the *Flood* is unique in the proliferation of figural motifs. In particular, he demonstrates a transparent sympathy for the struggling multitude, with whom he surely associates himself. This attitude finds confirmation in letters and poems, where he describes his struggle to paint the vast ceiling and, symbolically, the very scene of the *Flood*. He too labors with superhuman effort, like all the others, and his efforts may prove equally hopeless.

If there is ample evidence of Michelangelo's own, private interpretations of the human condition in the *Flood*, a similar strain may

be found in another Noah scene, the contiguous *Drunkenness*. Here the good son (the Bible version has two good sons), without looking, modestly covers Noah, who is lying out of control, with his genitals exposed, while the others look on sneeringly. This is a reversal of the incident of the old man saving the younger one since now the son comes to the aid of his father—not with the glass of water Lodovico had mentioned, but a coverlet. Michelangelo painted the fresco at the very time when his father was being mistreated by Giovansimone and Michelangelo came to his aid by severely chastising his sneering brother. Can we be far from Michelangelo's transliteration of the biblical account into his own family situation? Michelangelo, of course, is here the good son, who modestly covers the father's genitals. In an ironic, witty twist, Michelangelo shows all three sons just as nude as their father, and the cloth that the good son places on the old man is nearly transparent.

THE DEPICTION OF JULIUS

From the beginning problems arose, including technical ones related to the preparation of the surface for frescoing the *Flood*. In a letter of January 1509 to his father, Michelangelo expressed his dissatisfaction, complaining, "I am still in a state of grand confusion . . . because my work is not moving ahead in the manner that I believe it merits. This is due to the difficulty of the enterprise itself and, besides, because painting is not my profession," a familiar phrase he repeated again and again.

Michelangelo completed the first half of the ceiling in the summer of 1510, although Julius did not see the overall results from ground level until the following year, when that part of the ceiling was formally unveiled. However, from what he had been able to view from the scaffolding at different times, Julius was satisfied with the work, and gave Michelangelo the go-ahead by the fall of 1510 to paint the second half. Michelangelo must have been anxious to get the pope's approval for the demanding work, so when Julius expressed enthusiasm, the artist was euphoric. A cynical interpretation of Michelangelo's joy might suggest that the desire to please his patron was merely an attempt to ensure that he would be awarded the rest of the commission; but that reading does not take into account Michelangelo's self-imposed mission as an artist, his personal pride, and, of course, his profound hope to keep the door ajar to proceed with the Julius Tomb once the ceiling was finished.

Michelangelo made various private allusions to his patron in the fresco. The most obvious are the highly visible acorns protruding from the garlands that the *Ignudi* support. They refer to the oak tree, the emblem of Julius's family, the della Rovere ("of the Oak"). Acorns were ancient fertility symbols and the oak was the sacred tree of Jove, implicitly signified in the name Julius. The acorns were given special attention by Michelangelo, and he repeats them as part of the decoration of the imitation marble ribs of the superstructure. With the acorns Michelangelo inserted an inside joke, or *burla,* to amuse his *terribile* patron. Gigantic fertility symbols, those della Rovere acorns are shaped too much like the phalluses of the *Ignudi* holding them not to have been intentional. According to Tuscan slang, "prickhead" *(testa di cazzo)* is a favored insulting yet endearing appellation even today, especially in Michelangelo's Santa Croce section of Florence.

This kind of jocose engagement confirms Michelangelo's claims to intimacy with Julius, and the likelihood of the pope's secret visits to his workshop, despite their disagreement over the tomb. What can one say about the girl putto, an unheard-of type anyway, showing her fully developed bosom as she supports the nameplate of *Jeremiah?*

MICHELANGELO, *Ignudo.* Detail from Sistine Chapel ceiling.

After Michelangelo, copy of Michelangelo's Sistine Chapel ceiling. Detail: female "putto" supporting inscription, c. 1530.

Michelangelo could have dared to include such a pictorial artifice only with the tacit consent of the pontiff. This pungent witticism, a Tuscan trait, must have been precisely the element of Michelangelo's personality that drew the pope to him, and helps to explain why Julius was so angry when a companion of such appeal—not to mention a brilliant artist—left Rome in 1506 without permission.

In addition to symbols of Julius's family and the metaphorical references to him, did Michelangelo show any specific likenesses of Julius among the hundreds of figures painted on the ceiling? Though the artist was generally reluctant to render portraits, he may have placed the pope's face in some of the Sistine scenes, as Raphael did quite frequently in his frescoed rooms nearby in the Vatican Palace, painted around the same time. One of the most likely candidates as a secret portrait was also probably another inside joke to be appreciated most by painter and patron: the decapitated head of the Assyrian general Holofernes in the *Judith and Holofernes* pendentive. This has been wrongly proposed as a likeness of Michelangelo or as a representation somehow of the contemporary political conflict between pro- and anti-Florentine interests. In fact, the head resonates as a papal reference. A drawing, presumably a study for the cartoon, very close to the final fresco version has survived. That Michelangelo put the pope's head on a plate carried by a woman servant is a highly engaging possibility: the artist poking fun at the "prickhead" Julius, by showing him undone by a woman (he was known as a libertine).

A very recent experience might have sparked the joke. One of

MICHELANGELO, male head in profile, c. 1510.

MICHELANGELO, detail of the head of Holofernes from *Judith and Holofernes.*

MICHELANGELO, *Judith and Holofernes,* 1508–12.

the reasons that Michelangelo's *David* was moved to the front of the Signoria Palace in Florence was to replace Donatello's bronze *Judith and Holofernes,* a sculpture regarded as "unbecoming" because it was considered (by some) improper for a woman to dominate a man. The only element that might contradict the identification of Holofernes as Julius is its date of composition. If the fresco with the head was painted before the summer of 1510, Julius would not as yet have been shown as sporting a beard, which he only began to grow in October (following a long illness) as a reminder of the defeat of papal forces on the part of the French and the loss of Bologna on August 17, 1510. (He seems, incidentally, to have followed his namesake Julius Caesar, who let his beard grow after defeat at the hand of the same Gauls.) On the other hand, since Holofernes as a historical type appears wearing a beard in art, as Donatello portrayed him, Michelangelo may have had no alternative but to put one on him.

The two pendentive scenes, the *Judith* and the *David,* are regularly assumed to have been executed along with the rest of the "first" half of the ceiling; more specifically, they are regarded as having been painted after the *Flood,* so that would mean 1509 is the earliest possible date. But the chronology of the creation of individual parts of the Sistine ceiling is not confirmed by documentary evidence, while the stylistic indications are very difficult to unravel. All four pendentives could have been painted after the nine central histories, that is, after 1510 (and the pope's beard).

The question of chronology is, of course, related to assumptions about the scaffolding, because the kind of support Michelangelo built conditioned the order in which he approached the various segments of the ceiling. Modern scholars have been quite interested in the question of the scaffolding, but it has not yet been resolved. The newer theories adopted by the Sistine Chapel restoration team in the 1980s assume that Michelangelo devised a movable type of scaffolding, which ran or rather was pushed along the upper cornice

MICHELANGELO, drawing of a kneeling woman, c. 1510. • The theme of a woman holding the head of a man can represent either Judith with the head of Holofernes or Salome with the head of John the Baptist. In this drawing, Michelangelo seems to be treating the second theme. Here, instead of using Julius as the beheaded man, he substitutes his own likeness, which can be seen by turning the page to the side.

of the chapel. This far-fetched notion allows for certain suppositions about how he went ahead and in what order. But since this would have been a revolutionary (and really incredible) solution, it is hard to believe that no echo of it in the contemporary literature has survived. Indeed, there is a solid explanation why the movable scaffolding theory is untenable: Had the scaffolding been movable, allowing the artist to work on one section or bay at a time, the bays that had already been painted, except naturally the one he was then painting, would have been easily visible from the floor. In other words, the "unveiling" which occurred in 1511, when the pope had returned to Rome, would have been at best a monumental anticlimax. There would have been little reason for the pope and other dignitaries to struggle up the scaffolding to see Michelangelo's progress, since everyone would have already seen all but the most current scene. Considering Michelangelo's habit of secrecy about his art, it is not surprising that he was concerned that his enemies would be able to see his work in process; but they would have had to sneak into the chapel and climb up the scaffold to do so, which may be precisely what Raphael had done.

Michelangelo did not insert his own likeness among the approximately three hundred figures on the ceiling, as Signorelli had done in his frescoes at Orvieto Cathedral or as Raphael had done in his Vatican frescoes. This omission of both a self-portrait and a signature for the massive enterprise could be interpreted as inherent modesty in the context of a self-imposed mission. Along with the majestic and grand world view of the early history of man presented on the ceiling, time and time again the fabric of Michelangelo's private world is revealed. However, since the angels behind the Holy Family in the *Doni Tondo* referred to the donor whose name was Angelo, perhaps the proliferation of angels on the Sistine Chapel ceiling (and later in the *Last Judgment*) contains a similar reference. After all, Michelangelo, who once signed his name with angel wings, was an *Angelo* too. That may have been sufficient personal identification for him, if indeed the proposition has merit.

DEATH

Shortly after the ordeal of the Sistine ceiling, Julius II died in Rome: on the day of the Purification of the Virgin, February 2, 1513, when Michelangelo was thirty-eight years old. Julius's tomb, which had been the primary source of contention between the two men, gnawed at the artist's conscience until, after four decades of bickering and compromise with the della Rovere family, the tomb was finally completed. As it turned out, it was a mere shell of the early projects and was not placed in St. Peter's Basilica after all, but in San Pietro in Vincoli (St. Peter in Chains), a smaller church which had been assigned to Julius when he was made cardinal. But, for better or worse, Giuliano della Rovere and his tomb would remain very much on Michelangelo's mind for most of his life.

Il Magnifico was long gone, although memories of Michelangelo's relationship with him were never fully extinguished. Lorenzo's son Leo X, his nephew the future Clement VII, and his indirect heirs, including Duke Cosimo de' Medici, who would be the ruler of Florence at a later time, continued and treasured their predecessor's relationship with the artist. Michelangelo retained two sculptures he had made in the Medici Gardens for the rest of his life, perhaps as reminders of his first patron's affection and guidance. He also had the opportunity of seeing to the earthly remains of Lorenzo, while designing the Medici Tombs in the New Sacristy of San Lorenzo. In an early project he provided for a monument for il Magnifico, who never had a proper tomb. As the Medici Tombs were eventually carried out, however, the main place was given to the nephew, Giuliano, and the grandson, Lorenzo di Piero. But Lorenzo's bones were deposited in the New Sacristy beneath the Madonna Michelangelo had carved and the patron saints of the family, Cosma and Damiano.

Lodovico Buonarroti continued to exercise an impact upon his son long after his death on March 23, 1531. As he neared his own death decades later, Michelangelo made the quintessential declaration of filial affection and family allegiance by expressing his desire to be buried in Florence, in Santa Croce, close to the bones of his beloved father.

Michelangelo's very last efforts in life were devoted to carving an in-the-round *Pietà*. Rather than regarding it as "unfinished," the statue is more accurately described as "overfinished," for Michelangelo modified it constantly, even to the point of mutilation, virtually up to the moment of his death. Just over a month before he died, Michelangelo could no longer write his own letters, as "my hand no longer serves me" *(La mano non mi serve),* he said in a dictated letter to his nephew; but evidently he could still carve. This *Pietà,* found in his studio at the time of his death among his other Roman possessions, is now referred to as the *Rondanini Pietà.* Michelangelo hacked away at the block on and off for nearly a decade. An intimate friend and pupil of his final years, the sculptor/painter Daniele da Volterra, who won (or lost?) his place in history because he painted the loincloths on the nudes in the *Last Judgment,* witnessed the ancient master working on the *Pietà* for an entire Saturday, a mere six days before his death.

One historical detail which has escaped attention but which enriches an understanding of the interchanges between father and son concerns the destination of this late *Pietà.* It was not, as is usually assumed, conceived for Michelangelo's own tomb, but for his father's tomb, in which Michelangelo also wished to be deposited. As such, the fragmented, virtually flagellated Mary and Jesus should be regarded as the son's final desperate effort to win Lodovico's approval even beyond the grave. Michelangelo still sought to show his father, dead for thirty-five years, that sculpture was a dignified and noble endeavor. The artist was still continuing to struggle to obtain his father's admiration and his love—such a strong motivating force of his personal and professional life—to his last breath.

MICHELANGELO (?), possible self-portrait, c. 1545.

Epilogue:
A Celestial Triangle
at Macel de' Corvi

⬚⬚⬚

M ICHELANGELO almost certainly never knew Savonarola person-ally, though he had heard him speak from the pulpit, proba-bly many times, and we know that throughout his life he remembered the preacher's live voice *(restandogli ancora nella mente la memoria della sua viva voce)*. He studied Savonarola's writings on the Old and New Testament, which he held in high regard, according to Condivi. Michelangelo was not openly a Savonarolan, although members of his family and of his circle were. Nevertheless, Savonarola should be re-garded as another consistent strand in the artist's long life that can be traced to his youth but continued to affect him for the rest of his days. If any doubt remains that he was a devotee of the frate, the visionary tale told by a contemporary, Fra Benedetto Luschino, is vivid proof that even as much as fifteen years after Savonarola's death, Michelan-gelo was regarded by his followers as one of their own.

Benedetto, who had joined the Dominican order with the bless-ings of Savonarola himself, included the story in a treatise he com-posed when in prison for manslaughter. In it he referred to an event that had unfolded during the months immediately following Julius II's death. The treatise was written a few years after 1513, when the event had actually occurred, according to Benedetto. The portion concerning Michelangelo is a curious fantasy, but one that offers an insight into the artist at the end of the Julian years. The directness of the account is consistent with storytelling in the Tuscan countryside; besides, the flavors of the inexplicable, mysterious, and occult also reflect a facet of Michelangelo's thinking.

The exchange between two loyal Savonarolans begins when Agricola (Farmer) asks his companion Serpe (Serpent), "Tell me, I beg you, do you know a certain Florentine citizen of ours whose name is Michelangelo Buonarroti? The chap who today has the highest place among all mortals in the art of painting and sculpture."

"I certainly do know him," Serpe responds.

Agricola asks, "What is your opinion of him?"

"Without question, excellent; I consider him to be a singular, most honest man, God-fearing and in everything truthful," Serpe answers. "But why do you ask?"

Agricola replies, "Because in the year of Our Lord 1513, that is, during the first year Leo X had been elected, being in the city of Rome, and I believe, during the serene, summer night, outside . . . in the garden of his home, while praying and raising his eyes toward the sky, suddenly Michelangelo saw a marvelous, very large triangular sign, different in appearance from any usual comet in the sky."

He continues, "The sign was like a gigantic star, with three rays, or really tails, one of which extended toward the east and was of a splendid and resplendent color; it had the shape of a very clean silver wand [virga], or better, of a bronzed sword, and had at the top a circular form in the fashion of a ring. The second ray, or really tail, of this sign extended over the city of Rome and was of a bloody vermilion color. The third ray, completely the color of fire, extended in the direction of the city of Florence, that is, between the north and the west. At the end it was bifurcated and was of such extreme length

that it reached as far as Florence. So that thing appeared and was represented to the eyes of the man who had seen the thing. But I want
to tell about an agreeable action that the aforementioned Michelangelo did after having seen the celestial sign."

"And what agreeable thing did he do?" Serpe asks, taking the
lead.

"I will tell you," says Agricola. "Be aware that the same Michelangelo, when he had seen and considered the event, got the notion to
represent and paint this sign on a folio. He went quickly into the
house for a sheet [of paper], a pen and colors, and returned to the garden and represented the thing from the point at which it was being
observed. As he was finishing the representation, the aforementioned
sign disappeared from view."

Serpe, the straight man in this dialogue, remarks, "Oh, I would
be much pleased to see that design that he produced—even for a few
moments."

Agricola responds, "I have sketched it with my words; but if you
wish to see it, go and find the aforementioned sculptor, who presently
is to be found working in Florence, and in good faith he will show
you the design, and with humility he will confirm the truth of it all."

Serpe, changing the subject somewhat, continues: "I am sure that
you have sought to decipher what the sign might have meant."

Emphatically, Agricola answers, "You can be sure of it."

"And what have you concluded?"

"If I tell you what I have come up with, perhaps you will make
fun of it," Agricola replies cautiously.

Serpe answers, "I certainly will not make fun of what you say,
notwithstanding what you may guess."

"Well, then, what do you want to know from me?"

Serpe comes directly to his point: "What is your analysis of this
sign? What can be piously obtained other than it is not in disharmony
with the prophecies of Fra Hieronymo [Savonarola]?"

Agricola finally embarks upon his explanation: "Speaking to you with humility, according to certain reasonable discourses, it seems to me, barring proof to the contrary, that this sign signifies the tribulations of Rome, of Florence, and of all Italy, and that the barbarians will flagellate the Church, according to what our Prophet had predicted.

"And," continues Agricola, "note carefully that the heavenly triangular sign appears primarily to give notice of the number of the barbarians, that is, of the flagellators of our Italy, which must be three very powerful men: one French, namely, the King of France; another German, that is, the German Emperor; the third, the Emperor of the Turks. Our Prophet gave ample notice, while he was in the hands of his enemies, that these three generations would flagellate the Church and Italy. This, according to what appears in a certain trial [the trial of Savonarola in Florence in which he was sentenced to death by fire], though the evil interrogators would not permit its publication because it did not conform to their position; nevertheless, copies are to be found among some of our faithful friends. . . .

"The celestial sign that extends toward the east," Agricola proceeds, "it seems to me, denotes the unfaithful, to wit, the Turks. The circular ring or hook at the top appears to signify that they will be called to Italy by her sign, and by certain great teachers of the Christians, *sive manifeste, sive occulte,* and all this is not in discord with certain old prophecies that I have read. Besides, the circular form of the hook signifies the havoc these infidels will create over both goods and people, with young women taken into captivity as slaves. Additionally, the circular form and the reflecting color like silver, that is, of the splendid sword signifies that Rome will be encircled by iron, also by these infidels, who will make horse stalls of the churches and will do other terrible things, as our Prophet had often predicted. The fact that it is translucent signifies that when these Turks and Moors and other unbelievers are converted to the religion of Christ, they will be so full of virtuous faith that they will shine like a sun. And thus the prophetic words will be fulfilled. Now, what I have said is sufficient explanation of the sign, at least that part of it that reaches out toward the east."

He then explains the second ray as follows: "Concerning the bloody color that extends over the city of Rome, it seems to me overtly to signify the sword of the barbarians who will enter in that city, and the great spilling of blood without any regard for the level or dignity of any individual, as has been written in the sermons of our Prophet in diverse places.

"As for the third part of the Trinitarian sign, which extends with the color of fire as far as the city of Florence and which has the end bifurcated: this seems to me to signify the flagellation of Florence for having unfairly suppressed and burned the three Saints on the cross [probably referring to Savonarola and his two disciples at the stake]. It seems that the Florentines must receive just retribution at the unbending hand of God, as merits their very grave sins. For this thing, the sign of bifurcated fire, seems to me to signify Florence, which must be flagellated by two great fires, that is, by the material fire and by the fire of pestilence. In fact, the flagellation of Florence will be that much greater than that of the Castello di Prato, to the extent that the city of Florence is greater than the city of Prato."

The details about Michelangelo in this story are correct, which gives it greater authority for the modern historian. Michelangelo was indeed in Rome in 1513, and later, when the work was written, he indeed was living in Florence, where he began working for the Medici again. Thus, even if the supernatural theme was invented by Fra Benedetto, the fact that Michelangelo—at the time the most famous painter and sculptor in the world as a result of the *David* and the Sistine Chapel ceiling—was the protagonist, or at least the confirming testimony of the celestial sign, is a clear indication of his association with the movement surrounding the frate. Besides, circumstantial data supports the story's accuracy. And who would not wish to glimpse Michelangelo's design of the sign, even for a few moments; a remarkable "lost work" by the master?

The lodgings referred to in the story must be those at Macel de' Corvi, which translates as The Slaughterhouse of the Crows. It was there that the old painter Luca Signorelli visited Michelangelo to ask to borrow money in the very months when the vision was said to have occurred. We learn from Signorelli that Michelangelo, as was customary at the time, had his workshop in the house, which he maintained for fifty years, and where he died. At the time of Signorelli's visit and the mysterious appearance of the celestial triangle, Michelangelo was working on at least one of the *Slaves* (now in the Louvre) for the Julius Tomb, a commission that was turned over to him by the pope's heirs. Michelangelo must have had reasonably ample working space, large enough to permit carving the tomb figures. The *Moses,* which found its way to the final tomb as the *Slaves* did not, must also have been produced there.

Michelangelo kept up the house in Rome even while he was in Florence for extended periods during the late 1510s, in the 1520s, and the early 1530s. The modest structure stood in neglect until it was torn down to make room for a neoclassical monument dedicated to Vittorio Emanuele early in the twentieth century. But an idea of the house and the way Michelangelo lived in it can be deduced from a notarized inventory that was taken by a Roman official on Saturday, February 19, 1564, the morning after the master's death.

MICHELANGELO'S HOUSE
AT MACEL DE' CORVI

The inventory, at times tediously repetitive, as is the case with this type of document, is nevertheless fascinating because it brings us closer to the authentic Michelangelo. The formulaic wording begins with a Latin preamble and continues in Italian with Latin legalisms here and there. It allows us to walk through the colorless, even dreary, spaces and touch the modest furnishings that were an intimate part of Michelangelo's life. With them we can share, if only by osmosis, and nudge against the artist's daily physical world, where his thoughts, his inspirations, but also his trials, doubts, and moods reverberated. The inventory is an inadvertent prose poem, whose rhythmic repetitions reflect the mode of life and work that took place within the walls of the house and the studio attached to it:

The goods and money of the deceased gentleman Michelangelo Buonarroti.

In the Name of Our Lord, Amen. On Saturday, the 19th of the month of February 1564. This is an inventory of the real goods held in the home, the usual habitation of gentleman Michaelis Angeli Bonerote the Florentine, of good memory, most excellent sculptor when he lived; carried out by the gentleman Angelo Antonio de Amatis, substitute tax official, an agent of the most reverend governors [of Rome], and first,★

(A) *In the room where he used to sleep regularly:*

    (1) *A metal bed with a straw bed box, three mattresses, two covers of white wool and one of white lambskin.*

    (2) *A baldachin with its knot of white cloth.*

    (3) *A large wood credenza in which there are: (a) a long fur coat of wolf skin, old; (b) a rough woolen lion-colored blanket, heavily used; (c) another fur coat, half length, of wolf, with a cover of black cloth; (d) a mantle of fine black Florentine material, with sections of black lining inside, almost new; (e) a black lambswool tunic lined with black material, heavily used; (f) a mantle of black wool, lined inside, heavily used; (g) a rose undershirt with a rose silk border, heavily used; (h) two black Persian hats [ermesino negro]; (i) a long, pale-colored undershirt with a border of the same material, heavily used; (j) a cloth jacket [?gippone], heavily used; (k) a pair of white*

★I have added letters and numbers in the text to identify sections and parts for the benefit of the reader, although they do not appear in the original.

hose, heavily used; (l) a thick wool undershirt, heavily used; (m) white sheets, in number seven; (n) a large tablecloth. 2 canne and 6 palmi in length [= approximately 8 feet]; (o) another similar tablecloth, which measures 3 canni in length [= approximately 6 feet]; (p) another similar tablecloth that measures 2 canne and 6 palmi in length [= approximately 8 feet]; (q) another tablecloth of renso [?], 1 canna and just about a half in length [= approximately 4 1/2 feet]; (r) another large tablecloth of 1 canna in length [= approximately 3 feet]; (s) another tablecloth, square, old; (t) another similar one, old; (u) another similar one, thin; (v) 2 canne of thin cloth; (w) used shirts, in number nineteen; (x) new shirts, lined, in number five [Michelangelo's nephew Lionardo sent him shirts from Florence, in about 1540; Michelangelo wrote back that they were "so big that there is not a farmer around here who would not be embarrassed to wear them." Perhaps these are among the still "new," that is, never worn, shirts found at his death]; (y) a bust-length white cotton shirt; (z) a cotton shirt; (aa) handkerchiefs, in number fifteen; (bb) a pair of slippers; (cc) hand towels, in number five, old; (dd) face towels, in number three.

(B) In a room above:

(1) A bed with benches, tables, and a bed box filled with cotton, decorated with linens.

(2) A baldachin of cloth, old.

(3) Used sheets, three in number, hanging in the sun.

(4) Another sheet.

(C) In a room next to the one where Michelangelo slept:

(1) A bed with a bed box filled with straw.

(2) Two mattresses and two covers of white wool and their large sheets, used.

(3) *A pair of simple, iron wings, with springs* [for the sides of the bed].

(4) *A credenza where there are glasses, carafes, etc.: (a) six napkins, (b) a towel, (c) a tablecloth.*

(5) *An old box, inside which is a large mirror of metal and a cloth.*

(D) *In a room below, covered with a roof* [evidently Michelangelo's workshop], *where there are:*

    (1) *A statue of a St. Peter begun, roughed out, but not finished.*

    (2) *Another statue begun of a Christ and another figure above him, attached together, roughed out but not finished* [i.e., the *Rondanini Pietà*].

    (3) *Another statue, this one very small, of a Christ holding the Cross on his shoulders, not finished.*

    (4) *A trunk locked with a key and with a mattress around it* [in una stora?], *which is said to belong to a nephew of the aforementioned Nicolò Santi, just as in another room there is a desk* [studiolo] *tied with a cord, similarly of the heirs of that aforementioned messer Nicolò, as reports Antonio del Francioso of Casteldurante, formerly servant of the aforementioned Michelangelo, in a sworn statement* [et medio iuramento, tactis scripturis].

(E) *In the stall: A small brown horse of little value, its leather blanket, and reins, etc.*

(F) *Kitchen/pantry* [tinello]: *Some marbles and sponges, a jar, a half-size jar, three containers and six barrels, empty.*

(G) *In the basement: A half-barrel of vinegar and three containers, another five containers of water, two small spoons* [schiumarelli] *and a funnel* [imbottatore].

(H) *In messer Michelangelo's* [sitting] *room:*

    (1) *A large walnut box locked with a key and bound with seals.*

    (2) *Item, a cartoon, composed of several pieces glued together, upon which is drawn the plan of the Basilica of St. Peter's.*

(3) *Another cartoon, smallish, with the design of the facade of a palace.*

(4) *Another cartoon, where there is drawn a window of the Church of St. Peter's.*

(5) *Another cartoon composed of several pieces glued together, which, they say, is according to the model of San Gallo.*

(6) *Another cartoon where there are three sketches of tiny figures.*

(7) *Another cartoon, with drawings of a window and other things.*

(8) *A large cartoon, where there is a* Pietà *with nine figures designed, unfinished.*

(9) *Another large cartoon, where there are drawn and sketched three large figures and two children.*

(10) *Another large cartoon where there is drawn and sketched a lone large figure.*

(11) *Another large cartoon, where is drawn and sketched Our Lord Jesus Christ and the glorious Virgin Mary his mother.*

COUNTERSIGNED BY THE ROMAN GENTLEMAN
TOMASO DE' CAVALIERI, ON APRIL 7 1564
[*Fuit consignatum domino Thomeo de Cavaleriis romano,*
7 aprilis 64, ut infra]

[There were ten drawings in total, large and small]

(I) *The loggia on the ground floor:*

(1) *A forge with small handles.*

(2) *A large black leather valise.*

(3) *Two big benches.*

(4) *A largish saw.*

(5) *A box for feed.*

(6) *A certain quantity of wood, about 2 yards.*

(7) *A large table.*

(8) *The walnut box that was in the room where the aforementioned Michelangelo slept, before it was to be opened, was carefully observed and considered, and it was found sealed first with*

the sign of two different seals, attached with paper in five places, that is, with five long white strips with the impression of the aforementioned seals at the top of each strip of paper; and as far as can be seen, unchanged, intact and untouched. One of the seals was that of messer Thomeo de' Cavalieri, Roman gentleman, present and consenting under oath [presente et medio tactis scripturis, ita ricognoscente et attestante]; *and the other is of messer Diomede Leoni, Sienese, who lives in Rome, present and consenting under oath* [presente ita ricognoscente et attestante, medio iuramento, tactis scripturis].

And because it was recognized that originally there was attached another seal at the lock, that is, impressed in a triangle, and the paper there which was attached to the body and to the cover of the said box had been lifted, the same messer Thomeo said that it was the imprint of his own seal that, at the instigation of Antonio named above, recognizing the worsening health of messer Michelangelo, was put there by messer Camillo d'Arpino, teacher of that same messer Thomeo. Bonifazio de l'Auila, servant of messer Thomeo, Tuesday just past, was present when the sickness of Michelangelo began. And then, when the death of messer Michelangelo occurred, messer Thomeo said he tore it with his own hand in the presence of messer Diomede and of messer Daniele Ricciarelli da Volterra, and messer Mario son of the same messer Thomeo, and the above-mentioned Antonio, with the intention to seek to open the previously mentioned box to see what was inside. However, they were then resolved that it was judged better not to open it, but rather, to seal it, which they did, and wait for the arrival of the nephew of the aforementioned Michelangelo.

From this bland accounting we find insights about the dwelling in which Michelangelo spent nearly half his life, revealing his way of life, and the physical surroundings where the creation of his art took place.

Besides the garden mentioned in the story of the celestial triangle, which contained two fig trees, one for early fruit and another for later fruit, the house at Macel de' Corvi, located near the Church of Santa Maria di Loreto, consisted of two stories and a basement. There was the room where Michelangelo usually slept; and another next to it, the studio, which had a separate roof and must have been a fairly large space, higher than the rooms on the ground floor. A loggia on the ground floor opened onto the garden, near another room called "Michelangelo's room" in the inventory, probably his sitting room. The kitchen/pantry *(tinello)* also served as the dining area. There was at least one room on the second floor.

Although no pattern of luxury or high living emerges, the house at Macel de' Corvi seems to have been quite adequate for the un-married and childless sculptor, with rooms for an assistant or two as well as a servant. The inventory indicates that life in the house was as spartan as Michelangelo frequently claimed. He once told Condivi that "for a man as rich as I am, I always lived like a poor one." He ate little because he thought that heavy eating would cause him to sleep too much and lose time for work. We know of typical meals from his own handwritten notes, for example: "Two rolls, a pitcher of wine, a herring, ravioli, tortellini. . . . Some salad, four rolls, a round pitcher and a quarter bottle of sharp-tasting wine, a plate of spinach, four an-chovies, ravioli. . . . Six rolls, two bowls of fennel soup, a herring, a round pitcher of wine. . . ." Besides, Michelangelo was convinced that if he ate little, he would avoid headaches. Often he would not even stop working to eat, content with a piece of bread.

An air of minimum functionality seemed to pervade the place. One cannot help but think of the many times he complained to his family about his poor living conditions, whether in Bologna, Flo-rence, or Rome. In 1512, he wrote from Rome to his brother Buonarroto in Florence that "I do not have a penny and one can say that I am without socks and am naked," and in the same year he told his father that "I live poorly and do not take good care of my life or

MICHELANGELO, shopping list, 1518. • On the back of an
envelope Michelangelo has jotted down a food-shopping list
(or a record of food taken at an inn), which he whimsically
accompanies with ideograms of the objects purchased,
including two rolls, a pitcher of wine, a herring, and four
anchovies.

my honor . . . and I live with very great difficulty . . . I have been living here in Rome for fifteen years and I never had a decent hour, and
everything I did was to help you all." These complaints may contain
a degree of exaggeration, but there is little doubt that he was never
generous with himself, except perhaps when it came to his clothes,
and then only during a period in the late 1510s and 1520s when he
was in Florence. (He had two wolf-skin coats at the time of his
death.)

Everything in the house was oriented toward Michelangelo's
room and his working space, where there were drawings, models, and
cartoons, as well as some unfinished sculpture. He persisted in carving even to the edge of death, despite fatigue, failing eyesight, and
trembling hand. His last major public concern was the plans for St.
Peter's, which had become the vortex of his mission, now expanded
not merely to encompass the pictorial decoration of the Pauline
Chapel in the Vatican Palace but to give definition to the whole
structure of what was to be the central church of Christianity.

Further contemporary information about the drawings and cartoons that had been left behind, not to mention the sculptures, has
survived, including a letter by Daniele da Volterra (dated March 17,
1564). Of the four pictorial cartoons found by the men who inven-
toried the house, Daniele says that the *Christ* coincides with number
11 listed in the inventory. The *Mary and Christ* went to Tommaso de'
Cavalieri, who was a treasured friend of Michelangelo and who swore
that it had been donated to him by the artist while still alive. According to Daniele, this was the best among the four cartoons. The
second was one that Ascanio Condivi used to make a painting, if he,
Daniele, "remembered well," and corresponded to number 9 in the
inventory. This cartoon showed three large figures and two children
and was subsequently described as an *Epiphany;* it went to the notary.
The third was an *Apostle* which Michelangelo designed to go into St.
Peter's and which coincides with the inventory item 10, the "lone

large figure." Finally, there was the *Pietà*, which Michelangelo had just begun. "One can only apprehend the attitudes of the figures," Daniele said of the cartoon that corresponds to number 8, the *Pietà* with nine figures. Daniele informs us that all four cartoons had been dispersed. Two ended up with Michelangelo's nephew, Lionardo, on April 21, and the other two were claimed by Tommaso de' Cavalieri and the notary.

Daniele da Volterra also recalled some small drawings, including an *Annunciation* and a *Christ Praying in the Garden,* which Michelangelo had given to Jacopo del Duca, a fellow painter, before he died; but Lionardo managed to get them back in order to donate them to Duke Cosimo of Florence, who was anxious to own works by Michelangelo. Daniele does not mention the other drawings listed in the inventory but calls attention to the three unfinished sculptures: the *St. Peter* dressed in a papal habit; the *Pietà;* and a *Christ* who holds the Cross on his shoulders, similar to one Michelangelo made for the Minerva church in Rome decades before but smaller in size.

Anticipation on the part of those who attended the dying Michelangelo was intense, as the inventory relates. They wanted to open the walnut box which Michelangelo had guarded so jealously in life, but at the very last minute they decided against it, since Michelangelo's heir, his nephew, had not yet arrived in Rome. In the box were between 7,000 and 8,000 gold ducats, a considerable fortune by any calculation. Such hoarding is not untypical for the old, especially those who are alone and whose worst fear is indigence. Evidently, Michelangelo kept a nest egg for hard times. He might have chuckled to himself from time to time over Aesop's fable of the simpleton who owned the beautiful hen who laid golden eggs. Thinking that he would find even more gold inside the hen, the man killed her. To his horror, she was an ordinary hen inside. The lesson was to "be content with what one has," and Michelangelo had plenty.

What is surprising about the inventory is what was *not* there: no paintings at all, not even a sketch or a half-begun panel. This absence is telling, and indicates that the artist apparently had not used a brush for almost fifteen years. His most active phase as a painter was between 1504 and 1512, when he finished the Sistine Chapel ceiling, and afterward only in spurts. He regarded himself as a sculptor—as indeed he is named in the inventory—and even while he was painting in Rome, his family members addressed him as such.

In addition to the total absence of books, another important omission requires mention: not a single "pagan" painting, sculpture, or drawing appeared in the house; only works with religious subject matter (besides plans for St. Peter's and a drawing for a palace window, presumably for the pope or a cardinal) were found. Michelangelo surely sensed that his final hour was approaching and by then he was in a very different mood than when he continually complained about growing old. This change in perspective might help to explain the paucity of drawings and the total absence of overtly secular works. Duke Cosimo de' Medici's expectation that at Michelangelo's death he would come into possession of an accumulation of works by Florence's greatest artist would be frustrated. Indeed, Cosimo had for many years sought to persuade Michelangelo to return to Florence, but the call of his mission, now concentrated on St. Peter's, would not permit the old man's return.

Cosimo's ambassador in Rome, Serristori, wrote on February 19, saying that Michelangelo had died that very night. On orders from the duke, he had arranged for the inventory by an official of the governors of Rome to be taken that very morning. Cosimo feared that if any time was wasted, valuable works would disappear, which may have turned out to be the case. Serristori laments that there was very little there *(che furono poche),* and that "drawings were missing" *(e manco disegni).* His letter also informs Cosimo about the walnut box, which was "sealed with many seals," and goes on to report that the Roman official had opened it in the presence of Tommaso de'Cavalieri and Daniele da Volterra, who had been called by Michelangelo just before his death. Serristori also mentions the 7,000 or 8,000 ducats.

The drawings were Cosimo's true objective, and he had his men search high and low, but they located only the ten listed in the inventory. They reported extraordinary news to him: as for the expected stack of drawings, "it is said [here in Rome] that he [Michelangelo] had already burned them." Duke Cosimo was crushed; in his letter to Serristori of March 5, 1564, he said he was extremely disturbed by the loss of the rarest person in the world in his profession. But he was still more distressed upon learning that Michelangelo had not left any drawings (obviously the duke was not taking into account the handful that were found).

"It seems hardly a worthy act on his part to have set fire to the drawings," the duke lamented.

What motivated Michelangelo to put the torch to possessions that he had so passionately accumulated over the years? Later critics have suggested that the artist did not want to unveil the struggle present in them. An alternative explanation may be closer to the truth. The voice of Savonarola may still have been in his ears and the written words of the prophet still on his mind in those last days. When the frate called for a burning of the vanities, many artists joined to heap their own "pagan" works on the fires, among them Sandro Botticelli. Michelangelo, still quite young, was away from Florence at the time and could not participate. But with the end at hand seven decades later, he gathered together his much-guarded drawings and cartoons, over which he had been especially secretive, and set them to flames. Could some have been too pagan or sexually explicit? We shall never know. But the ritual was Michelangelo's final act in the exhausting mission that had propelled him through his long life. "In death everyone is made equal"—*La morte pareggia tutti.*

MICHELANGELO, drawing of hand holding book, 1547(?).

A Note on Sources

Because this is not a scholarly book in the usual sense, but is intended as an interpretation of the personality of Michelangelo, sources and citations for the various assertions made are not provided. They are readily available, especially the well-known biographies by Condivi and Vasari; the letters written by, to, or related to Michelangelo; and contemporary histories of the period by Machiavelli and Guicciardini, among others. The complete citations for these works appear in the Bibliographic Note.

From time to time, less accessible references are occasionally offered in the Notes that follow, as well as commentaries, translations, or analyses that were not considered fitting to be incorporated into the text. Furthermore, as the result of an irresistible urge on the part of the author to touch upon various oblique points, additional scholarly issues and asides have been included in the Notes.

Perhaps a word should be reserved for the inclusion of many proverbs in translation and in the original (to maintain their flavor). These are for the most part Tuscan sayings that were—and continue to be—an integral part of normal human exchange. Some of them derive specifically from Michelangelo's letters, while others were common to the period or are known through their continuous usage. One can still find an insistent dependence upon such proverbs, especially in small towns and villages. Conversations with two older men living in the foothills of Montalbano in the area around Vinci and Lamporecchio have provided me with direct exposure to this heavy reliance upon adages in daily intercourse. Their language and the wisdom and experience from which these proverbs derive are, I suggest, very much a part of Michelangelo's mind-set or, if you wish, his *cultura*.

The translations from the Italian are largely my own, although I would like to acknowledge James M. Saslow's *Poetry of Michelangelo: An Annotated Translation* (New Haven and London, 1991).

Bibliographic Note

The single most important source of documentation and bibliography before 1962 is P. Barocchi's edition (with notes) of Giorgio Vasari, *La Vita di Michelangelo nelle redazioni del 1550 e del 1568,* 5 vols. (Milan–Naples, 1962). This exemplary publication contains not only the vital bibliography of studies in all languages but also complete and authoritative transcriptions of contemporary texts and documents. It should be regarded as the starting point for any serious investigation of Michelangelo; see, in particular, the Bibliography in vol. I, pp. 313–76. For more recent bibliography, see the various indices, including that of RILA and the Art Index; and for works in English, a collection of essays selected by William Wallace: *Michelangelo, Selected Scholarship in English,* 5 vols. (Hamden, Conn.: Garland, 1995). Special mention should also be made of the bibliographies collected in E. Steinmann and R. Wittkower, *Michelangelo-Bibliographie, 1510– 1926* (Leipzig, 1927), and Liutpold Dussler, *Michelangelo. Bibliographie, 1927–1970* (Wiesbaden, 1974).

Also of prime importance are the collections of letters written by

Michelangelo, those written to him, and those written about him, as well as his *ricordi*, which are found in: P. Barocchi, K. L Bramanti, and R. Ristori, eds., *Il Carteggio Indiretto di Michelangelo*, vol. I (Florence, 1988), vol. II (Florence, 1995); P. Barocchi and L. Ciulich Bardeschi, eds., *I Ricordi di Michelangelo* (Florence, 1970; P. Barocchi and R. Ristori, eds.), *Il Carteggio di Michelangelo*, 3 vols. (Florence, 1965–73). A curious but not unhelpful study is P. Barocchi, S. Maffei, G. Nencioni, et al., eds., *Michelangelo. Lettere. Concordanza e indice di frequenza*, 2 vols. (Pisa, 1994).

Modern scholarship owes a debt to Giovanni Poggi, whose various publications are basic and whose archives are housed in the library of the Istituto Nazionale di Studi sul Rinascimento, located in Florence's Palazzo Strozzi. Other evidence that should be considered can be found in Michelangelo's poetry, for which see J. M. Saslow, *The Poetry of Michelangelo: An Annotated Translation* (New Haven and London, 1991), with references to the various editions and translations, and another more recent translation by C. Ryan, *Michelangelo: the Poems* (London, 1996).

John Addington Symonds's *Life of Michelangelo Buonarroti*, 3rd ed., 2 vols. (London, 1899) remains valuable; but in my view the most rewarding modern biography is that of Giovanni Papini, *La vita di Michelangiolo nella vita del suo tempo* (Milan, 1949; English trans. L. Murname, New York, 1952). R. Liebert's *Michelangelo: A Psychoanalytic Study of His Life and Images* (New Haven, 1983), offers insights, as does M. and R. Wittkower's *Born Under Saturn* (New York, 1964) and L. Schneider Adams's *Art and Psychoanalysis* (New York, 1994). A collection of essays of considerable variety can be found in M. Salmi, ed., *Michelangelo artista, pensatore, scrittore* (Novara, 1965; English trans. *The Complete Work of Michelangelo*, 2 vols., London, 1966). Michael Rocke's *Forbidden Friendships: Homosexuality and Male Culture in Renaissance Florence* (New York and Oxford, 1996) provides richly documented background to the question, accompanied by an ample bibliography.

As for the art, the most useful is still the five volumes of C. de Tolnay, *Michelangelo* (Princeton, 1944–60), and for the drawings, C. de Tolnay, *Corpus dei disegni di Michelangelo,* 4 vols. (Novara, 1975–80), as well as A. Perrig's contrarian *Michelangelo's Drawings: The Science of Attribution* (New Haven and London, 1991), which might be seen in distinction to M. Hirst's *Michelangelo and His Drawings* (New Haven and London, 1988). Among the older monographs, that of Charles Heath Wilson, *Life and Works of Michelangelo Buonarroti* (London, 1876 and later editions) deserves special attention. Alessandro Parronchi's various studies of Michelangelo's early career are always illuminating.

Modern writers who have devoted their attention to Michelangelo and his multifaceted career include: J. Ackerman; G. Agosti; S. Alexander; P. Barolsky; R. Clements; S. J. Freedberg; S. Freud; C. Frommel; C. Gilbert; E. N. Girardi; F. Hartt; H. Hibbard; S. Levine; F. Mancinelli; E. Panofsky; C. Seymour, Jr.; J. Shearman; L. Steinberg; D. Summers; W. E. Wallace; K. Weil-Gariss Brandt; J. Wilde; E. Wind; and H. Wohl.

Notes

❈

PROLOGUE: A DIVINE MISSION

1 *referred to as "divine":* Bernardetto Minerbetti, bishop of Arezzo, in writing to Vasari on October 4, 1551, mentions "chel divino Michelangelo" and "e si come io conosco per miracoli tutte l'opere che *miracolosamente* [*sic*] escono delle sue mani." In K. Frey, *Il Carteggio di Giorgio Vasari* (Arezzo, 1941), I, p. 306. For other references and in general, see also P. Barocchi, ed., Giorgio Vasari, *La Vita di Michelangelo,* II, pp. 21–23.

In letters from 1553 (October 14 and 28), Vasari refers to Michelangelo as "il mio raro et divinissimo Vecchio." Cf. Frey, *Carteggio,* I, pp. 371 and 378. A decade earlier, we have a letter of December 1, 1543, from the writer Doni to Michelangelo, which reads in part: "O divino uomo, tutto il mondo vi tiene per un oracolo, che dal nostro intendere nascono così famose opere . . . certo che io vi tengo per uno Iddio, con licenzia della nostra fede, perchè si come Domenedio ebbe fatto Adamo di terra, soffiò lo Spirito della vita in esso, così voi . . . quei figuroni morbidi e musculosi . . . gridando 'Michel Agniolo Divino, Michel Agniolo Divino.' "Aretino, in a letter also written to Michelangelo concerning the *Last Judgment,* begins his cynical criticism with the phrase "for someone who is said to be divine" *(per esser divino).* These references and others have led P. Barocchi (in Vasari, *La Vita di Michelangelo,* II, Commento, p. 23) to observe that "divine Michelangelo" was a constant mode of reference for the master by midcentury.

2 *An artist . . . "must maintain":* Francesco d'Olanda, *Dialoghi Michelangioleschi di Francesco d'Olanda,* ed. A. M. Bessone Avreli (Rome, 1953), p. 136. Helmut Wohl tells me that a good deal of what is attributed to the artist in this book is the invention of its author, the Portuguese painter Francesco d'Olanda, according to his most recent research.

4 *Michelangelo lay:* Letter from the priest Don Giovanni di Simone, written from Florence to Leonardo di Buonarroto in Rome, on March 18, 1564. The body was deposited, apparently beside the Chapel of the Cavalcanti, where Donatello's marvelous *Annunciation* is still in place. For this letter, see the Archive of Giovanni Poggi housed in the Library of the Istituto Nazionale di Studi sul Rinascimento (Palazzo Strozzi, Florence), with the Library's reference XIV, B, n. xiii, and G. Daelli, *Carte Michelangiolesche inedite* (Milan, 1865), pp. 50–53. The letter provides other information about the arrival of the body in Florence as well. Also in the Poggi Archive *(loc. cit.)* is the transcription of an earlier letter, that of March 4, 1564, written by the same priest, likewise addressed to Leonardo, in which Don Giovanni says he was happy to have learned that Michelangelo had received the last rites: "I sacramenti della S. Chiesa con buonissimo conoscimento e contritione."

MICHELANGELO AND LORENZO IL MAGNIFICO

11 *Through Condivi, Michelangelo narrated:* Condivi gives the recipient of the dream as a court musician, but as already implied by other scholars, including Robert Liebert, it must have been Michelangelo himself. In addition to the evidence of Michelangelo's thoughts generally as offered by Condivi, one should also consider some direct quotations from Michelangelo that were recorded after the publication of Condivi's life of the artist. Here remarks and corrections by the master have been preserved, for which see Ugo Procacci, "Postille contemporanee

in una esemplare della vita di Michelangelo del Condivi," *Atti del Convegno di Studi Michelangioleschi, Roma-Firenze, 1964* (Rome, 1966), pp. 279–94.

17 *For il Magnifico, that meant:* My reading of the evidence runs at variance both to P. Barolsky and to W. E. Wallace, "The Myth of Michelangelo and Il Magnifico," *Source,* XII, no. 3 (1993), pp. 16–21 and elsewhere. These scholars along with others believe that Michelangelo manipulated his account of events to fit his own goals. While it would not surprise me that some of the details here and there have been embellished by Michelangelo in collusion with his biographers, such as Michelangelo's claim that he had arranged for his father to have a civil service position at the customhouse *(dogana)*, the matrix is historically accurate as he looked back on earlier events in his life. The arrangements for Michelangelo's apprenticeship with Ghirlandaio, in my view, suggest a direct association with Lorenzo, so much questioned by both Barolsky and Wallace, who in particular reject the possibility that Michelangelo lived in il Magnifico's household. Admittedly, this might have been unusual, but then both Lorenzo and Michelangelo were unusual. And after all, Bertoldo di Giovanni had a room of his own in the palace, while in the next century so did the sculptor Baccio Bandinelli.

19 *Michelangelo's first excursion:* As with other incidents or events in the early life of Michelangelo, the copying of Schongauer's print is not confirmed by contemporary documents. A purist might therefore question the veracity of the account as it appears in the biographies. On the other hand, the very nature of contemporary documentation would speak against finding absolute proof. One would have to find, for example, a *ricordo* by Granacci confirming that he had indeed given Michelangelo the print to copy, or the account books of a seller of art supplies *(speziali)* in Florence listing payments dating from, say, 1487, when Granacci is described as paying for colors that were to be "passed on to his friend Michel Agnolo to paint a panel." The chances that such information was registered at all, or if registered, that it would have been preserved, are effectively nil. Additionally, to reject a story of this kind, repeated by Michelangelo through Condivi, merely to leave a void, is not particularly productive.

In this book, I am inclined to accept such assertions, especially where there is confirmation in contemporary letters. If the claims have a decisive effect upon our understanding of Michelangelo, which the Schongauer copy hardly seems to have, caution is, of course, in order.

26 *Two fairly complete life-size:* A. Parronchi, *Opere Giovanile di Michelangelo* (Florence, 1973), pp. 3–18, has suggested that the statue of that subject, the so-called Marsyas "rosso" in the Uffizi, can be identified with a statue that was once in the Medici Gardens, and that the head might actually have been a restoration by the young sculptor. More specifically, according to this scholar, the head might have been the head of an old faun that Michelangelo is known to have made among his first works in the gardens, and that has never been convincingly identified, much less recovered. Parronchi himself has second thoughts about his very engaging proposal.

Of the two large-scale versions of the theme owned by the Medici, one was of white marble and the other of red marble, which showed the strained muscles more dramatically. A recent scholarly presentation on the two statues can be found in F. Caglioti, "Sui restauri per le antichità dei primi Medici: Mino da Fiesole, Andrea del Verrocchio e il 'Marsia rosso' degli Uffizi," *Prospettiva, 73–74* (April 1994).

43 *The collection also contained:* They would be termed "Byzantine" today. The language in the inventories (ASF, MAP, no. 163, fol. 61v of Piero di Cosimo of 1464) is "una tavola greca di pietra fine," or "una tavola greca di musaico," and the subjects were sacred images, including an *Annunciation,* a *Christ and the Last Judgment, Mary and the Twelve Apostles,* a *St. Michael,* the *Passion of Christ,* a *St. Nicholas,* and a bust of *St. John.* These tiny objects were highly valued: from 20 to 100 florins.

57 *the example of Donatello:* Nor should it come as a surprise that Donatello was actually regarded as something of a painter as well as his generation's leading sculptor, though not a single picture by him survives. The elegantly designed stained-glass window for the Duomo shows the *Coronation of the Virgin.* According to B. Cellini, ed. P. Scarpellini, *La Vita, I Trattati, I Discorsi* (Milan, 1967), p. 564: "il detto Donatello dipinse bene." Ghiberti was apparently also skilled in painting, while

Masaccio probably made sculptures of terra cotta and perhaps of wood (see J. H. Beck, "Masaccio's Early Career as a Sculptor," *Art Bulletin*, LIII [1971], pp. 195ff.). Condivi has Michelangelo say that there was only one thing wrong with Donatello: that he did not have the patience to properly give the finishing touch to his work *(ripulir le sue opere: si sorte che, riuscendo mirabili a vista lontana, da presso perdevano riputazione).* Is this not an oblique self-criticism? In the postilla, published by Procacci, *op. cit.*, p. 287, we find that Michelangelo modifies his criticism for Donatello's *Judith and Holofernes* in particular, adding that when works are good, finishing refinements are not necessary. The transcription of the note is: "Errò, doveva dire Iuditta et Oloferne e che quando son buone non ci occorre tanti pulimenti."

59   *whose sculptures . . . he saved:* This unusual episode was brought to light by J. Beck and M. Fanti in "Un probabile intervento di Michelangelo per la 'Porta Magna' di San Petronio," *Arte antica e moderna,* 27 (1964), pp. 349–54.

61   *The Head of a Faun:* A reference to this piece, purported to be contained in an inventory of the Medici Guardaroba of 1669, reads as follows: "una maschera di marmo d'un satiro di mano di Michelangelo Buonarroti suo primo lavoro fatto d'anni 16 incirca, alto 1/3 [braccia]." The word is "mask" rather than "head," and its rather small dimensions, about 8 1/2 inches in height, makes the attribution of this object— which has been conflated with a piece once in the Bargello but that ended up in Russia after World War II—questionable. Furthermore, the mask is without distinction, though that in itself might not be an absolute deterrent to the attribution, considering Michelangelo's age and experience at the time.

64   *of what Michelangelo would be producing:* Among the more feeble critical suggestions is one that would posit a meaningful rapport between the central figure in the relief with his right arm raised and the Judging Christ from the *Last Judgment,* forty years on.

66   *A classical flavor:* Michelangelo's *Battle* relief should be a touchstone for any early sculptural works one might seek to attribute to him, because of its authenticity and the sheer number of types and poses he used in it, which can be employed in comparisons.

71 *The Hercules is assumed:* M. Hirst, *The Young Michelangelo* (New Haven and London, 1988), pp. 17 and 72, n. 11, and the *Carteggio Indiretto,* II, appendix 2 and note 1, pp. 497–500. Alessandro Parronchi has very recently published a *Hercules* that was brought to the United States following World War II, from France, which he asserts is Michelangelo's lost *Hercules.* It was known and photographed in the 1970s when it was purchased by a New York art dealer, but has since disappeared, as least for now. Since I have not seen the work, I prefer to reserve judgment, although the suggestion is certainly engaging and feasible, and the piece is illustrated here on p. 71.

72 *Although there have been diverse candidates:* See my paper, "Benedetto di Leonardo da Maiano e Michelangelo giovane," in *Giuliano e la bottega dei da Maiano. Atti del Convegno Internazionale di Studi* (Florence, 1994), pp. 176–81. It is necessary emphatically to remove the Casa Buonarroti *Crucifix* from Michelangelo's oeuvre because it is so misleading in reconstructing a clear understanding of his early career and continues to be a peg on which to hang other works even further removed from Michelangelo.

75 *and Contessina:* There is a vague implication in the literature that Michelangelo had a special affection for Contessina; see, e.g., the sensitive and insightful book by G. Papini, *Michelangelo: His Life and His Era,* trans. L. Murnane (New York, 1952), p. 56. She married Piero Ridolfi in 1494 and moved to Rome. Their son, Cardinal Niccolò Ridolfi, was on close terms with Michelangelo, who produced the bust of *Brutus* for him.

MICHELANGELO AND HIS FATHER, LODOVICO

80 *Accompanied by two:* See G. Poggi, "Della prima partenza di Michelangelo Buonarroti da Firenze," *Rivista d'arte,* IV (1906), pp. 33–37. In a letter from Ser Amadeo to his brother, the sculptor Adriano di Giovanni de'Maestri, known as Adriano Fiorentino (a pupil of Bertoldo), Amadeo says, "Sapi che Michelangelo ischultore dal giardino se n'è ito a Vinegia sanza dire nulla a Piero, tornando lui in chasa mi pare che Piero l'abia auto molto male." This letter is revealing for a variety of

reasons, one of which is that it underscores the inherent accuracy of Condivi's account, while it confirms the fact that Michelangelo at a young age was already being watched by artists in Florence.

92 *Was there a moral lapse:* That the episode of the *Cupid* was essentially a self-constructed and self-perpetuated myth, one of many, as is sometimes claimed, is disproved by the contemporary letters referred to in the text.

112 *Botticelli's brother, Simone Filipepi, left a favorable: Cronica di Simone Filipepi,* published in P. Villari and E. Casanova, eds., *Scritti di Fra Girolamo Savonarola, con nuovi documenti intorno alla sua vita* (Florence, 1898), pp. 453ff. All the subsequent citations from Simone come from this edition.

122 *In early September 1501:* If the statue had a "chest," it must have had a certain form before Michelangelo ever got his hands on it, a fact which supports the difficulty attributed to his task by Condivi and Vasari. That is, Michelangelo was dealing with a block that had not only been roughed out (possibly badly at that) but had also been carved to some degree already. The church officials referred to the block as handed over to Michelangelo as "quella figura chiamata *David,*" so it had an iconographic identity as an object already; but was it the prophet David or the youthful David?

A theory has surfaced that it was not Donatello's but Verrocchio's *David* that was in the courtyard of the Palazzo Signoria at the time of the deliberations, for which see F. Caglioti, "Donatello, i Medici e Gentile de' Becchi: un po' d'ordine intorno alla 'Giuditta' (e al 'David') di Via Larga, III," *Prospettiva,* 59 (1995). Either way, there is little difference in terms of my treatment here.

135 *Doni, a year younger:* I have used the research of Alessandro Cecchi, "Agnolo e Maddalena Doni Committenti di Raffaello," in M. Sambucco Hamoud and M. Letizia Strocchi, eds., *Studi su Raffaello* (Urbino, 1984), pp. 429–39, *Atti del Congresso internationale di studi,* Urbino-Firenze, April 6–14, 1984. See also A. Hayum, "Michelangelo's Doni Tondo: Holy Family and Family Myth," *Studies in Iconography,* 7–8 (1981–82), pp. 209–51. A. Natali, "L'Uamo Nuovo. Postseritto per il Tondo Doni," in idem, *La Piscina di Betsaida. Movimenti nell'arte fiorentina del Cinquecento,* Florence-Siena, 1995, pp. 31–42. As usual, the unpublished

carte of Giovanni Poggi have been helpful. Doni, who died in 1539, had a distinguished career of public service as *priore,* as one of the Dodici Buonomini, and as head of the Misericordia. In a family letter from later in the century, the painting is described as being by the hand of the *maestro de maestri,* that is, Michelangelo.

139 *Michelangelo was commissioned:* A recent paper on the two works is A. Cecchi's "Niccolò Machiavelli o Marcello Virgilio Adriani? Sul programma e l'aspetto compositivo delle 'Battaglie' di Leonardo e Michelangelo, per la Sala del Maggior Consiglio in Palazzo Vecchio," *Prospettiva,* 83–84 (1996), pp. 102–15.

MICHELANGELO AND POPE JULIUS II

147 *the fable of the viper:* Other misogynist proverbs include: "He who speaks the word 'woman' speaks of trouble" *(Chi disse donna, disse guai);* "He who has a wife has woes" *(Chi ha moglie, ha doglie);* "He who takes a wife loses half his brain; the other half goes for radishes" *(Chi prende una moglie perde la metà del cervello; l'altra metà se ne va in radici);* "He who takes a wife deserves a crown of patience; he who takes two deserves a crown of insanity" *(Chi prende una moglie, merita una corona di pazienza; che ne prende due, merita una corona di pazzia).* This litany of sayings that circulated in Tuscany was part of the "culture" Michelangelo would have shared.

152 *and much later, he conducted:* Biblioteca Laurenziana, Archivio Buonarroti, n. 30a, fol. 107r. (unpublished). We have the following payment: "Addì xvi detto [March 1518, modern] soldi xii d. vi piccoli, portò Pietro detto [garzone], dise per dare a quello che sta nel charnaio di Santa Maria Nuova, per fare notomia."

154 *to conduct a moral life:* The reference is here to the *Dialoghi Michelangioleschi di Francesco d'Olanda,* IV, p. 136. The Italian text, which is of course a translation from the Portuguese, reads: "Non basta ad un pittore per imitare in parte la venerabile immagine del Signor Nostro, essere un grande maestro, ma deve tener buona vita, e se possibile, essere santo, acciocchè il suo intelletto sia ispirato dallo Spirito Santo." Even if Francesco recreated this thought, it conforms with what was known about Michelangelo and is fittingly applied to him.

155 *He took the name:* Sixtus IV, the very model of a nepotistic pope in the true meaning of the word, raised his nephew Giuliano to the cardinalate, as well as the son of his sister, Lucchina, Girolamo Basso; and also Piero Riario (†1474), the son of another sister (Jolanda), a high liver in Rome who had ingratiated himself with his uncle by engineering his election as pope in the first place. Among other cardinals in the della Rovere line were Raffaelle (Sansoni) della Rovere (†1521), Michelangelo's short-time patron, who was a grand-nephew of the pope, and two other grand-nephews, Cristoforo (†1478) and Domenico (1501), brothers, who were the sons of the pope's brother Giovanni. In the same family line, but raised by Julius II, were the two sons of his own daughter, Lucchina: Sisto (†1517) and Galeotto (1508).

Julius II's brother Giovanni was married to Caterina di Montefeltro, heir to the duchy of Urbino, which was passed on to their son Francesco Maria della Rovere, the pope's favorite nephew. Another brother of the pope, Leonardo, duke of Sora, had been married to Giovanna, the illegitimate daughter of Ferrante of Naples. Count Girolamo Riario, brother of Cardinal Piero, violently sought to regain papal lands, and was instrumental in the infamous Pazzi Conspiracy in 1478 to murder Lorenzo il Magnifico and his brother Giuliano. Cardinal Raffaelle Riario was an accomplice; he was saying mass in the Duomo during the murder.

159 *according to conventional wisdom:* The remarks of Giovanni Papini in his biography (*Michelangelo,* p. 113), sum up the general view on the subject: "The two men [i.e., Julius II and Michelangelo] had a curious affinity of nature: they were so similar in boldness of temperament, carried to the sublime, to the terrible, to anger and to passion, that their friendship was as tempestuous as the love of two giants which seems at moments to resemble hate."

161 *the artist's precipitous flight from Rome:* The essential details of the story of Michelangelo's flight are confirmed by the letters between the pope and the Signoria, as well as in Soderini's correspondence. There are discrepancies and changes of emphasis in the various accounts, which are all, except for one, based upon recollection long after the event. Although Michelangelo's memory was said to have been excellent, it is

hardly surprising that he was confused by a few minor details. Even the best witnesses at trials have the same problem.

Probably Michelangelo's letter to Giuliano da Sangallo is the most authoritative, since it was written hardly two weeks after the event. Further, in a point that seems to have been overlooked, the letter was in essence intended for Julius, since Michelangelo asks Giuliano to show his letter to the pope *(Or voi mi scrivete da parte del Papa; e così al Papa legierete questa)*. It seems unlikely that he would have lied about the circumstances, as is sometimes suggested, when the pope himself knew them firsthand or could very easily control them.

172 *Michelangelo proved to be:* The list of Michelangelo's artist friends is long. Only a few more need be mentioned: the architect Simone del Pollaiuolo; Pietro Rosselli, a mason-turned-architect; and Giovanni Michi, Pietro d'Argenta, and L'Indaco, who were pupils or assistants of Michelangelo over the years. L'Indaco's company was particularly treasured by the artist; they ate together frequently because Michelangelo appreciated his sense of humor (for which see Vasari, *Vita,* III, p. 682).

178 *to meet the pope:* Cf. F. Malaguzzi Valeri, *L'Architettura a Bologna nel Rinascimento* (Rocca S. Casiano, 1890), p. 100. R. Tuttle, "Julius II and Bramante in Bologna," in A. Emiliani, ed., *Le Arti a Bologna e in Emilia dal XVI al XVII secolo* (Bologna, 1982), p. 3, concludes that Julius II resided in Bologna on two occasions, a three-month period during the winter of 1506–07 (when Michelangelo went to see him), and a nearly five-month one during the winter of 1510–11, when Michelangelo made at least one and perhaps more visits to the pope there.

180 *After a few months:* See W. E. Wallace, "Michelangelo's Assistants in the Sistine Chapel," *Gazette des beaux-arts,* 110, no. 2 (1987), pp. 203–16, far and away the most comprehensive treatment of the subject. Wallace tends to lump together, however, the technical assistance that Michelangelo obtained from Piero Rosselli and Giuliano da Sangallo, the unskilled labor of assistants like Pietro Urbano and Giovanni Michi, and the work of trained painters. Since much has been made of Vasari's report that Michelangelo undertook the grueling task of executing the frescoes without any assistance whatsoever, Wallace's claim that Michelangelo had more than a dozen assistants who are known to have

collaborated with him in the Sistine Chapel may be an antidote. On the other hand, Wallace has been unable to prove that Michelangelo had serious and significant collaboration in the actual painting, so for me, Vasari remains uncorrected.

Among actual painters who were at times available, especially during the organizational stage, but also for transferring cartoons, first and foremost was the artist's friend Francesco Granacci, as well as Giuliano Bugiardini, Jacopo di Sandro (known as il Indaco Vecchio), Agnolo di Donnino, and Aristotile da Sangallo. They stayed only a few months and were sent away without doing much at all.

While I have no intention of rehearsing here the issues surrounding the recent restoration of Michelangelo's frescoes in the Sistine Chapel (1980–94), for which see J. Beck with M. Daley, *Art Restoration: The Culture, the Business, the Scandal* (enlarged edn., New York, 1996), the implications of Wallace's article to the effect that there were many collaborators are consistent with the line taken by the Vatican's restoration team. To reconstruct their rationale: If there were many inept hands around and involved, then passages that appear now after the cleaning to be weak could be assigned to them. Some, then, of the rather shabby-appearing portions should be relegated to assistants, and not to alterations that could have occurred from the harsh intervention, which is the Beck-Daley point of view. Though incidental passages may have been done by assistants, one would be hard-pressed to find any identifiable share of the actual histories or the main figures by helpers. See also J. Beck, "Michelangelo's Pentimento Bared," *Artibus et Historiae,* 24 (1991), pp. 53–64; "The Final Layer: 'L'ultima mano' on Michelangelo's Sistine Ceiling," *Art Bulletin* (September 1988), pp. 502–03; and "SOS per Michelangelo," *Europeo,* 21, May 26, 1990, pp. 96–97.

185 *did not require explanation:* This does not apply to the scenes on the Medallions, whose subjects still puzzle specialists.

190 *The identity of the Ignudi:* There is an interesting parallel with Nanni di Banco's *Assumption of the Virgin* relief on the Porta della Mandorla, where at least four categories of angels assist in the scene, representing different age groups. We can be virtually certain that Michelangelo ad-

mired this carving, one of the wonders of Florentine fifteenth-century sculpture.

193 *and the seventh:* For my analysis and the general situation on the identification of this scene, see J. Beck, "Michelangelo's Sacrifice on the Sistine Ceiling," in J. Monfasani and R. G. Musto, eds., *Renaissance Society and Culture. Essays in Honor of Eugene F. Rice, Jr.* (New York, 1991), pp. 9–18. An additional observation seems appropriate: it would be strange, for example, not to have the *Cain and Abel Offering* or at least a reference to Cain and Abel on the ceiling.

One further bit of evidence points to the identification of the sacrifice scene as indeed representing the *Cain and Abel Offering* and not the *Sacrifice of Noah*. A sixteenth-century engraving depicts a colored wax in relief of Michelangelo's paintings in the Sistine Chapel in which elements from the ceiling were incorporated in a unified composition with the *Last Judgment*. The relief has long since disappeared, but its author, the Reverend Jacomo Vivio of Aquila, published his engraving along with a lengthy description of his unique relief. On this remarkable object, see G. Pausa, "Giacomo Vivio dell'Aquila ed i suoi bassorilievi in cera stuccata, a colori," *l'Arte,* 9 (1906), pp. 449–52. Vivio's description of his sculpture is found in his *Discorso Sopra la Mirabil Opera di Basso Rilievo di Cera Stuccata, con colori scolpita in Pietra Negra* (Rome, 1590), pp. 22–23. The relevant section reads as follows:

"Dimostratione del sesto ottangolo. Vedesi in questo ottangolo Abel e Caim, fratelli, e figliuoli di Adamo offerire al Signore nell'altare; però Caim avaro, et ingiusto come Agricoltore offeriva delle pichi trite e senza frutto al Signore, ma Abel, giusto offeriva à Dio delli più grassi animali della sua gregge, e perciò molto acceto l'era il suo sacrificio: onde Caim per invidia della gratia e bontà del fratello crudelmente l'uccise; e per questo havendo ricevuto da Dio la sentenza della maledittione, vagabondo, e disperso faccia del Signore ando sempre."

211 *It was not:* In a letter written by the prete Simone on March 18, 1564, to Lionardo (for which see Poggi, XIV, B, n. xiii), and from other sources, we know that an earlier *Pietà*—or more accurately a *Deposition*—the one that ended up in Florence and is presently in the Museo dell' Opera of the Duomo, was intended for his father's tomb. This

work includes a vague self-portrait of Michelangelo as Nicodemus. For reasons that are not altogether clear, Michelangelo mutilated the work, and sold it off to an assistant. Perhaps he had some difficulty with the stone, or was not satisfied with the results as they were turning out. Significantly, there was no commission for it or for the *(Rondanini) Pietà,* which he was working on just before he died. The latter must have been a replacement for the *Deposition,* and was also intended for his father's tomb. It is significant that there is no reference to himself in the *Pietà,* unlike the *Deposition.* In fact, the portrait reference to Michelangelo himself might have made him uneasy, and was one of the reasons for his dissatisfaction with it.

Epilogue: A Celestial Triangle

215 *the exchange between two loyal Savonarolans:* I have translated the text as given by Barocchi/Vasari, IV, pp. 2028–30. See also Aldo Fortuna, "Cronologia Michelangiolesca," *Il Vasari,* XV–XIX (1957–61), doc. no. 433, with interesting notes.

231 *What motivated Michelangelo:* According to information gathered by his nephew Lionardo, who was not an eyewitness, Michelangelo made two fires in his last days *(lui stesso in due volte, abruscio ogni cosa).* Cf. K. Frey, *Der literarishe Nachlass Giorgio Vasaris,* II (Munich, 1930), p. 82. As Hirst in *Michelangelo and His Drawings,* pp. 17–18, reminds us, Michelangelo had destroyed others of his drawings on previous occasions.

Acknowledgments

Conversations with artist friends about "our" master, foremost among them Roberto Barni in Florence and Judah Goldstein in New York, in the past few years have been most helpful in the realization of this book. Exchanges with other artists, including Umberto Buscioni, Milo Lazarevic, and Jan Sawka, have also been helpful. Extremely beneficial has been the sharing of ideas with graduate and undergraduate students at Columbia University, including Denise Budd and Alessio Assonides. I am particularly indebted to my assistant, Lynn Catterson, for her constant help, her good spirit, her intelligence, as well as her own affection for Michelangelo. I have benefited from exchanges with art historians, particularly Paul Barolsky and Mark Zucker; the latter offered innumerable suggestions for refining my text. Mark is a remarkable reader. Rab Hatfield, who is currently preparing a book on Michelangelo's finances, kindly allowed me to consult his material. I also benefited from a reading at a late stage by Dr. Maria Grazia Pernis, while Ann Adelman make a sizable contribution with her sensitive copyediting. Finally, dealing with Don Lamm, my patient editor at W.W. Norton, has been an education all by itself.

FEBRUARY 1998
FLORENCE

Credits

⬚⬚⬚

p. 5: Donatello, *Marzocco*. Florence, Bargello. p. 9: Study of *Madonna and Child*. Paris, Louvre. Courtesy Réunion des Musées Nationaux. p. 15: Donatello, *David*. Florence, Bargello. p. 18: Leonardo da Vinci, Lorenzo profile head. London, © Her Majesty Queen Elizabeth II. Royal Collection Enterprises, Ltd. p. 19: Schongauer, Martin, *Temptation of St. Anthony,* detail. Washington, National Gallery of Art, Rosenwald Collection. p. 22: Donatello, *St. George*. Florence, Bargello. p. 27: Roman artist, *Marsyas.* Florence, Uffizi. p. 29: (top and bottom [detail]) Michelangelo copy after *Profile Portrait of Alessandro, Count of Canossa.* London, © British Museum. p. 30: Michelangelo, *Battle of Cascina.* London, © British Museum. p. 31: Raimondi, Marcantonio, *The Climbers.* Poughkeepsie, Vassar College Art Gallery, gift of Mrs. Felix M. Warburg and her children. p. 41: Bertoldo di Giovanni, *Medal of the Pazzi Conspiracy.* Florence, Bargello. p. 47: Farnese Cup. Naples, Italy, Museo Archaeologico Nazionale/Bridgeman Art Library, London/New York. p. 49: Masaccio, *Shivering Boy.* Florence, Santa Maria del Carmine, Brancacci Chapel. p. 50: da Volterra,

Daniele, *Portrait Bust of Michelangelo.* Florence, Casa Buonarroti. p. 53: Michelangelo, study after Masaccio's *Tribute Money.* Munich, Staatliche Graphische Sammlung. Foto Marburg/Art Resource, NY. p. 56: di Cosimo, Piero, *Giuliano da Sangallo.* Amsterdam, © Rijksmuseum-Stitching. pp. 58–59: Michelangelo, block sketches. London, © British Museum. pp. 64–65: Michelangelo, *Battle of the Centaurs.* Florence, Casa Buonarroti. p. 68: Michelangelo, *Madonna of the Steps.* Florence, Casa Buonarroti. Alinari/Art Resource, NY. p. 74: Botticelli, Sandro, *Adoration of the Magi.* Florence, Uffizi. p. 82: della Quercia, Jacopo, *Creation of Eve.* Bologna, San Petronio, main portal. p. 102: Michelangelo, letter to his father. Florence, Casa Buonarroti. pp. 114–15: da Vinci, *Map of Tuscany* (detail). London, © Her Majesty Queen Elizabeth II. Royal Collection Enterprises, Ltd. p. 117: Rustichi, drawing of Duomo. Florence, Biblioteca Seminario Arcivescovile. p. 121: Michelangelo, drawing for the bronze *David.* Paris, Louvre. Courtesy Réunion des Musées Nationaux. p. 122: Raphael, study after Michelangelo's *David.* London, © British Museum. p. 126: Donatello, *Judith and Holofernes.* Florence, Piazza della Signoria. Scala/Art Resource, NY. p. 136: (top [detail] and bottom) Michelangelo, *Doni Tondo.* Florence, Uffizi. p. 153: Michelangelo, *Bacchus.* Florence, Bargello. pp. 156–57: After Michelangelo, project for the Julius Tomb. Berlin, Kupferstichkabinett, Staatliche Museen zu Berlin— Preußischer Kulturbesitz. p. 160: Raphael, *Portrait of Julius II* (detail). Florence, Uffizi. pp. 162–63: Michelangelo, studies for *Slaves,* Julius Tomb. Oxford, Ashmolean Museum. p. 173: *Laocoön.* Vatican State, Vatican Palace. p. 175: Michelangelo, Bruges Madonna. London, © British Museum. p. 179: Sistine Chapel before frescoes. Vatican State, Vatican Palace. Alinari/Art Resource, NY. pp. 182–83: Michelangelo, *Sistine Chapel.* Vatican State, Vatican Palace. Scala/Art Resource, NY. p. 186: Michelangelo, composition sketch for the Sistine Chapel ceiling. London, © British Museum. pp. 188–89: Michelangelo, studies for three *Ignudi.* London, © British Museum. p. 192: Michelangelo,

Creation of Adam. Vatican State, Vatican Palace. Alinari/Art Resource, NY. pp. 200–201: (top left [detail] and bottom) Michelangelo, *The Flood.* Vatican State, Vatican Palace. Alinari/Art Resource, NY. p. 204: Michelangelo, detail of *Ignudo* from Sistine Palace ceiling. Vatican State, Vatican Palace. Alinari/Art Resource, NY. p. 206: (top) Michelangelo, male head in profile. Florence, Uffizi. p. 207: (center [detail] and bottom) Michelangelo, *Judith & Holofernes.* Vatican State, Vatican Palace. Alinari/Art Resource, NY. p. 208: Michelangelo, kneeling woman. Paris, Louvre. Giraudon/Art Resource, NY. p. 213: Michelangelo, self-portrait? Private collection. p. 227: Michelangelo, shopping list. Florence, Casa Buonarroti. p. 232: Michelangelo, drawing of hand. Rome, Biblioteca Apostolica Vaticana.

Index

Page numbers in *italics* refer to illustrations.

Abraham (Donatello), 23
Academy (Florence), 3, 4, 75
Adoration of the Magi (Botticelli), 74, *74*
Adoration of the Magi (Leonardo), 32
Agostino di Duccio, 120–22
Alberti, Leon Battista, 62
Alcibiades, 151
Alexander VI, Pope, 76, 111, 112
Alidosi, Francesco, 177
Ancestors of Christ (Michelangelo), 184, *185,* 186, 187, 188, 195, 196
Annunciation (Donatello), 240*n*
Annunciation (Michelangelo), 229

Antonio del Francioso of Casteldurante, 223
Apostle (Michelangelo), 228–29
Apostles (Michelangelo) (painting), 180
Apostles (Michelangelo) (sculpture), 120
Arca di San Domenico (Niccolò dell'Arca), 83, 84–86, 108–9
Aretino, Pietro, 2, 168
Argenta, Piero d', 113, 248*n*
Ariosto, Lodovico, 2
Arnolfo di Cambio, 83
arrabbiati, 111
Arte della Lana (Wool Guild), 122, 123–24

Ascension of Christ (Donatello), 46
Assumption of the Virgin (Nanni di
    Banco), 249*n*–50*n*
astrology, 6, 7, 141, 149, 154
Attavante (miniaturist), 131
Autobiography (Cellini), 49–50

Bacchus (Michelangelo), 69, 89, 92,
    97, 101, 103, 116, 134, 141,
    153
Baccio da Montelupo, 49, 85–86,
    119
Baldassare del Milanesi, 90, 91, 92
Bandinelli, Baccio, 130, 241*n*
Baptism of the Neophytes (Masaccio),
    49
Baptistery (Florence), 34, 80, 81
Barbaro, Ermolao, 76
Bartolommeo della Porta, 108
Bartolommeo della Rocca, 111
Battle Between Dragons and Lions
    (Uccello), 44
Battle of Anghiari (Leonardo), 30,
    130, 139, 142
Battle of Cascina (Michelangelo),
    30, 31, 44, 48, 130, 139,
    142, 178
Battle of San Romano (Uccello),
    43–44
Battle of the Centaurs
    (Michelangelo), 61, 62–67,
    64, 68, 69, 90, 243*n*
Bellini, Gentile, 80
Bellini, Giovanni, 2, 80
Belvedere Palace, 173–74

Benedetto da Maiano, 57, 119,
    147
Bernardo di Marco, 128
Berni, Francesco, 2, 114
Bertoldo di Giovanni, 33–34, *41,*
    54–55, 60, 61, 66, 241*n*
Bibbiena, Piero Dovizi da, 13–14
Bible, 133, 184–202, 215
Boccaccio, Giovanni, 93–94, 143
Bologna, 14, 15, 78, 80–86, 108–9,
    165–67, 175, 178, 207,
    248*n*
Borgia, Cesare, 91
Borgia, Rodrigo, 76, 111, 112
bottega, 17, 19–20, 67, 118
Botticelli, Sandro, 12, 17, 21, 33,
    74, *74,* 108, 117, 126–27,
    132, 145, 152, 155, 180,
    231
Bound Slave (Michelangelo), 156
Bramante, Donato, xvii, 97, 155,
    176–77, 178, 189
Brancacci Chapel, 48–49, 118
Brazen Serpent (Michelangelo), 189
bronze casting, 34, 166
Bruges Madonna (Michelangelo),
    174, *175*
Brunelleschi, Filippo, 32, 39, 45
Brutus (Michelangelo), 244*n*
Buonarroti, Brigida, 104
Buonarroti, Buonarroto (brother),
    3, 97, 98, 103, 113, 167,
    174, 197
Buonarroti, Francesca (mother),
    5–8, 70, 79, 197

Buonarroti, Francesca (niece), 197

Buonarroti, Francesco (uncle), 9, 16, 23

Buonarroti, Giovansimone (brother), 98, 101, 169, 202

Buonarroti, Lionardo (brother), 97, 98, 99, 103

Buonarroti, Lionardo (nephew), 3, 6, 67–68, 152–54, 197–98, 222, 225, 229, 251*n*

Buonarroti, Lucrezia degli Ubaldini da Gagliano, 99, 103

Buonarroti, Michelangelo, *see* Michelangelo Buonarroti

Buonarroti, Sigismondo (brother), 16, 98

Buonarroti Simoni, Lodovico di Leonardo (father), 9–23
    correspondence of, 99–100
    death of, 211–12
    Michelangelo's artistic aspirations opposed by, 9, 16–17, 21–23, 99–100, 101, 135
    Michelangelo's relationship with, xv, xvi–xvii, 98–105, 116, 138, 169, 199, 202, 211–12, 211*n*
    as *podestà*, 5
    tomb of, 211–12, 250*n*–51*n*
    Via del Bentaccordi house of, 3–4, 9, 61, 244*n*

buon fresco, 184

Caesar, Julius, 207

Caffaggiolo, 40, 73, 78

Cain and Abel Offering (Michelangelo), 193, 194, 250*n*

Cancelleria, 96

Candlestick Angel (Michelangelo), 83

Canossa family, 28, 29

cantiere, 18

capomaestro, 56

Caprese, 4–5

"Cardiere, il," 12–13

Careggi villa, 13, 72

Carrara marble quarries, 157–59, 161, 164, 172, 174

Casa Buonarroti, 3–4, 9, 61, 244*n*

cassoni, 45

Caterina (Michelangelo's supposed lover), 150

Catholic Church, 94–95

Cavalcanti family, 89

Cavalieri, Tommaso de', 3, 224, 225, 228, 229, 230–31

Cellini, Benvenuto, 23–24, 49–50, 130, 143

Charles VIII, King of France, 80, 111

Christ (Michelangelo) (drawing), 228

Christ (Michelangelo) (sculpture), 229

Christ Praying in the Garden (Michelangelo), 229

Church of the Holy Apostles, 3

Cibò, Franceschetto, 38, 76

Cisti, Consiglio d'Antonio, 104

Clement VII, Pope, xvi, 38, 98, 170, 210

Columbus, Christopher, 148
Company of the Assumption
    (Assunta), 3
Condivi, Ascanio, xiv–xv, 6, 11, 61,
    63, 69, 71, 80, 92, 109, 127,
    144, 151–52, 158, 165, 171,
    191, 193, 228, 240n, 241n,
    243n, 245n
Confraternity of San Giovanni
    Decollato, 3
Confraternity of the Tre Magi, 75
Constantine I, Emperor of Rome,
    96
contracts, xiv, 123, 157
Convent of San Giovanni
    Evangelista a Boldrone, 197
copybooks, 19–20
Corniole, Giovanni, 131
Cosimo I, Duke of Florence, 38,
    67–68, 210, 229, 230–31
Creation of Adam (Michelangelo),
    190, 192–93, 192
Creation of Eve (Jacopo della
    Quercia), 82
Creation of Eve (Michelangelo),
    192–93, 194, 195
Creation of the Sun and Moon
    (Michelangelo), 192
Credi, Lorenzo di, 108, 118, 131
Cronaca (Filipepi), 145
Crucifix (Michelangelo), 244n

Daniel (Michelangelo), 187, 188
Daniele da Volterra, 3, 50, 211,
    225, 228, 229, 230–31

Dante Alighieri, 85, 117, 149
David (Donatello), 15, 15, 120,
    125, 132, 133, 245n
David (Michelangelo), 85, 90, 96,
    118–35, 122, 141–42, 158,
    168, 205–7, 219, 245n
David (Michelangelo), Leonardo's
    drawing of, 131–32, 132
David (Michelangelo), Raphael's
    study after, 122
David (Michelangelo) (bronze), 34,
    120
David (Verrocchio), 245n
David and Goliath (Michelangelo),
    189, 207
Decameron (Boccaccio), 93–94
Dei, Benedetto, 78
della Robbia, Andrea, 131
Della Robbia family, 108
della Rovere, Francesco, xvii,
    154–55, 180, 247n
della Rovere, Galeotto Franciotti,
    161
della Rovere, Giuliano, see Julius II,
    Pope
della Rovere, Leonardo, 154
della Rovere, Lucchina, 161
Deposition (Michelangelo),
    250n–51n
desco da parto, 138
Desiderio da Settignano, 60, 68
Dioscuri, 96
disegno, 33–34
Divine Comedy (Dante), 117, 149
Dolce, Lodovico, 168

Dominicans, 112
Donatello:
 Medici patronage of, 15, 28, 42
 Michelangelo influenced by, 23,
  33–34, 39, 49, 57, 59–61,
  69–70, 120, 133, 243n
 as painter, 242n
 as sculptor, 15, 27, 46, 55, 68
 see also individual works
Donati, Lucrezia, 42
Doni, Angelo di Francesco,
  135–36, 138, 246n
Doni, Maddalena, 136
Doni Tondo (Michelangelo),
  135–39, 137, 178, 190,
  196, 209
drawing of Michelangelo's David
  (Leonardo), 131–32, 132
Drunkenness of Noah
  (Michelangelo), 193, 201–2
Duomo (Florence), 32, 34, 56, 73,
  81, 83, 109, 112, 117, 120,
  122, 123, 125, 126, 127
Dying Slave (Michelangelo), 156

Egidius of Viterbo, 159
Epiphany (Michelangelo), 228
Este, Isabella d', 91
Expulsion of Adam and Eve from
  Paradise (Masaccio), 48
Eyck, Jan van, 33

Fall of Adam and Eve and the
  Expulsion from Paradise
  (Michelangelo), 193, 194

Farnese Cup (Tazza Farnese), 46–47,
  47
Fattucci, Giovan Francesco, 164
favola d'Orfeo, La (Poliziano), 25
Feast of Herod (Donatello), 46,
  69–70
Ficino, Marsilio, 24, 41, 73, 74,
  143, 147
Filarete, Francesco di Lorenzo,
  124–25
Filipepi, Simone, 112, 145
Fiore di Virtù, 147
Fiorentino, Adriano, 244n
Firenzuola, 40
Flood (Michelangelo), 171–72, 193,
  198–202, 200, 202, 207
Florence:
 artistic movements in, 81
 bonfire of the vanities in,
  109–10, 231
 defenses of, 40
 description of, 78–79
 expansion of, 39
 Medici rule in, 14–15, 63, 72,
  76, 77, 80–81, 86–87, 108,
  110, 133, 134
 Michelangelo's separations from,
  14, 72, 77–86, 93, 142–43
 republican rule in, 14–15, 86,
  108, 110, 112, 119–20, 133,
  134
foreshortening, 177, 189, 191
Fra Angelico, 1, 32–33, 39, 44–45,
  48
Franciscans, 11, 112, 155

frescoes, 18, 47–48, 52, 117–18,
155
of Sistine Chapel ceiling, 20–21,
171–72, 176–80, 184, 202,
248n–49n

Galatea, Francesco, 16
Galli, Jacopo, 89, 116, 172, 174
Galliena (weaver), 129
garzoni, 20, 54
Gates of Paradise (Ghiberti), 34, 116
Gauricus, Pomponius, 135
Ghiberti, Lorenzo, 34, 81, 116,
242n
Ghirlandaio, Benedetto, 20, 129
Ghirlandaio, Davide, 20, 129
Ghirlandaio, Domenico, 9, 17–21,
24, 49, 51, 52–53, 54, 61,
67, 92, 129, 155, 171, 178,
180, 241n
Ghirlandaio, Ridolfo, 19
Giambellino, see Bellini, Giovanni
Giotto, 43, 50, 78
Gonzaga family, 159
Granacci, Francesco, 18, 19, 21, 49,
131, 171, 179, 241n, 249n
Greek sculpture, 27–28, 34, 43, 60,
62, 84, 88–89, 91
Guicciardini, Francesco, 41, 42, 76

Hall of the Great Council (Sala del
Maggior Consiglio), 30–31,
130, 142, 168
Head of a Faun (Michelangelo), 61,
62, 243n

Henry VII, King of England, 51
Hercules, 46
Hercules (Michelangelo), 70–71, 71,
244
Hercules Killing the Hydra
(Pollaiuolo), 46
Hercules Squeezing Antaeus to Death
(Pollaiuolo), 46
Hercules Victorious Over the Lion
(Pollaiuolo), 46
Hippocrates, 143
Holy Family, 136, 138
homosexuality, 144–47, 149–54
Hospital of Santa Maria Nuova,
152
Hospital of Santo Spirito, 72, 152

Ignudi (Michelangelo), 188, 189,
190, 191, 192, 195, 203,
204, 249n–50n
Indaco, L', 248n
see also Jacapo di Sandro
ingegno, 6
Innocent VIII, Pope, 37, 38, 76, 111
in-the-round sculpture, 61, 66, 70,
97

Jacopo del Duca, 229
Jacopo della Quercia, 58–59,
81–82, 82, 83
Jacopo di Sandro (il Indaco
Vecchio), 249n
Jeremiah (Michelangelo), 187, 203
Jonah (Michelangelo), 187, 192
Judgment of Paris (Uccello), 44

Judith and Holofernes (Donatello),
15, 124–27, *126,* 131, 133,
205–7, 243*n*
Judith and Holofernes
(Michelangelo), 189,
205–7, *206, 208*
Julius II, Pope, 154–67
death of, xv, 210, 216
Laocoön acquired by, 173–74
Michelangelo's bronze statue of,
34, 96, 166–67, 175
Michelangelo's estrangement
from, 161–66, 171, 176,
177, 205, 247*n*–48*n*
Michelangelo's reconciliation
with, 165–67, 175, 178
Michelangelo's relationship with,
xv, xvi, xvii, 105, 154–80,
203, 205
as patron, xvii, 142, 155
physical appearance of, 155–56
portraits of, 155, 157, 159–61,
160, 202–7, *206*
Sistine Chapel ceiling and, 167,
175, 181, 202–7, 208, 209
as *terribilità,* 156–57, 159–67, 203
Tomb of, 156–59, *156,* 161–66,
172, 175, 176, 177, 178,
179, 203, 210, 220

Landino, Cristofano, 40
Laocoön, 26, 172–74, *173*
Last Judgment (Michelangelo), 27,
168, 184, 185, 190, 209,
211, 243*n,* 250*n*

Last Supper (Leonardo), 139
Lazzaro of Pavia, 75
Leo X, Pope, xvi, 5, 12, 14, 15, 24,
36, 37–38, 53, 75, 80–81,
94, 134, 149, 169–70, 210,
216
Leonardo da Vinci:
apprenticeship of, 53
David as viewed by, 128, 131–32
Medici patronage of, 28, 38
Michelangelo compared with,
xv, 1, 2, 3, 53, 152
Michelangelo's relationship with,
28–32, 118
reputation of, 28, 32, 118
as sculptor, 119
sculptors as viewed by, 23
sexuality of, 147, 148, 152
see also individual works
lettuccio, 45
Leibert, Robert, 240*n*
Life of Michelangelo (Condivi),
xiv–xv, 6, 11, 61, 63, 69, 71,
80, 92, 109, 127, 144,
151–52, 158, 165, 171, 193,
228, 240*n,* 241*n,* 243*n,*
245*n*
Lioni, Pierleone, 75
Lippi, Filippino, 117–18, 129, 132
Lives of the Artists (Vasari), xiv, 1–2,
6, 61, 81, 127, 245*n,* 248*n,*
249*n*
Loggia dei Lanzi, 127, 128, 129,
131
Lomazzo, Giovanni Paolo, 168

Lorenzo il Magnifico, profile head
(Leonardo), *18*
Lo Scheggia, 44
Luschino, Benedetto, 215–19

Machiavelli, Niccolò, 41
Madonna (Donatello), 46
Madonna and Child (Donatello),
46
Madonna and Child (Michelangelo),
9
Madonna of the Rocks (Leonardo),
32
Madonna of the Steps
(Michelangelo), 61, 62–63,
67–70, *68*
Magi, 73–74
Manetti, Giovanni di Gianozzo,
145–46
Mantegna, Andrea, 33
Marcus Aurelius, Emperor of
Rome, 96
marquetry, 44
Marsyas, 26–27, *27,* 51, 242*n*
Mary and Christ (Michelangelo),
228
Marzocco (Donatello), *5,* 129, 131
Masaccio, 32, 43, 48–49, 50, 118,
243*n*
Medal of the Pazzi Conspiracy
(Bertoldo di Giovanni), *41*
Medici, Clarice Orsini de', 5, 25
Medici, Contessina de', 37, 38, 75,
150, 244*n*

Medici, Cosimo de', xvii, 14, 15, 26,
28, 39–40, 42, 62, 73–74
Medici, Giovanni de', xvi, 5, 12,
14, 15, 24, 36, 37–38, 53,
75, 80–81, 94, 134, 149,
169–70, 210, 216
Medici, Giovanni dell Bande Nere
de', 38
Medici, Giovanni di Bicci de', 39
Medici, Giovanni di Pierfrancesco
de', 15, 38, 87, 112
Medici, Giuliano de', xvii, 24–25,
36, 41
Medici, Giuliano de', duke of
Nemours, 12, 15, 24, 37,
38, 75, 80–81, 134, 210–11
Medici, Giulio de', xvi, 38, 98, 170,
210
Medici, Lorenzo de' (the
Magnificent), 35–47
art collection of, 42–47, 124
birth of, 74
court of, 24–26, 40–41
death of, 64, 71, 72–76, 79, 108
family of, 12–15, 24, 37–38
funeral of, 75–76
jousting enjoyed by, 43–44
as *Maestro della Bottega,* 36
Michelangelo's dream about,
11–16, 76, 240*n*
Michelangelo's relationship with,
xv, xvi, xvii, 14, 16–17, 21,
35, 39, 43, 48, 51, 76, 79,
97, 170, 210, 241*n*

palle emblem of, 44, 72, 134
as patron, xvi, 36, 39–42, 43, 62,
  63–64, 66, 76
personality of, 37, 42
physical appearance of, 36
political power of, 35–39, 41–42,
  63, 76, 87, 106
ring worn by, 73, 74–75
Rome as viewed by, 94, 143
salver of, 45–46
Savonarola and, 106, 107–8,
  113
tomb of, 210–11
Medici, Lorenzo de', duke of
  Urbino, 148–49, 211
Medici, Lorenzo di Pierfrancesco
  de', 15, 86–88, 89, 91, 92,
  111, 112, 115–16, 117, 120
Medici, Lucrezia de', 37, 38, 75,
  150
Medici, Lucrezia Tornabuoni de',
  36, 46
Medici, Luigia de', 37, 38, 150
Medici, Maddalena de', 37, 38, 75,
  76, 150
Medici, Picarda Bueri de', 39
Medici, Pierfrancesco de', 42
Medici, Piero de' (the Gouty), 26,
  46
Medici, Piero de' (the
  Unfortunate), xvi, 11–16,
  24, 37, 38, 71, 75, 80–81,
  87, 110, 112, 115
Medici bank, 35, 37, 41–42

Medici Gardens, 15, 23, 24–28, 32,
  33–34, 48, 54, 61, 62, 72,
  77, 88, 114–15, 171, 180,
  210, 242n
Medici Palace, 13, 14, 35, 39,
  42–47, 69–70, 77, 114–15,
  180, 241n
Medici Tombs, 39, 44, 55, *59,* 76,
  210–11
Melozzo da Forlì, 155
mezzo relievo, 63, 66
Michelangelo (goldsmith), 130
Michelangelo Buonarroti:
  adolescence of, xvi, 61
  anatomy studied by, 72, 152
  ancestry of, 16, 28, 29
  apprenticeship of, 9, 16–34,
    51–54, 178, 241n
  as architect, 97, 228, 230
  artistic development of, xvi, 6,
    9–10, 16–34, 39, 51–61, 62,
    66, 67, 88–89, 97, 113, 118,
    167
  biographies of, xiv–xv
  birth of, 4–6
  in Bologna, 14, 15, 78, 80–86,
    108–9, 165–67, 175, 178,
    248n
  broken nose of, 47–51, 80, 118,
    168
  celestial sign observed by,
    215–20
  chronology of, xix–xxvi
  Colossus project of, 158

Michelangelo Buonarroti *(continued)*
commissions of, 67, 70–71, 72,
83, 89, 97, 103, 116–17,
119, 120, 122, 156, 157,
175, 176–78, 220
correspondence of, xiv, 67, 84,
87–90, 98–102, *102,*
104–5, 168–69
death of, 3, 220, 230–31, 240*n*
as "divine," xiii, 1–4
documentation on, xiii–xiv
drawings by, 16, 29, 33–34, 53,
61, 171, 205, 223–24,
228–31, 251*n*
early works of, 18–19, 61–72,
83, 85, 87–93, 243*n*
education of, 9, 16
enemies of, 164–65, 176–77,
178
family as important to, 10, 97,
98, 101, 103–4, 138–39,
142–43, 168–69, 197–202,
211
father figures of, xv–xvii
finances of, 10, 89, 100–101,
104–5, 116, 142, 169, 229
in flight from Rome (1506),
161–66, 176, 177, 205,
247*n*–48*n*
as Florentine, 3, 4, 9, 14, 78–79,
85–86, 93, 95, 116
forgery accusation against, 87,
90–93
friendships of, 77–78, 170–72,
248*n*

funeral of, 3–4, 75
generosity of, 2, 36, 104–5, 169,
171
genius of, xiii–xiv
horoscope of, 6, 7
influences on, 24–34, 48, 49,
51–61, 69–70, 81–85
inventory of possessions of,
220–25
Latin studied by, 16, 25, 43
Macel de' Corvi house of,
220–31
models used by, 152
as painter, 9–10, 16–21, 23–24,
51–54, 60, 135, 139, 156,
166, 178–79, 190–91, 202,
219, 229–30
personality of, 21, 156–57, 159,
171–72
physical appearance of, 50, 80
Platonic relationships of, 151–52
political views of, 109, 113, 134,
143
property owned by, 10, 105
religious faith of, 109, 143, 151
reputation of, xiii, xiv–xv, 56, 86,
97, 105, 114, 116–18, 135,
139, 141–42, 219
reticence of, 143, 174, 180, 209,
231
in Rome, 85, 86, 87–114,
142–43, 172–231
rural background of, 9–10
as sculptor, 9, 20, 21–24, 28,
54–61, 97, 99–100, 101,

116, 135, 141–42, 156, 171, 219, 230
self-portraits of, *208, 209–10, 213, 251n*
as self-taught, 51–61, 68, 72
sexuality of, 143–54
shopping list of, *227*
"single stone" rule of, 97, 112, 134
sonnets of, 94, 105, 113, 150, 197
as *terribilità,* 156–57, 159, 161–72
unfinished projects of, 64, 67, 71
in Venice, 14, 80, 81
vulnerability of, 101
wet nurse of, 6–9, 70
work schedule of, 96–97
workshop of, 220, 223, 226
see also individual works
Michelozzo di Bartolommeo, 42
Michi, Giovanni, 248n
Mini, Antonio, 34
Mino da Fiesole, 26, 27
Mirabilia urbis Romae, 95–96
Monciatto, Francesco, 125
Montefeltro, Federico da, Duke of Urbino, 15
Moses (Michelangelo), 156–57, 168, 220

Nanni di Banco, 59, 249n–50n
Nasi, Bartolomea de', 42
Niccolò dell'Arca, 83–85, 87
Nifo (astrologer), 149
Nudes (Michelangelo), 190–91, 195

oil painting, 33, 138
On Sculpture (Gauricus), 135
Operai del Duomo, 120
Orlando Furioso (Ariosto), 2
Orsanmichele, 34, 116

Pacchierotto, 145
Palazzo Signoria, 30–31, 119, 124–26, 129, 134, 139, 142
Palazzo Vecchio, 134
Papini, Giovanni, 247n
Paris di Grassis, 159
Parronchi, Alessandro, 71, 244n
Pazzi Conspiracy (1478), 36, 41, 247n
perspective, linear, 32, 45, 47, 48
Perugino, Pietro, 53, 118, 131, 132, 155, 180
Petrarch, 46
Piazza della Signoria, 110, 112
Piccolomini Altar, 51, 120
Pico della Mirandola, Giovanni, 24, 25, 40–41, 76, 108
Piero di Cosimo, 21, *56,* 117, 131, 155
Pietà (Michelangelo) (sculpture), 69, 85, 97, 100, 103, 112–14, 116, 122, 134, 141, 143–44
Pietà (Michelangelo) (drawing), 229
Piffero, Giovanni, 130
Piombo, Sebastiano del, 169–70, 171
Pisa, 40, 111, 125
Pisano, Giovanni, 60, 83

Pisano, Nicola, 60, 82–83
Plato, 24
Platonic Academy, 24
Pliny, 173
Poggi Imperiale, 40
Poggio a Caiano villa, 39, 54
Poliziano, Angelo, 11, 24–26, 27,
    40, 63, 76, 108
Pollaiuolo, Antonio del, 46, 49,
    155
Pollaiuolo, Piero del, 46, 49
Pollaiuolo, Simone del, 108, 131,
    176, 248n
Pontormo, Jacopo, 147
Popolani, 15, 120
Porta Magna (San Petronio), 59, 81
Portrait Bust of Michelangelo
    (Daniele da Volterra), 50
Portrait of Giuliano da Sangallo
    (Piero di Cosimo), 56
Portrait of Julius II (Raphael), 155,
    159–61, 160
Portrait of Savonarola, 106
practica, 123
Prato, 134, 219
Profile Portrait of Alessandro, Count
    of Canossa (Michelangelo),
    29
Punishment of Haman
    (Michelangelo), 189–90
putti, 185–86, 190, 203–5, 205

quarries, marble, 40, 157–59, 161,
    164, 172, 174
quattrocento, 55

Raimondi, Marcantonio, 31
Raphael:
    apprenticeship of, 53, 132
    Michelangelo compared with,
        1, 2, 8, 23, 53, 132, 167–68
    as painter, 132, 136, 155, 205,
        209
    personality of, 167–68
    sexuality of, 152
    see also individual works
relics, 94–95
reliefs, 53, 61, 62–70
Renaissance:
    architecture in, 39, 96
    painting style of, 32
    quattrocento of, 55
Riario, Raffaelle, 88, 89, 90, 92, 96,
    103, 116, 142, 247n
Riccio, Andrea, 128
ricordi, xiv, 100, 241n
Ridolfi, Niccolò, 244n
Ridolfi, Piero, 38, 150, 244n
Roman sculpture, 26–27, 34, 43,
    60, 62, 66, 84, 88–89, 91,
    93, 96, 172–74
Rome:
    corruption in, 93–95
    Michelangelo in, 85, 86, 87–114,
        142–43, 172–231
    Michelangelo's flight from
        (1505), 161–66, 176, 177,
        205, 247n–48n
    sights of, 95–96
Rondanini Pietà (Michelangelo),
    211–12, 223, 229, 251n

Rosselli, Cosimo, 17, 117, 126, 155, 176, 177, 178
Rosselli, Pietro, 248*n*
Rossellino, Antonio, 68, 120–22
Rucellai, Bonda, 6
Rucellai, Paolo, 89
Rustichi, *117*
Rustici, Giovan Francesco, 131, 132

Sacrifice of Noah (Michelangelo), 193, 250*n*
St. Antoninus, 150
St. Bartholomew, 27
St. Bernardino of Siena, 94–95, 149
St. Francis (Michelangelo), 51
St. Francis of Assisi, 5
St. George (Donatello), 23, *23,* 34, 116
St. Jerome in His Study (van Eyck), 33
St. John the Baptist, 3, 18, 123, 138, 146
St. Mark (Donatello), 23, 34
St. Paul (Masaccio), 43
St. Peter (Masaccio), 43
St. Peter (Michelangelo), 229
St. Peter's basilica, 57, 97, 155, 178, 228, 230
Sala del Maggior Consiglio (Hall of the Great Council), 30–31, 130, 142, 168
Salvestro (jeweler), 129
Salviati, Jacopo, 38, 150

San Donato a Scopeto monastery, 32
Sangallo, Antonio da, 56, 129–30
Sangallo, Francesco da, 56, 115, 172–73
Sangallo, Giuliano da, xvii, 55–57, 97, 118, 127–35, 142, 155, 164–65, 171–73, 176, 178, 248*n*
San Giovanni in Laterano, 95
San Giovannino (Michelangelo), 87
San Lorenzo church, 28, 32, 75, 110
  New Sacristy of, 39, 44, 55, 76, 148, 170, 210–11
  Old Sacristy of, 39, 44
San Marco church (Florence), 75
  Convent of, 32–33, 73–74, 106
  Library of, 39
San Marco church (Venice), 80
San Petronio basilica, 59, 81–82, 96, 175
San Petronius (Michelangelo), 83, 85
San Pier Maggiore church, 3–4
San Pietro in Vincoli, 156, 210
San Procolus (Michelangelo), 83, 85
Sansovino, Andrea, 119, 131
Santa Croce basilica, 4, 203, 211
Santa Maria di Popolo church, 161
Santa Maria Novella church, 17–18, 52, 73, 76
Santi, Nicolò, 223
San Tommaso church, 147

Santo Spirito Crucifix
    (Michelangelo), 71–72
Sassetti Tombs, 55
Savonarola, Girolamo, 39, 106–12
    execution of, xvi–xvii, 106, 110,
        112
    Lorenzo de' Medici and, 106,
        107–8, 113
    Michelangelo's relationship with,
        106, 109, 113, 215–19,
        231
    opposition to, 103, 108, 109,
        111, 112
    political influence of, 86
    portrait of, 106
    preaching by, 107, 108, 109,
        110–12, 110, 215
    sexuality as viewed by, 144–47,
        149–50
Savonarola Preaching, 110
Scala, Bartolommeo, 54
scarpellino, 23
Scheggia, 146–47
schiacciato, 63, 69
Schongauer, Martin, 18–19, 19,
        51–52, 241n–42n
secco, 184
Seers (Veggenti) (Michelangelo),
        184–85, 187–88, 190, 195,
        198
Separation of Light and Darkness
        (Michelangelo), 184, 192
Separation of the Land and the Waters
        (Michelangelo), 192, 193
Sera, Neri di Miniato del, 6

Serristori (Cosimo's ambassador),
        230–31
Settignano, 8–9, 10
Sforza, Ascanio, 91
Sforza, Galeazzo Maria, Duke of
        Milan, 45
Sforza, Lodovico (il Moro), Duke
        of Milan, 32
Shivering Boy (Masaccio), 48, 49
Sibyls (Michelangelo), 68, 70
Signorelli, Luca, 2, 155, 180, 209,
        220
Simone, Giovanni di, 240n
Sistine Chapel ceiling
        (Michelangelo), xv, xvi,
        xvii, 176–210
    artistic style of, 156, 180, 181,
        184, 219
    assistants for, 57, 175, 180,
        248n–49n
    commission for, 175, 176–78
    frescoes of, 20–21, 171–72,
        176–80, 184, 202,
        248n–49n
    iconography of, 34, 113, 125,
        179–202
    illustrations of, 179, 181, 185,
        186, 188, 189, 192,
        200–201, 204, 205, 206,
        208
    Julius II and, 167, 175, 181,
        202–7, 208, 209
    older frescoes and, 155, 180
    restoration of, 207–9, 249n
    scaffolding for, 203, 207–9

Sixtus IV, Pope, xvii, 154–55, 180, 247*n*

Slaves (Michelangelo), 156, *162,* 220

Sleeping Cupid (Michelangelo), 67, 87, 89–93, 245*n*

Socrates, 151

Soderini, Francesco, 165–66

Soderini, Piero, 119–20, 130, 135, 136, 165, 166, 172

sodomy, 144–47, 149–50

Stanze per la giostra del magnifico Giuliano de' Medici (Poliziano), 24–25

Strozzi, Giovanni di Marcello, 136

Strozzi, Laudomia, 144

study after Masaccio's *Tribute Money* (Michelangelo), *53*

study after Michelangelo's *David* (Raphael), *122*

syphilis, 148–49

tempera painting, 33, 138

Temptation and Fall of Adam and Eve (Masaccio), 48

Temptation of St. Anthony (Schongauer), 18–19, *19,* 51–52, 241*n*–42*n*

Three Figures (Raimondi), *31*

Tiberius, Emperor of Rome, 96

Titian, 1, 2

tondo, 45, 135, 136

Tornabuoni family, 17, 24, 36, 46

Torrigiani, Pietro, 48–51, 168, 174

Torso Belvedere, 174

Trajan's Column, 96

Tribute Money (Masaccio), Michelangelo's study after, *53*

Tuscany, map of (Leonardo), 114

Uberti, Fazio degli, 77

Uccello, Paolo, 32, 43–44

Urbano, Pietro, 248*n*

Vasari, Giorgio, xiv, 1–2, 6, 55, 61, 81, 127, 245*n,* 248*n,* 249*n*

Venice, 14, 80, 81

Verrocchio, Andrea del, 26, 27, 28, 49, 53, 245*n*

Virgil, 26

Vivio, Jacomo, 250*n*

Volpaia, Lorenzo della, 128

Wool Guild *(Arte della Lana),* 122, 123–24

Zachariah (Michelangelo), 185, 187, 188, 189

Zuccone (Donatello), 23